Analyzing
Philosophical
Arguments

Chandler Publications in

PHILOSOPHY

Ian Philip McGreal, *Editor*

Analyzing Philosophical Arguments

AN INTRODUCTION TO
PHILOSOPHICAL METHOD

IAN PHILIP McGREAL

Sacramento State College

CHANDLER PUBLISHING COMPANY

124 Spear Street

San Francisco, California 94105

TO MY FATHER,
MICHAEL R. McGREAL,
MATHEMATICIAN,
FROM WHOM I INHERITED MY LOVE OF ANALYSIS

CONTENTS

PREFACE

An introduction, by demonstration, to the philosophical analysis and criticism of arguments is an introduction to philosophy itself. No man in his senses would approach philosophy without going, first of all, to the great philosophers; but no one will understand and appreciate philosophy who considers the great arguments while failing to employ the critical arts of philosophical analysis: attention to the uses of terms, discovery and clarification of meanings, logical examination of the structure of claims and arguments, and appraisal of premises.

Unless in studying the writings of the great philosophers one makes the effort to examine the arguments line by line in order to discover as precisely as possible *what* is being claimed, *how* it is being claimed, and whether what is said is *justified,* one does not really study, criticize, or even read what the great philosophers have written.

For to read philosophy at all, one must read it critically. A philosophical work should be approached with both respect and caution—respect for the fame of the philosopher, a fame which, through the ingenious practice of his art, he has probably earned; and caution because, through the exercise of his persuasive talents, the philosopher can beguile us into accepting propositions which, in

xi

our right mind and in a "cool hour," to use Bishop Butler's phrase, we would not dream of accepting.

Through the critical examination of the arguments devised by our greatest philosophers we gain a new appreciation of their genius; at the same time we discover the vulnerability of even the most resourceful of those who have used language to describe—in the most illuminating and persuasive manner possible—the world of common experience and concern. Only through the practice and understanding of the philosophical art, which involves the creative use of language for the sake of making new perspectives eloquent and appealing, can a student of philosophy hope to confront philosophy itself: that abstruse, paradoxical, ridiculous, shocking, enlightening, and profoundly important expression of man's concern to say what the world means to him.

A method of philosophical analysis and appraisal is implicit in the work of every philosophical critic, but there is no use pretending that philosophers agree in their views as to what that method ought to be. Hence, this set of demonstrations begins with an explicit account of the method—hardly revolutionary—by which the arguments of the philosophers are here analyzed and appraised. I believe that the account makes explicit the techniques of analysis and construction by which philosophers, whether authors or critics, must operate; but my essay on method is itself a philosophical claim to which a discerning reader may want to take exception. In any case, the body of the book is the set of ten demonstrations of philosophical analysis and criticism; and just as medical students can profit from the mistakes of the surgeon who shows them how to dissect the corpse, so students may profit from whatever errors and injudicious steps may be exhibited in the ten critical examinations which follow.

Adequate selections from the works of the philosophers whose arguments are examined will present to the reader the original arguments with the force and security provided by an ample context. Each exercise in analysis begins with the attempt to isolate the philosopher's basic claim. In the process of abstracting that claim and comprehending its function, the reader is introduced to the philosophical arts. Through attention to the demonstrations the student first of all becomes aware of the need to study a philosophical text closely in order to determine the philosopher's use of terms, for it quickly becomes evident that the *meaning* of a claim (which may be a terminological suggestion in disguise) depends on the philosopher's *use of terms*. In turn, the *logical structure* of a claim depends on the *meanings* of terms, and the range of possibilities for the speculative metaphysician (he who would venture to describe what, because of logical barriers, lies beyond the limits of empirical investigation) depends on the *logical structure* of what is said.

As the reader follows the analytic demonstrations of which this book is mainly composed, he discovers, *in use,* the terminology, the techniques, the analytic and constructive arts of the philosophical critic. Insofar as the demonstrations are revealing, philosophy becomes once again, as it was for the philosophers whose arguments are here examined, a fresh and lively experience, a stimulating and challenging intellectual game—but more than a game: as Ludwig Wittgenstein has suggested, "a way of life."

No single criticism of a philosophical argument will exhaust the possibilities for illuminating comment on the work at hand, for the critic's understanding of what a philosopher says is limited by the critic's own perspective and style. Philosophical writings, like other works of literary art, have nuances of meaning that escape the attention of even the most conscientious and thorough of critics. Realizing this truth and my own limitations, I have advanced the accounts of my analysis and criticism *not* to provide the last word, but to make available concrete examples, in detail, of what a philosopher does when he reads philosophical arguments critically. Each analysis, then, is but "an" analysis of the argument under consideration, and the reader is invited to criticize the demonstrations by considering alternative interpretations and analyses of the arguments.

In each case I conclude my criticism of the argument being examined by commenting on general features of the argument, with the aim of suggesting that even when a great philosopher errs he is worth studying. As the critic, I attempt to determine whether an argument is valid or invalid; I consider whether I am prepared to grant the truth of the premises; but then I ask whether—even in those cases involving invalid inferences and unacceptable premises—there does not remain an illuminating insight which, when modified to satisfy my criteria of acceptability, might by its value overcome whatever formal deficiencies have been involved in its expression.

The logical symbolism used in several of the demonstrations is on an elementary level; in every case the symbolism is explained and a "translation" into English is provided. The logical diagrams, devised for this series of critical demonstrations, clarify the matter further by *showing,* through the use of easily comprehended symbols, the logical structure of the argument under consideration. The discussion is such, however, that even if one disregards the symbolism, the content and direction of the analysis are entirely clear.

If this book has a moral, it is this: although the logical analysis of arguments is always an important part of philosophical criticism, the central problem for the philosophical critic is that of deciding whether, everything considered, he finds the philosopher's descriptions acceptable. Since an argument is a persuasive device by which the philosopher seeks to win assent to his account of what concerns him, the critic proceeds with caution; for language as used by a great philosopher becomes a new phenomenon, the understanding of which may open up novel and significant perspectives for the critical reader.

I should like to acknowledge with gratitude the critical encouragement I have from time to time received, in connection with my study of philosophical method, from C. J. Ducasse (under whom I studied at Brown University, and whose book on method, *Philosophy As a Science,* deserves more attention than it has so far received), John Wisdom (who graciously was willing to correspond about James's squirrel), and my colleagues at Sacramento State College: Jean Faurot, Leon Miller, Edward T. Bartlett, and Perry Weddle.

Analyzing
Philosophical
Arguments

I

PHILOSOPHY AND
PHILOSOPHICAL METHODS

The term "philosophy" has been used in various ways, and consequently the word has various meanings. We are here interested in the activity to which our attention is called by the present-day, academic use of the term as shown, for example, in the catalogs of American colleges. We are not concerned with philosophy as *the search for wisdom*—a definition suggested by literally translating the Greek *philosophia* (φιλοσοφία) as "the love of wisdom"—although we agree that philosophy can assist the wise man in his search. (Unfortunately, philosophy can also be used to give confidence to the fool.) Nor are we concerned with philosophy in the broad sense of the term as created by the early Greek use of the word; philosophy, according to our use of the term, is not science, nor does it include any of the natural sciences. (We do not deny that the philosopher may systematically acquire knowledge about the uses and meanings of terms and about the logical structure of statements.) Nor are we interested in philosophy as the attempt to provide the basic beliefs and principles of an organization, a meaning implicit in the practice of speaking about the "philosophy" of a business firm. (However, we do not deny that among the basic beliefs and principles of an institution or organization may be beliefs and principles capable of "philosophical" justification, as we would use the term.)

A definition of the term "philosophy," according to its modern, academic use, is possible, but it may be possible only at the expense of ruling out certain kinds of investigation and decision which are on occasion designated as "philosophical," or of including certain kinds of activity not ordinarily called "philosophical" by professional philosophers and others who use the term "philosophy" in the way here mentioned. It would nevertheless be illuminating and useful to define the term, even though the definition were to some extent not a *report* of meaning but a *suggestion* as to the meaning which, in a specified, disciplined use, the term "philosophy" might profitably have.

But prior to making the effort to give a general description—perhaps not entirely precise but nevertheless helpful—of the activity to which the term "philosophy" in its current, academic use calls attention, we must review the various sorts of activities, the various kinds of inquiry and construction, covered by the word in its use. *Semantical construction* (the making of a *definition,* the stipulating of a meaning of a term), if it is not to be entirely arbitrary, must be disciplined by the results of *semantical analysis or investigation* (the inquiry into the *meaning* of a term in use). Semantical analysis, in turn, depends upon the results of *pragmatical analysis and decision* (the investigation and consequent limitation of the *use, or uses,* of a term in question).

Only if, as the late Ludwig Wittgenstein suggests in his *Philosophical Investigations,* we "look and see" how expressions involving the use of the term "philosophy" work in our language, and only if we notice the great multiplicity and variety of problems and methods we call "philosophical," can we begin to appreciate the creative effort—and, even, temerity—that is needed to construct a definition, a setting of the limits and mode of the application of the term, which *emphasizes the resemblances* to be found among problems called "philosophical" and *obscures the differences.*

Let us, then, begin the examination of the traditional fields of philosophy by giving samples of the sorts of questions that are ordinarily designated as "philosophical." The questions will be arranged here according to the usual classification suggested by the uses of the names for the various fields.

THE PROBLEMS OF PHILOSOPHY

The traditional fields of philosophy include: ethics, esthetics or the philosophy of art, logic, metaphysics, epistemology, philosophy of religion, philosophy of science, philosophy of politics, philosophy of mind, philosophy of history, philosophy of education, philosophy of man, philosophy of language, and philosophy of philosophy.

ETHICS: How can a person decide what he *ought* to do? What is *duty*? Can *moral obligations* conflict with *social obligations*? When is an act *morally right*? Isn't *morality* merely a matter of *opinion, sentiment, or custom*? What is the difference, if any, between a *morally right act* and a *morally obligatory act*? Is there a *moral law* for all men? What is a *moral law*? Is *knowledge about values* possible? What is a *voluntary* act? Is man's *will free or determined*? Is it possible to reconcile *individual interests* with *public interests*? What is *value*? What is *goodness*? *evil*? Is there anything which is *good for its own sake*? Does *moral value* take precedence over *artistic value*? Is *pleasure* or happiness *good on its own account*? Is there any such thing as *moral intuition*? Are values *relative* or *absolute*? *Subjective* or *objective*?

ESTHETICS or the PHILOSOPHY OF ART: What is *fine art*? Is art play or work? Is the work of art physical or not? What is *beauty*? Is beauty *objective or subjective*? Are *all* works of art *beautiful*? What is *esthetic contemplation*? How is the *value* of a work of art to be determined? Is *universality of appeal* a criterion of great art? What is *literature*? What distinguishes *prose* from *poetry*? What is *tragedy*? *comedy*?

LOGIC: When is an argument *sound*? What is *validity*? What are the *principal forms* of valid arguments? *How* can the validity of an argument be *determined*? What is the difference, if any, between a *statement* and a *proposition*? When is a statement the *contradictory* of another? the *contrary*? What relation does the *form of an argument* bear to the *uses of language*? What is the difference between *deductive* and *inductive* reasoning? What are the principal logical *fallacies*? What is the difference between a *formal fallacy* and a *material fallacy*? How can *logical paradoxes* be resolved? How are *symbols* used to show and to analyze the forms of arguments? Are the *laws of thought,* the principles of logic, *natural laws*?

METAPHYSICS—Problems of ONTOLOGY: What is *being as such*? Can a *study of* the being of things reveal generic features that belong to God? Is being *limited* or *unlimited*? Does being as such have a *cause*? Are there *various kinds* of being? Are there *levels* of being?

METAPHYSICS—Problems of COSMOLOGY: *How* did the *universe begin* to exist? Did the universe have a beginning? Is there a *sufficient reason* for everything that exists? Is everything *composed* of some *basic material*? Is the nature of any one thing *internally related* to the nature of everything else? What is an *individual* thing? What is the relation of *universals* to *particulars*? Is the *universe finite* or *infinite*? What is *space*? What is *time*? What are the *categories of the real*? What is *causation*?

EPISTEMOLOGY (often referred to as a branch of metaphysics): What is *knowledge*? *How* is knowledge *possible*? Is knowledge of the *external world* possible? What is *perception*? What is *sensation*? What is the *relation* of what is *given* in sensation *(sense data)* to the *objects sensed*? What is *truth*? Are there *kinds* of truth? What is a *proposition*? What is a *belief*? What is *evidence,* and when is it *sufficient*? What is *an idea*? a *concept*? Are there *universals*, and, if so, what are their relations to *particulars* or *individuals*? Is *intuition* a way of knowledge? What is it to *know* something *directly*? What is the difference between *a priori* and *a posteriori* truths? What is the difference between *analytic* and *synthetic* propositions? Are *synthetic a priori* propositions possible? Are *analytic* statements *necessarily and universally true*? If so, why? What is the difference, if any, between a *logical truth* and a *factual or empirical truth*?

PHILOSOPHY OF RELIGION: What is *religion*? Is a religion *without the belief in God* possible? What is God? Could there be more than one god? Does God *exist*? Is God *love*? Is God *being* or *a being*? Is God *omnipotent*? *omniscient*? *benevolent*? What is *prayer*? Is *prayer* a kind of *communication*? What is *worship*? *ritual*? *Is there* any such thing as *the soul*? *What* is the *soul*? Is the soul *immortal*? Is there a *heaven?* a *hell?* Is man *born evil?* Did God *create* man? Is it possible to *prove* that there is a God? What is *faith?* What is a *person?* What is a *spirit?* Are there *angels?* Are *angels physical* beings? What is a *mystical* experience? What is *sin?* Is man *free?* If God is omnipotent, omniscient, and all-good, *how is evil possible?*

PHILOSOPHY OF SCIENCE: What is *science?* What is scientific *method?* How are scientific *principles* established? What is *induction?* What is *evidence?* What is *matter? energy?* How are *natural laws* discovered? How are *probability* judgments justified? What is *verifiability?* What is a *cause? effect? condition?* What is *measurement?* How is a *standard* of measurement decided upon? Are empirical judgments *relative?* What is an *event?* Are *space* and *time* relative to methods of observation? What is a *scientific theory?* How is a theory verified?

PHILOSOPHY OF POLITICS: What is *politics?* What is a *state?* a *government?* What are the *kinds* of government? How can governments be *established?* What is a *ruler?* Are some men born with the *right to rule?* What kind of government is *best?* How is the *value of government* to be determined? What would be the character of an *ideal state?* What is a *civil law?* Should a *representative* elected by the people serve the opinions of the people, or their interests, or what he thinks is right, or his own interests, or what? When is *civil disobedience* justifiable? What is *tyranny?* What is a *democracy?* Can laws be *wrong?* What relations obtain, or should obtain, between the *executive, legislative,* and *judicial* branches of government? Are there *inalienable rights?* Are some truths concerning government *self-evident* truths?

PHILOSOPHY OF MIND: What is the *mind?* What is the *relation* of *mind* to *matter,* and of the mind to the *body?* Is the *knowledge of other minds* possible? What are the *contents* of *consciousness?* What is *consciousness?* Is a *pain physical* or *mental?* Is a *behavioristic analysis* of mind adequate to explain all mental operations? Is *consciousness* nothing but a *brain process?* Are all *thoughts private?* What are *emotions?*

PHILOSOPHY OF HISTORY: What is *history?* Is *history* a *science* or an *art,* or neither? What constitutes *historical evidence?* How can a *historical claim* be *justified?* Are so-called "periods" and "eras" merely the *inventions* of historians? Can historical findings be *objective*? How is the historian to distinguish between the *causes* and the *conditions* of significant change? Does the *historical process* have a *character* or *direction*? Is *social change* initiated by *individuals,* or are individuals merely the products of social conditions? Are there *historical laws*?

PHILOSOPHY OF EDUCATION: What is *education?* What are the *goals* of education? What is a *teacher?* a *scholar?* What is the *learning process?*

PHILOSOPHY OF MAN: What is *man?* Do human beings have a *fixed nature* or *essence?* Are all men *rational?* What is *rationality?* Were men *created* by God? Can a man *make his own character?* Is human *freedom* an *illusion?*

PHILOSOPHY OF LANGUAGE: What is a *language?* What is a *sign?* a *symbol?* What are the various *functions* of language? What is a *meaning?* Are there *kinds* of meaning? Is meaning *relative to interpreters?* What is the relation of the *uses* of language to its *meanings?* What is a *word?* Is it possible to *discover the meaning* of an expression? How is the meaning for a sign *stipulated?* Is a sign an *object* or an *event?* What is the relation between a *sign* and the *signified object?* How are signs related to *ideas, beliefs, motions, things?* How can signs be related to one another *without reference to meanings?* How are the *rules of grammar* determined? How are signs related to the *interests* of their users?

PHILOSOPHY OF PHILOSOPHY: What is *philosophy?* Is philosophy a *science* or an *art,* or neither? What is *analytic* philosophy? Must philosophy be concerned with *language?* Are all meaningful philosophical claims *verifiable?* Is *metaphysics* possible? Does philosophy *synthesize* the results of *scientific inquiry?* Does philosophy have a *therapeutic function* in that it cures the difficulties that arise from *misusing ordinary language?* What is *speculative* philosophy? What is *ethics? logic? esthetics?*

These are some of the traditional problems of philosophy; they are problems which have been described as "philosophical" by professional philosophers and teachers of philosophy; and they are problems to be encountered in courses dealing with the history of philosophy or with the introduction to philosophical problems.

But the problems of philosophy are not limited to the traditional or "classic" problems. Some of the questions cited under the heading "philosophy of man" and some under the heading "philosophy of philosophy" are the products of recent philosophical work—the former, of existentialism; the latter, of linguistic philosophy and, in particular, of Wittgensteinian philosophy. And anyone who attends to the work presented in philosophical journals or professional treatises of various sorts which are concerned with problems said to be "philosophical" will find that the particular problems with which philosophers are presently engaged are expressions of recent interests and reflect sophisticated and technical perplexities. Thus, philosophers have lately attempted to examine such matters as conditionals contrary to fact, negative existentials, and performative utterances; and they have asked such questions as "Can computers think?", "Is a private language possible?", "What do we discover when we examine the various uses of the word 'real'?", and "Is it misleading to claim that only sense data are perceived directly?"

Some especially interesting problems that show the direction of current philosophical interests have been presented by the British philosophical journal *Analysis* in a series of competitions: "What sort of 'if' is the 'if' in 'I can if I choose'?", "What is the difference between saying how you feel and showing by your words how you feel?", "If a distraction makes me forget my headache, does it make my head stop aching or does it only stop me from feeling it aching?", "How can one wish to have been Napoleon?", "Can I *decide* to do something immediately without *trying* to do it immediately?", "Does it make sense to suppose that *all events,* including personal experiences, could occur in reverse?", "Is it possible that one and the same individual object should cease to exist and, later on, start to exist again?", "If I carefully examine a visual after-image, what am I looking at and where is it?"

A consideration of such problems leads one to decide that although the problems of philosophy have traditionally been classified according to subject matter, it would be more helpful—because more illuminating with regard to the methods of resolution—to classify problems according to the kinds of investigation and decision the satisfactory answering or handling of the questions calls for. The further realization that all philosophical problems involve for their resolution *linguistical* considerations—analyzing and deciding upon the uses, meanings, and forms of statements—suggests how such a division, according to methods of resolution, can be accomplished.

(We note here that although recent twentieth-century philosophy has emphasized, on the one hand, the importance of linguistical analysis, and, on the other, the importance of abandoning the search for meaning and, instead, creating meaning through gratuitous and active commitment, philosophers have always been concerned both with language and with definitive action. Furthermore, although philosophers have lately been accused of being more concerned about their language and their attitudes than about the world and the practical affairs of men, they suffer from such misleading charges in company with their professional colleagues over the ages.)

THE METHODS OF PHILOSOPHY

Contemporary philosophy has been very much influenced by philosophers whose revolutionary works have, in one way or another, contributed to the understanding of philosophical method. Among the most influential of such philosophers have been G. E. Moore, whose work emphasizes the philosophical relevance of ordinary language and common sense; Bertrand Russell, who has shown that logic can be a creative as well as an analytic instrument; Ludwig Wittgenstein, who dreamed of showing the structure of the world through the exhibition of logical form, and who then destroyed his own dream through a grand exhibition of the multiplicity of uses, defying summation, to which language can be put; John Wisdom, who with an illuminating wit has ironically written of the ironic power of philosophical discourse; A. J. Ayer, whose insistence on relating philosophical claims to sense experience has perpetuated the tough-minded pragmatism which Americans know through C. S. Peirce; Gilbert Ryle, whose work on systematically misleading expressions has provided philosophy with a fresh understanding of its own linguistical malpractices; Rudolf Carnap, who has attempted to discipline semantical and syntactical analysis; Charles L. Stevenson, who has performed the chastening act of making evident the emotive meaning of value judgments and moral utterances; and John Austin, who by meticulously exposing the actual operations of language has humiliated those who supposed that they had accomplished something significant through the use of what Austin called "a certain special, happy style of blinkering philosophical English."

It may be argued that despite the profound influence of such illuminating books as Ayer's *Language, Truth, and Logic,* Wittgenstein's *Tractatus Logico-Philosophicus* and *Philosophical Investigations,* and Wisdom's *Philosophy and Psycho-Analysis,* no general outline of philosophical method, at once simple enough to make the matter clear and complex enough to do justice to the myriad of operations within philosophy, has emerged. Each of the authors on philosophy has tended to emphasize one kind of philosophical activity at the expense of other, undeniable aspects of the philosophical art. Philosophy involves analysis and attention to language, but there are various kinds of linguistical analysis, and the kinds assume a certain order relative to a vocabulary of classification. Philosophy involves, or sometimes involves, metaphysical speculation; but speculation depends upon analysis and must itself be disciplined. Philosophy involves construction through decision; but construction, if it is to be effective, must rest upon analysis and conventional discourse. Philosophy is often critical; but to be responsibly critical, one must systematically uncover the series of discoveries and decisions which preceded the making of the philosophical claim being criticized, and one must be creatively philosophical oneself.

Philosophy, we find, is a complex kind of activity, and philosophers are adept at invention (both linguistical and metaphysical) and at covering the traces of their creative work. It is no wonder, then, that some philosophers have despaired of ever being able to describe philosophical practice by laying bare the methods philosophers use in the resolution of problems. But the order is there; one needs only to "look and see." Through a careful examination of philosophical arguments—and it really does not matter whether the arguments we choose be "classic" or contemporary, although the former are historically more significant and come closer to matters of human concern—we discover the characteristic features of philosophical analysis and construction, features which we can mark through the use of a vocabulary fashioned for that purpose.

The terminology which, as influenced by Charles Morris and others, we have devised to present our account of philosophical method is such that, *by its use,* there are four and only four kinds of philosophical problems: (1) *pragmatical* problems, those which can be resolved by discoveries or decisions as to the *uses* of certain expressions; (2) *semantical* problems, those which can be resolved by discoveries or decisions as to the *meanings* of terms or expressions; (3) *logical* problems, those which can be resolved by discoveries or decisions as to the *formal structure* of statements; and (4) *metaphysical* problems, those which can be resolved by decisions (which would be, at this level, commitments *on faith*) as to the truth or falsity of propositions the truth values of which are not (because of logical restrictions) determinable by empirical investigation.

Before attempting to classify some of the traditional problems by using this methodological vocabulary, we shall consider these distinctions at greater length and examine some examples of problems of each type. This introductory account will be supplemented in the course of analyzing and criticizing the ten classic arguments which provide the material for our introduction to the problems and methods of philosophy. Our initial claim is that *philosophical* problems are soluble either *pragmatically* (by attention to the *uses* of language), *semantically* (by attention to the *meanings* of expressions), *logically* (by attention to the *forms* of statements), or *metaphysically* (by *acts of faith* with regard to the truth value of logical possibilities).

THE ORDER OF PHILOSOPHICAL INVESTIGATIONS AND DECISIONS

Whatever the problem which confronts the philosopher, he must begin, *if* he is to resolve his problem, with *pragmatical investigation;* that is, he must begin by attempting to *discover,* through investigation of the contexts in which the language of his problem is used, *how* that language is used. Even if the question by which he expresses his problem is one which the philosopher asks himself, he must first of all determine (*if* he is to proceed systematically, knowledgeably, and not haphazardly) (a) *what he is doing with the language of his question,* and (b) *what it is he wants to discover and decide with regard to that language.* In short, he must discover (a) how the language of his question is used, and (b) what kind of question it is.

The philosopher must investigate his use of language even though he may not know that he is doing so; he must discover how he uses the language of his question and what he is using it for, even though it may never occur to him to consider his problem as one having something to do with language.

It is possible to proceed linguistically, that is, by paying attention to the uses, meanings, and forms of certain expressions, without knowing that one is doing so, for philosophical problems may be expressed either linguistically or nonlinguistically: they may be expressed so as to be clearly recognizable as having something to do with language, or they may be expressed as if they were about nothing other than the "world." But no philosopher can systematically resolve a philosophical problem—for example, the problem of determining the nature of man—without considering, through analysis, the sort of entity meant by a term used to designate the subject matter of the problem.

To ask "What is the essential nature of man?" is to ask something like "Where shall I draw the line in defining the term 'man,' relative to my use of that term?" A philosopher may put the problem to himself in the first way, but he resolves it only by attending to the matters he would have to attend to if he proceeded systematically to handle the problem as expressed in the second (linguistical) way.

When Wittgenstein, in Section 65 of the *Philosophical Investigations,* imagined someone's asking him to say what the essence of language is, to explain what is common to the various "language-games," he replied that language-games have no common feature, that "they are *related* to one another in many different ways." To illustrate the method which led him to this conclusion, Wittgenstein (Section 66) then considered "the proceedings that we call 'games,' " and asked, "What is common to them all?" The suggestion is that the question "What is the essence of games?" functions as the question "What is common to all games?" functions; in turn, the latter question, when translated into a linguistical (and, in this case, semantical) question, becomes: "What is common, if anything, to the proceedings we call 'games'?" Wittgenstein's answer, as most persons who have any interest in philosophical method know, is that if you *"look and see,"* you will find that there is nothing common to all those proceedings called "games"; "And the result of this examination is: we see a complicated network of similarities overlapping and crisscrossing: sometimes overall similarities, sometimes similarities of detail."

We call the kind of examination which Wittgenstein undertook— and which he repeated throughout his philosophical investigations and invited his readers to undertake—*pragmatical investigation.* Pragmatical investigation (or analysis) is the activity of attempting to discover how certain expressions are used. The term "games" is used (usually) to *refer* to various kinds of activities; the term has a *descriptive function.* But when one attempts to describe what is common to games (in other words, to make clear the meaning of "games," to give the essence of games), one discovers (so Wittgenstein claimed) that there is nothing common to all games. The pragmatical investigation showed the futility of attempting to resolve the semantical problem of making clear the meaning of "games" (which is how one handles the problem of getting at the essence of games). Or, we should say, the investigation showed (or was presumed to show) that one cannot *by investigation alone* resolve the semantical problem as to the meaning of *"games"* (the essence of games). But there is still the opportunity, which Wittgenstein tended to ignore or overlook, of constructing a definition of "games" by the use of which one could give a definitive (but creative) answer to a question about the essence of games. One might take advantage of the ambiguity of such a term as "amusing," or one might, by stipulation, rule out many of those cases now conventionally called "games." The decision to use a term (or expression) in a certain way is a *pragmatical decision*; the statement of the rule by which the principle (if any) of the decision is made clear is a semantical statement, the result of a *semantical decision.*

The question as to whether it is ever advisable to construct definitions which are based on the results of pragmatical investigation, but which are creative in that they go beyond or limit the class of entities ordinarily designated by the term being defined, is a practical question, best answered by consideration of the particular circumstances confronting the philosopher: What does he stand to gain or lose by framing a meaning, say of the term "games," which is at variance with the meaning of the term as actually employed? The current fashion of parading paradigm cases (prime examples) and showing, without describing, their similarities and differences is a sign of the present ascendancy of pragmatical investigation—the result, in all probability, of Wittgenstein's influence. But there is no reason why philosophers should continue to elect to remain at this first level of philosophical work, and there is no reason for supposing that the majority of philosophers ever have remained or will choose to remain at that level. At the same time one must recognize the chastening effect of pragmatical investigation when, in the hands of a master like John Austin, it is used to check the creative extravagance of philosophers who attempt, without properly disciplining themselves by grounding their work in linguistical analysis, to undertake tasks which call for philosophical construction.

The order of philosophical investigations and decisions can be summarized as follows:

1.1 *Pragmatical investigation:* the examination of the functioning, in context, of the expressions involved in the statement of a problem;

1.2 *Pragmatical construction* (by decision): the decision as to how expressions involved in a problem are henceforth to be used;

2.1 *Semantical investigation:* the analysis, preparatory to the framing of a definition, of *common features* of matters designated by a term in use, or of features that can be *said* to be common because of the utility of certain terms or expressions that can be used to designate a number of things which, although not precisely alike in kind, not even generically, nevertheless bear certain "family resemblances" —as Wittgenstein calls them—to one another;

2.2 *Semantical construction* (by decision): the framing of a definition which, although grounded in use, may to some extent (even radically) modify the ordinary use of the term defined;

3.1 *Logical investigation:* the analysis of the formal structure of statements that (by steps 2.1 and 2.2) have been semantically clarified;

3.2 *Logical construction:* the decision to govern the use of an expression so as to retain a certain logical form of that expression;

4.1 *Metaphysical investigation:* a study of the logical possibilities within an area logically closed to empirical investigation;

4.2 *Metaphysical construction:* the commitment by faith to the truth or falsity of a statement shown by logical analysis, or declared by logical decision, to be a contingent statement not subject to empirical confirmation. (Such a statement would be neither tautologous, that is, true by logical form; nor self-contradictory, false by logical form.)

What makes this order necessary? Why is the metaphysical built upon, but not exhausted by, the logical? Why is the logical built upon the semantical, the semantical upon the pragmatical, and the pragmatical upon the philosopher's use of language?

The answer involves reference to logical connections established by the description of philosophical order:

1. The *pragmatical* depends upon the user's use of language because no expression has a use abstracted from its use in some person's discourse.

2. The *semantical* depends upon the *pragmatical* because the meaning of an expression depends upon the use of the expression; an expression cannot be meaningful unless it is used.

3. The *logical* depends upon the *semantical* because the form (logical structure) of an expression depends upon the meaning of the expression; an expression cannot have a structure unless meaning, itself contingent upon use, fixes that structure.

4. The *metaphysical* depends upon the logical because logical restraints prohibit empirical resolution of the problem of deciding upon the truth value of a statement which logical analysis and decision determine as contingent.

Consider the question "What is a tumbler?" One might ask, "What is the nature of tumblers? What is their essence?" Perhaps one assumes that if a number of things are tumblers, they must have something in common; one then asks, "What is common to all tumblers?" Or one might put the question linguistically, as a semantical question, "What is the meaning of the term 'tumbler'?"

But how would it be possible to *discover,* or with some basis in ordinary discourse to *decide upon,* the meaning of the term "tumbler" if there were no specific instances of the use of the term to which one could refer? If the question is to be answerable, it must be complete; it must involve a reference, whether implicit or explicit, to some body of usage. (When in his *Philosophical Investigations* Wittgenstein invited the reader to consider the proceedings called "games," he added, "I mean board games, card games, ball games, Olympic games, and so on.") To indicate the use of the term "tumbler," one might say, "The tumblers are now doing cartwheels"; or, if that were not the use in question, one might say, "The tumblers are singing in the trees; I mean—those birds"; or "The tumblers—those glasses on the table"; or "The tumbler in that lock, for example"; or "That part of the washing machine"; and so on. A person may know how to use a word; he may be able to give examples of his use of the term; but he may not be able to make the meaning clear through a definition. We know how to *use* the word "spiral," but can we give its meaning in a definition? We can pragmatically exhibit our use of the term, but can we semantically clarify its meaning? If it is possible to define the meaning of a term—if the meaning of a term is something definable in that the term is used as a sign by which one calls attention to a number of things that can be covered by a definitive description—it is possible only because the term has a use to which the semantical analyst can refer. Thus, prior to analyzing the meaning of an expression, the semantical analyst must undertake pragmatical analysis; before deciding on a definition (which may, to some extent, broaden or narrow the class of things to which the use of the term calls attention), the philosopher must attend to the discourse in which the term is at work.

If the term "tumbler" has a use subject to investigation, there is some body of discourse to which one can refer; if there is a body of discourse, there is someone who has used the term. *A question about use is made clear by reference to the discourse which illustrates that use.*

If the term "tumbler" has a meaning, it has a use subject to investigation. *A question about meaning is made clear by reference to the use in question.*

Now, to appreciate the dependency of the logical upon the semantical, the relation of form to meaning, consider the statement "Not all men are men." What is the logical character of that statement? Only by determining its logical character can we be sure whether or not the proposition sets forth a possibility. If the term "men" means the same thing in both instances, the sentence is a contradiction in terms; but *does* the word "men" mean the same thing in both instances? The statement cannot be *nobody's* statement: it must have a use, and the term "men" must have a use, but not necessarily the same use, both times it is used in the statement. Pragmatical investigation might show that the term "men" in its first appearance was being used to designate human beings; in its second appearance, the term (vocable) was being used to designate *courageous* human beings: "Not all men are *men.*—Not all men are *really* men!" The definition of "men" as first used would differ from the definition of "men" as used on the second occasion within the statement. Semantical construction (decision and possible refinement), based upon the results of semantical investigation (the search for "common" features), itself based upon pragmatical investigation (the analysis of the function of the terms in use), would make the difference of meanings clear, and upon logical analysis the contingent character of the statement would be made evident. "Must God be omniscient?" We ask, "What is the meaning of 'God' and 'omniscient,' as you are using the terms?" (Semantical question, put linguistically.) The questioner is not able to answer the semantical question, perhaps. We ask, "How are you using the terms? Show me how." (Pragmatical question and injunction.) If we decide upon answers to our semantical questions, we can decide upon an answer to the logical question. But since the answers to our semantical questions depend upon the answers to our pragmatical questions, we examine the relevant uses of terms; we begin with pragmatical investigation.

Thus, if an expression has a logical form, it has a meaning subject to investigation. *A question about logical form is made clear by reference to the meanings involved.*

But *the meanings depend on the uses of terms.*

And *the uses of terms are exhibited in somebody's discourse.*

Finally, metaphysical commitment (if it is not to be immediately vulnerable) requires logical investigation and decision because a commitment by faith to the truth or falsity of a statement logically closed to empirical testing involves the implicit claim that there are logical restrictions upon empirical investigation and, furthermore, that the statement represents a logical possibility but not a necessity. The statement is neither analytically (logically) true nor false, but contingent.

For example, the metaphysical claim that *the soul survives the death of the body* cannot itself survive as a metaphysical claim unless the terms of the claim are used in such a way that the statement of the claim is both *meaningful* (semantical investigation based on pragmatical investigation will show whether it is), and *contingent* (to be settled by logical analysis based on semantical decisions), and *not empirically soluble because of logical restrictions* (to be uncovered by logical analysis). To show that the statement "The soul survives the death of the body" is contingent would involve clearing up the meanings of the terms "soul," "death," "survives," "body," and of the statement as a whole by considering, first of all, the use of the statement and, thus, the degree to which the statement and its terms have descriptive functions. If definitive descriptions can be devised to summarize those functions—if the meaning is made clear in this way— logical structure is then determinable; *only* if the meaning of the statement is made clear is the logical structure determinable.

Thus metaphysical commitment, if it is to be philosophically justifiable, demands most in the way of preparation for its defense. The metaphysical claim is, methodologically speaking, the most complex sort of philosophical claim, for, although it is fundamentally an expression of faith, it is also, at least implicitly, a logical, hence semantical, hence pragmatical claim.

The order of philosophical composition, then, is the following: pragmatical, semantical, logical, metaphysical. Each stage involves an investigative (analytic) and a constructive phase; but since one need not go beyond the investigative phase if the problem does not demand it, the philosopher may stop at any one of the eight stages of philosophical practice.

A *critic* who concerns himself with a metaphysical claim (or with what is purported to be a metaphysical claim) should first of all determine whether the series of vocables which is intended to be an expression of a claim is, in fact, a linguistically effective utterance. He determines whether the expression exhibits a use of language by undertaking *pragmatical investigation*. If the expression has a use and the philosopher consents to that use or modifies it (one hopes, with the consent of the person who ventures the claim), he has passed to the stage of *pragmatical decision* (or *construction*). The critic must then determine, by looking for common features in the use (*when* the meaning *is* the use) or among the entities designated by the terms (*when* the terms have a designative or descriptive function), whether or not there is a ground for saying that the terms of the expression and the expression itself are meaningful and definable. His inquiry is at the third stage: *semantical investigation* (or *analysis*). The fourth stage is to settle on definitions *(semantical decision or construction)*. The fifth stage is to undertake *logical analysis* of the statement. Then, having committed himself to a certain logical form (as the result of a *logical decision*) and having found (if he has) that the statement is neither tautologous nor self-contradictory but contingent in logical character, the critic seeks to determine whether the logical possibility which the statement expresses is one which, because of logical barriers, is closed to empirical resolution (seventh step: *metaphysical investigation,* a logical investigation undertaken in the effort to discover the area within which faith must operate if the problem is to be resolved). If the critic agrees that the matter is open for metaphysical commitment, he may then declare his own commitment. Either he agrees in faith with the proponent of the original claim (in which case the critic assents to the claim), or he differs in faith (in which case he denies the claim).

We do not suggest that a philosopher might not begin his philosophical effort with the *making of a claim*. But if a philosopher begins with a claim, he must attend to the uses, meanings, and forms of the statements he uses if he is to *defend his claim philosophically.*

One final matter in connection with the order within philosophy: Why does semantical construction (for example) depend on semantical analysis? Could not a philosopher, in making a claim in regard to essence, simply invent—without any attention whatsoever to any conventional uses of a vocable—a definition for that vocable? A man *could* do this: make up definitions out of the blue, without recourse to usage. But no claim as to the essence of the matter would then be regarded as a philosophical claim—or, at least, as a responsible philosophical claim. Philosophical claims concerning essences, that is, semantical claims, are interesting and provocative because the philosopher who presents the claim is in effect suggesting that he has isolated, from the multiplicity of cases designated by a certain term, some "common" feature. Maybe what the philosopher claims is the result of a certain amount of word play or usage refinement; maybe what he says is striking because it throws language into a new gear—but whatever he does in the framing of his definitions, he works *from* some conventional usage of terms. He may not *hold* to that usage; but at least, in some way or other, he counts on it. Entirely novel terms may be useful as technical terms in the exposition of a claim, but the claim cannot be concerned with the essence which that novel definition picks out. When we ask, "What is beauty?" or "What is justice?" we will not accept answers which rest on purely arbitrary and wholly novel definitions. The ideas which philosophers make clear are the ideas which some conventional discourse provokes.

PHILOSOPHICAL STYLE

Still to be considered are matters of philosophical style—not matters of individual literary style, but matters of formulation, questions as to the way in which something philosophical is said.

Let us consider an amusing and perplexing problem drawn from an essay entitled "What Pragmatism Means" (from *Pragmatism,* 1907) by the American philosopher William James:

Some years ago, being with a camping party in the mountains,

I returned from a solitary ramble to find every one engaged in a ferocious metaphysical dispute. The corpus *of the dispute was a squirrel—a live squirrel supposed to be clinging to one side of a tree-trunk; while over against the tree's opposite side a human being was imagined to stand. This human witness tries to get sight of the squirrel by moving rapidly round the tree, but no matter how fast he goes, the squirrel moves as fast in the opposite direction, and always keeps the tree between himself and the man, so that never a glimpse of him is caught. The resultant metaphysical problem now is this:* Does the man go round the squirrel or not? *He goes round the tree, sure enough, and the squirrel is on the tree; but does he go round the squirrel?*

Consider the problem before reading further. How would you answer the question, and how would you argue in defense of your answer? What kind of philosophical question is being asked?

James goes on:

In the unlimited leisure of the wilderness discussion had been worn threadbare. Every one had taken sides and was obstinate; and the numbers on both sides were even. Each side, when I appeared, therefore appealed to me to make it a majority. Mindful of the scholastic adage that whenever you meet a contradiction you must make a distinction, I immediately sought and found one, as follows; "Which party is right," I said, "depends on what you practically *mean by 'going round' the squirrel. If you mean passing from the north of him to the east, then to the south, then to the west, and then to the north of him again, obviously the man does go round him, for he occupies these successive positions. But if on the contrary you mean being first in front of him, then on the right of him, then behind him, then on his left, and finally in front again, it is quite obvious that the man fails to go round him, for by compensating movements the squirrel makes, he keeps his belly turned towards the man all the time, and his back turned away. Make the distinction, and there is no occasion for any further dispute. You are both right and both wrong, according as you conceive the verb 'to go round' in one practical fashion or the other."*

Although one or two of the hotter disputants called my speech a shuffling evasion, saying they wanted no quibbling or scholastic

*hair-splitting, but meant just plain honest English "round," the major-
ity seemed to think that the distinction had assuaged the dispute.*

*I tell this trivial anecdote because it is a peculiarly simple example
of what I wish to speak of as* the pragmatic method. *The pragmatic
method is primarily a method of settling metaphysical disputes that
otherwise might be interminable. Is the world one or many?—fated or
free?—material or spiritual?—here are notions either of which may or
may not hold good of the world; and disputes over such notions are
unending. The pragmatic method in such cases is to try to interpret
each notion by tracing its respective practical consequences. What
difference would it practically make to any one if this notion rather
than that notion were true? If no practical difference whatever can be
traced, then the alternatives mean practically the same thing, and all
dispute is idle. Whenever a dispute is serious, we ought to be able to
show some practical difference that might follow from one side or
the other's being right.*

(In his comment on the problem, James describes what he calls
"the pragmatic method" of settling disputes he calls "metaphysical."
He speaks of trying "to interpret each notion by tracing its respective
practical consequences." To trace out the practical consequences of
a "notion" and to discover how the term in question is being used—
how it functions, practically, as a linguistical instrument—are practically the same thing: what James calls "the pragmatic method" we
call "pragmatical investigation." The questions which James, in line
with tradition although somewhat wryly, calls "metaphysical"—including the problem of the man and the squirrel—are questions we
call "pragmatical." In contending that these so-called "metaphysical"
problems are "serious" only when some practical difference follows
from "one side or the other's being right," James shows his concern
with what we have decided to call "pragmatical" method.)

Notice that the *questioner,* the man who provokes philosophical
discussion by asking, "Does the man go round the squirrel?" cannot
be using the word "round" in either of the senses James spelled out:
either to mean traveling a path which encloses the path traveled by
the squirrel, that is, going to the west, north, east, and south of the
squirrel (or vice versa), in which case, the man surely goes round

the squirrel, and there is no problem—or to mean "being first in front of him, then on the right of him . . . ," and so on, in which case, the man obviously does *not* go round the squirrel, and again there is no problem. We realize that the man who asks the question might not himself be bothered by the problem the question poses; he might be a teacher, or a gadfly. The question he asks is effective philosophically because it leaves the question of the use of the term "round" open; it is as if the questioner had asked, "Should we say that the man goes round' the squirrel?" Or he might have mentioned the word "round" with a rising inflection, so as to show that the problem is one of deciding on the use of the term: "Does the man go *round* the squirrel?" But by asking, in the tone one might use to ask a factual question, "Does the man go round the squirrel?" attention is diverted from the pragmatical problem involved, although every effort to resolve the problem involves pragmatical decisions.

The pragmatical problem arises because the case is not one to which any "plain, honest English 'round' " applies. Ordinarily we would say that a man goes "round" (or "around") anything he circles, but the imaginary case is peculiar in that the squirrel keeps making "compensating movements." The case is like any ordinary case of going around something in that the man circles the thing in question: why not say that the man goes "around" the squirrel? But the case is different from the usual case in that the squirrel makes compensating movements, and this difference would be significant if, say, we were attempting to get "around" him to look at a spot on his right-hand side; so why not say that the man does *not* go "around" the squirrel? Each way of talking has its advantages, but each way also leaves something out.

The quarrel comes from not recognizing the problem as pragmatical and from disagreeing as to what ought to be said in describing the situation. The question is *pragmatical* because it is a question as to how the word "round" ought to be used under these circumstances not covered by any habitual mode of description. We might say that the question *breeds an ambiguity* in that the word "round" (or "around"), not ordinarily ambiguous, shows its potentiality for ambiguity. The man who asked the question was clever in that he saw how some philosophers would be tempted to talk the one way, some the other—precisely because, in this case, conventional usage cannot come into play, and yet there are important distinctions to be made.

Philosophers are like artists in that philosophers attempt to fashion persuasive and illuminating descriptions of "reality"—of whatever provokes their interest. But if a philosopher decides to say, "Philosophers are literary artists who aim at expressing new truths about matters of common experience and concern," the philosophical critic replies, "But notice the differences! *Are* philosophers *artists*? Are they *really* artists? Is their experience truly *common*? Is any truth really *new*?" Ordinarily, neither the philosophical critic nor the critical philosopher is inclined to make the pragmatical issues explicit by asking, "*Ought* we to describe philosophers—that is, those to whom we call attention through our use of the term 'philosophers'—as 'artists'? Wouldn't that be misleading? Wouldn't that obscure the differences between those we call 'philosophers' and those we call 'artists'? Might it not be better to examine the multiplicity and variety of activities in which those we call 'philosophers' are engaged?"

Philosophers *tend* (although in this age of self-conscious linguistical philosophy they need not do so) to make their claims, ask their questions, and offer their criticism as if they were concerned not with language but with the *world*. And, in fact, *we might decide to say,* philosophers *are* concerned with the world, but their concern is not to get at the facts—they know the facts already—but to see the world better, to understand it from the new perspectives and in the new dimensions and with the new emphasis which novel, persuasive, and illuminating descriptions make possible. To get at the world, to fix the objects of his investigations, to isolate "essences," to find possibilities, impossibilities, and necessities, and to discover the barriers with which logic confronts faith, the philosopher must use, and attend to the uses of, language.

Every philosophical question and every philosophical claim can be stated in a way which makes explicit the linguistical problem involved, but every problem can also be stated, and more frequently is stated, in a way which hides—sometimes deliberately, sometimes not—the linguistical aspect of the problem.

PRAGMATICAL QUESTIONS

The question "How is the mind related to the body?" is often taken as an invitation to consider how one *thing,* the mind, is causally or spatially related to another *thing,* the body. But the question can be put, "How is what we call 'the mind' related to what we call 'the body'?" or, even better, "How is our use of the term 'mind' related to our use of the term 'body'?" The suggestion that mind is a function of the organism, or, alternatively, that we use the term "mind" in talking about the capacity of an organism to add numbers, to draw conclusions, and so forth, is more likely to come up once the problem is understood linguistically, pragmatically.

The questions of which the British philosopher John Wisdom is so fond, questions like "Is he sane or is he not?", "Was he negligent or was he not?", "Are men ever really free?" are pragmatical questions in *nonlinguistical* form. (Of course, his examples are not always expressions of philosophical problems; the point of them is to show, indirectly and somewhat ironically, that philosophical problems are often matters to be settled by making a judgment as to which of various alternative descriptions, apparently conflicting, might best be used in cases in which an appeal to ordinary usage does no good.) Put *linguistically,* pragmatical problems, in question form, become: "Everything considered, should we say that the man goes 'round' the squirrel?", "Taking all the known facts into account, would it be more illuminating to describe him as 'sane,' even though the term would then be used in a somewhat unconventional way, or to describe him as 'insane,' although that term, too, would have to be used unconventionally?", "Should we call philosophers 'artists' or shouldn't we?"

SEMANTICAL QUESTIONS

In Book I of Plato's *Republic* Socrates asks Cephalus, ". . . as concerning justice, what is it?" and he suggests that justice must be more than speaking the truth and paying one's debts, for:

Suppose that a friend when in his right mind has deposited arms with me and he asks for them when he is not in his right mind, ought I to give them back to him? No one would say *that I ought or that I should be right in doing so,* any more than they would say *that I ought always to speak the truth to one who is in his condition* . . . . (Emphasis added.)

When Cephalus says, "You are quite right," Socrates replies, "But then . . . speaking the truth and paying your debts is not a correct definition of justice." Here, as elsewhere, Socrates quite properly identifies questions as to the *nature* of something with questions as to the *meaning of certain expressions in use.*

Put *nonlinguistically,* semantical problems, expressed as questions, have the form: "What is justice?", "What is philosophy?", "What is man?", "What is fine art essentially?", "What is the essence of beauty?", "What is the nature of science?", "What is being as being?", and the like.

Put *linguistically,* the questions become: "What is the meaning of the term 'justice,' as that term is used in the following instances . . .?", "What is the meaning of the term 'philosophy,' as that term is used . . .?", and so on.

The question considered by Wittgenstein as to the *essence* of games was treated by him as a call for whatever is *common* to all games. Like the question "What is language? What is the essence of language, or of language-games?", which prompted the discussion as to the essence of games, the question concerning the essence of games is *semantical.* The point of Wittgenstein's discussion is that it would be better to undertake the pragmatical survey of the great variety of activities called "games" than to make the effort to find any characteristic common to them all. The problem is semantical, but Wittgenstein refused to handle it semantically for the reason that when he *looked* at games, he *saw* no common element, and he refused to take advantage of the vagueness and ambiguity of certain terms (such as "amusing") in the construction of definitions presumably *reporting* common elements. Nevertheless, definitions which are not misleading are possible, provided the definitive description acquires the wealth of meaning that comes from pragmatical illumination.

LOGICAL QUESTIONS

Philosophical claims about what is necessary, possible, or impossible, when stated *nonlinguistically,* take the following forms (among others): "The soul *must* be immortal," "God *necessarily* exists," "Men *can* err," and so forth. Logical questions take a corresponding form: "Is the soul necessarily immortal?", "Is it possible that God does not exist?", "Can men err?", and so forth.

What are such questions about? As influenced by the nonlinguistical expression of the problems, a student might answer that such questions are about the *soul,* and *God,* and *man.* But when the questions are put *linguistically,* one realizes that it is more illuminating, more revealing of what one has to examine if the questions are to be answered, to say that such questions are about *terms,* such as "soul," "God," and "man," and about their logical relations: "Is the statement 'The soul is immortal,' that is, 'If there is a soul, then it is immortal,' logically true? Would a denial of the statement be self-contradictory?", "Is the statement 'There is a God' logically true? logically false? Is it a meaningful, contingent statement?" "Is it a contradiction in terms to state 'Men err,' or is it no part of the meaning of the term 'men' that the entities so designated be incapable of error?"

Again we see that the resolution of logical problems involves the resolution of semantical problems, and that the resolution of the latter, in turn, involves the resolution of pragmatical problems.

In summary: a philosophical claim about a *necessity* is properly and methodologically understood when it is understood as attributing necessity not to the *state of affairs* to which the statement of necessity refers, but as attributing necessity (logical truth) to a *statement* of the matter. To say that "*S* (some *state of affairs*) is *necessary*" is to imply that " '*S*' (a *statement* of that state of affairs) is *logically true,* analytically true, true by form, true by definition, tautological." To say that a certain state of affairs is *impossible* is, in effect, to say that a statement of that state of affairs would be a contradiction, a logically false statement, capable of being shown, by logical analysis, to be false. To say that a state of affairs is *possible* is to contend that the statement of that state of affairs would *not* be a contradiction.

METAPHYSICAL QUESTIONS

The question "*Is* there a life after death?" (as distinguished from the *logical* question "*Could* there be life after death?") is a *metaphysical* question provided that the language of the question is so used that the question is *meaningful* and refers to a *contingency* which, because of logical barriers, is not open to empirical investigation. Put linguistically, the question becomes: "Is the statement 'There is a life after death,' as used in such-and-such a way, contingent in that it is not logically true or false; would it be contradictory to state, 'We have resolved by empirical investigation that the statement "There is a life after death" is factually true,' and how do you, in faith, stand committed with regard to the truth or falsity of the statement 'There is a life after death'?"

What kind of logical barrier stands in the way, if it does, of empirically resolving the question of "life" after death? Perhaps, relative to the use of the term "evidence," *nothing counts as evidence* in support (or denial) of the claim: neither sounds in the night, erratically behaving objects, wisps of foglike substance in the cemetery, nor anything else. Perhaps, for the man who asks the question, nothing could settle the matter other than the experience of finding himself, as a person, surviving the corruption of his body. Thus, for him as a human being no scientific resolution of the problem is possible, since for him no observation in *this* life counts as a source of evidence bearing on the problem.

What kind of logical barrier stands in the way, when it does, of empirically resolving the question as to *whether unobserved objects exist?* Ordinarily, in nonphilosophical contexts, the question as to whether an unobserved object (say, an automobile, a coat, or a wallet) "exists" does *not* come up. The question is whether the object, which is presently unobserved, is where one left it; or the question is as to where the object is. But the philosophical concern is not a practical one. The philosophical question "Do unobserved, unperceived objects exist?" is asked in such a way that the subject matter of the problem may be said to be *objects* "defined" as *unobserved.* The problem becomes intriguing because one *could not,* by observation, determine that the observed objects were, while being observed, observed to be unobserved. The question as to whether there are such objects, defined as unobserved, becomes a metaphysical question: the logical barrier to empirical resolution is the barrier set up by using the term "unobserved objects" semantically. The egocentric predicament is a logical predicament which makes metaphysics possible.

We are now in a position to appreciate the claim that the classification of philosophical problems by *subject matter* is misleading in that it obscures the linguistical aspects of philosophical problems. A question that appears to be about *souls* may be about the *use* of the term "soul," the *definition* of the term, the *logical structure* of statements in which the term appears, or *contingent matters* beyond the range of empirical resolution. Consequently, the attempt to achieve resolution of a problem about souls proceeds effectively only when it is disciplined by attention to the linguistical problems involved. *Decisions,* based upon *investigation,* have to be made with regard to the *uses* of various critical terms; and then, perhaps (depending on the philosophical type of problem), decisions have to be made concerning definitions, logical form, and matters that, because of logical restrictions, challenge faith.

Let us look at some of the problems cited under the heading "metaphysics" at the beginning of the chapter. The question "What is being as such?" ordinarily functions as a *semantical* question; the problem is to define (or at least to relate the meaning of the term to its uses) the term "being"; no act of faith is needed. The question "Can a study of the being of things reveal generic features that belong to God?" is a *logical* question; the answer depends on the decision to define the term "God" by making reference to characteristics said to be "common" to the things called "things." The question "Is the universe finite or infinite?" may very well be asked *pragmatically;* the problem then would be to decide whether, everything considered, one is to describe what one calls the "universe" as "finite" or "infinite." Of course, such a question—that is, such a set of terms—may be used in such a way that the question is one for physics, not philosophy; or it may be asked in such a way that the problem does indeed call for speculation and a leap of faith. But if discovering the character of a problem depends on discovering the *use* of the language by which the problem is expressed, then no *list* of "questions" can make clear the various kinds of philosophical problems. A classification of problems according to the kinds of inquiry and decision needed to resolve them would be more helpful; but the task of making such a classification involves careful attention to the linguistical perplexities, usually hidden, which give rise to the questions. Hence, the best way to appreciate the character of philosophical questions and claims is to analyze philosophical arguments *one by one*. By moving critically into the context in which a philosophical claim is made and defended, one learns, through understanding and participation, how the philosopher uses language in the attempt to throw the world into a new and revealing perspective.

QUESTIONS FOR DISCUSSION

1. The claim is made that *all* philosophical problems involve linguistical issues and that a classification of philosophical problems by the use of the terms "pragmatical," "semantical," "logical," and "metaphysical" would be more helpful in directing attention toward the method of resolution than classification by subject matter would be. Can you think of any problem, which would generally be called "philosophical," that does not appear to be either pragmatical, semantical, logical, or metaphysical?

2. What kinds of logical restrictions make metaphysical problems possible? (Or, are those critics right who claim that there are no legitimate metaphysical problems?) Distinguish between logical restrictions and practical restrictions on observation.

3. In what way, if at all, do linguistical problems have something to do with the "world"? What is to be gained, if anything, by a survey of the various ways in which an expression *is* used? What might be gained by a consideration of the ways in which an expression *might well* be used?

4. Classify the following questions according to the level at which they could *first* be resolved. (Thus: if a question *could* be resolved pragmatically, although a semantical analysis might further illuminate the matter, classify the question as pragmatical; if a pragmatical survey would not be sufficient to yield a response to a question, but a definition would count as an adequate answer, classify the problem as semantical; and so on.) Consider what kind of problem would *ordinarily* be expressed by a given question. As an additional exercise, consider what kinds of problems might conceivably be expressed by the question; that is, by the interrogative expression cited. You may use the letters "P," "S," "L," and "M" as abbreviations.

1. Can God do the impossible?
2. What is the essential nature of man?
3. What is an angel essentially?
4. Is a handsome man beautiful?
5. How many angels can dance on the head of a pin?
6. Do angels ever dance on the heads of pins?
7. Will virtue be rewarded in the afterlife?
8. What is truth?
9. Are some momentous questions really trivial?
10. Are some insane men saner than some politicians?
11. Is man lost in a universe which is meaningless to him?
12. Can one play chess without the queen?
13. Could a triangle have a missing side?
14. If there is motion, must there be things capable of motion?
15. Has the time of your death been determined?
16. Are you fated to die at a certain time?
17. If God is all-perfect, how is evil possible?
18. Does "I ought" imply "I can"?
19. Is our idea of a physical thing our idea of its effect on our senses?
20. Is knowledge really possible?
21. Are all men self-seeking egoists?
22. Is any man ever really free?
23. When a tree falls in the forest and no one is around, does it make a noise as it falls?
24. Does a coat in a closed closet, in the darkness, have any color?
25. Is it true that some souls go to Heaven and that others go to Hell?
26. Could a man think he was Napoleon and yet be sane?
27. Doesn't the existence of God follow from the fact that God is love and that some men love their fellowmen?
28. Do women know some things by intuition?
29. Is the world flat or round?

30. Is the world really round?
31. Can we ever discover whether the color of a sensation is the same color as the object sensed?
32. Does an afterimage have more than one side?
33. Is truth subjective or objective?
34. Is truth relative or absolute?
35. Are values subjective or objective?
36. Isn't justice merely a matter of opinion?
37. Doesn't the existence of God follow from the fact that the ear is beautifully designed to make hearing possible?
38. Is the ear designed to make hearing possible?
39. Does God love all men?
40. Could God be dead?
41. Does religion involve faith in the supernatural?
42. Must not the universe have had a beginning?
43. Is virtue worthwhile on its own account?
44. Can a metaphysical theory be disproved?
45. Is everyone subconsciously, if not consciously, selfish?
46. Can you ever really know what another person is thinking?
47. Are there any self-evident truths?
48. Is murder ever morally justifiable?
49. Are our decisions free or determined?
50. Does man have a conscience?

II

MILL

SOME KINDS OF PLEASURE ARE
MORE DESIRABLE AND MORE VALUABLE
THAN OTHERS—*a pragmatical claim*

MILL'S ARGUMENT

The creed which accepts as the foundation of morals "utility" or the "greatest happiness principle" holds that actions are right in proportion as they tend to promote happiness; wrong as they tend to produce the reverse of happiness. By happiness is intended pleasure and the absence of pain; by unhappiness, pain and the privation of pleasure.

*   *   *   *

Now such a theory of life excites in many minds, and among them in some of the most estimable in feeling and purpose, inveterate dislike. To suppose that life has (as they express it) no higher end than pleasure—no better and nobler object of desire and pursuit— they designate as utterly mean and groveling, as a doctrine worthy only of swine, to whom the followers of Epicurus were, at a very early period, contemptuously likened . . . .

*   *   *   *

MILL'S ARGUMENT • 33

. . . *But there is no known Epicurean theory of life which does not assign to the pleasures of the intellect, of the feelings and imagination, and of the moral sentiments a much higher value as pleasures than to those of mere sensation. It must be admitted, however, that utilitarian writers in general have placed the superiority of mental over bodily pleasures chiefly in the greater permanency, safety, uncostliness, etc., of the former—that is, in their circumstantial advantages rather than in their intrinsic nature. And on all these points utilitarians have fully proved their case; but they might have taken the other and, as it may be called, higher ground with entire consistency. It is quite compatible with the principle of utility to recognize the fact that some kinds of pleasure are more desirable and more valuable than others. It would be absurd that, while in estimating all other things quality is considered as well as quantity, the estimation of pleasure should be supposed to depend on quantity alone.*

If I am asked what I mean by difference of quality in pleasures, or what makes one pleasure more valuable than another, merely as a pleasure, except its being greater in amount, there is but one possible answer. Of two pleasures, if there be one to which all or almost all who have experience of both give a decided preference, irrespective of any feeling of moral obligation to prefer it, that is the more desirable pleasure. If one of the two is, by those who are competently acquainted with both, placed so far above the other that they prefer it, even though knowing it to be attended with a greater amount of discontent, and would not resign it for any quantity of the other pleasure which their nature is capable of, we are justified in ascribing to the preferred enjoyment a superiority in quality so far outweighing quantity as to render it, in comparison, of small account.

Now it is an unquestionable fact that those who are equally acquainted with and equally capable of appreciating and enjoying both do give a most marked preference to the manner of existence which employs their higher faculties. Few human creatures would consent to be changed into any of the lower animals for a promise of the fullest allowance of a beast's pleasures; no intelligent human being would consent to be a fool, no instructed person would be an ignoramus, no person of feeling and conscience would be selfish and base, even though they should be persuaded that the fool, the dunce, or the rascal is better satisfied with his lot than they are with theirs. They would not resign what they possess more than he for the most complete satisfaction of all the desires which they have in common with him. If they ever fancy they would, it is only in cases of unhappiness so extreme that to escape from it they would exchange their lot for almost any other, however undesirable in their own eyes. A being of higher faculties requires more to make him happy, is capable probably of more acute suffering, and certainly accessible to it at more points, than one of an inferior type; but in spite of these liabilities, he can never really wish to sink into what he feels to be a lower grade of existence.

* * * *

. . . It is better to be a human being dissatisfied than a pig satisfied; better to be Socrates dissatisfied than a fool satisfied. And if the fool, or the pig, are of a different opinion, it is because they only know their own side of the question. The other party to the comparison knows both sides.

* * * *

. . . It may be questioned whether anyone who has remained equally susceptible to both classes of pleasures ever knowingly and calmly preferred the lower, though many, in all ages, have broken down in an ineffectual attempt to combine both.

From this verdict of the only competent judges, I apprehend there can be no appeal. On a question which is the best worth having of two pleasures, or which of two modes of existence is the most grateful to the feelings, apart from its moral attributes and from its consequences, the judgment of those who are qualified by knowledge of both, or if they differ, that of the majority among them, must be admitted as final. And there needs be the less hesitation to accept this judgment respecting the quality of pleasures, since there is no other tribunal to be referred to even on the question of quantity. What means are there of determining which is the acutest of two pains, or the intensest of two pleasurable sensations, except the general suffrage of those who are familiar with both? Neither pains nor pleasures are homogeneous, and pain is always heterogeneous with pleasure. What is there to decide whether a particular pleasure is worth pur-

*chasing at the cost of a particular pain, except the feelings and judg-
ment of the experienced? When, therefore, those feelings and judgment declare the pleasures derived from the higher faculties to be
preferable* in kind, *apart from the question of intensity, to those of
which the animal nature, disjoined from the higher faculties, is susceptible, they are entitled on this subject to the same regard.*

*   *   *   *

*It has already been remarked that questions of ultimate ends do
not admit of proof, in the ordinary acceptation of the term. To be
incapable of proof by reasoning is common to all first principles, to
the first premises of our knowledge, as well as to those of our conduct.
But the former, being matters of fact, may be the subject of a direct
appeal to the faculties which judge of fact—namely, our senses and
our internal consciousness. Can an appeal be made to the same faculties on questions of practical ends? Or by what other faculty is cogni-
zance taken of them?*

*Questions about ends are, in other words, questions what things
are desirable. The utilitarian doctrine is that happiness is desirable,
and the only thing desirable, as an end; all other things being only
desirable as means to that end. What ought to be required of this
doctrine, what conditions is it requisite that the doctrine should ful-
fill—to make good its claim to be believed?*

*The only proof capable of being given that an object is visible
is that people actually see it. The only proof that a sound is audible is
that people hear it; and so of the other sources of our experience. In
like manner, I apprehend, the sole evidence it is possible to produce
that anything is desirable is that people do actually desire it. If the
end which the utilitarian doctrine proposes to itself were not, in theory
and in practice, acknowledged to be an end, nothing could ever convince any person that it was so. No reason can be given why the general happiness is desirable, except that each person, so far as he believes it to be attainable, desires his own happiness. This, however,
being a fact, we have not only all the proof which the case admits of,
but all which it is possible to require, that happiness is a good, that*

each person's happiness is a good to that person, and the general happiness, therefore, a good to the aggregate of all persons.

*   *   *   *

And now to decide whether this is really so, whether mankind do desire nothing for itself but that which is a pleasure to them, or of which the absence is a pain, we have evidently arrived at a question of fact and experience, dependent, like all similar questions, upon evidence. It can only be determined by practiced self-consciousness and self-observation, assisted by observation of others. I believe that these sources of evidence, impartially consulted, will declare that desiring a thing and finding it pleasant, aversion to it and thinking of it as painful, are phenomena entirely inseparable or, rather, two parts of the same phenomenon—in strictness of language, two different modes of naming the same psychological fact; that to think of an object as desirable (unless for the sake of its consequences) and to think of it as pleasant are one and the same thing; and that to desire anything except in proportion as the idea of it is pleasant is a physical and metaphysical impossibility.

[From *Utilitarianism* (1861) by John Stuart Mill (1806–1873).*]

AN ANALYSIS OF MILL'S ARGUMENT

1. THE BASIC CLAIM

Philosophical hedonists agree in claiming that pleasure is good for its own sake. Most hedonists also insist that pleasure is the *only* "intrinsic" good, the only thing worthwhile on its own account, whether or not the *consequences* of being pleased and of having done whatever was necessary to secure pleasure are also worthwhile according to the amount of further pleasure secured. But Mill is distinctive among the philosophical hedonists in that he claims not only that pleasure is the only thing "desirable" as an end, but also that pleasures

Edition used: Liberal Arts Press, Inc., The Bobbs-Merrill Co., Inc., 1957.

vary in quality and that qualitative differences sometimes account for *differences in value,* even in cases in which no quantitative difference can be discovered. In Mill's own words, "some kinds of pleasure are more desirable and more valuable than others." Mill adds, "It would be absurd that, while in estimating all other things quality is considered as well as quantity, the estimation of pleasure should be supposed to depend on quantity alone," and we thereby know that, according to Mill, *it is a difference of quality that makes some pleasures more valuable than others.*

The basic claim may be broken down into a number of separate, but related, claims:

There are pleasures.
Pleasures are sometimes equal in quantity.
Pleasures equal in quantity are sometimes different in quality.
Some pleasures different in quality from other pleasures and equal in quantity to the others are more valuable because of the qualitative difference.

2. THE BASIC ARGUMENT

Mill's argument in support of his claim that qualitative differences make some pleasures more valuable or desirable than others consists primarily of an appeal to the experience of his readers and to their sense of the propriety and accuracy of Mill's descriptions of the matters with which he is concerned. He offers a definition, operational in character, of what is meant by the expression "difference of quality" as he uses that expression; and he also provides an account of the procedure by which one can determine whether or not something in question is desirable. But the operational definitions are offered in preparation for an "appeal to the faculties which judge of fact"; Mill's case does not rest on his definitions.

Let us suggest, by abstraction from the text, the character of Mill's basic argument:

1. "[There are] pleasures of the intellect, of the feelings and imagination, and of the moral sentiments [and] of mere sensation." "[There are] mental [and] bodily pleasures . . . ." "[There are] a beast's pleasures . . . ."

2. "... on the question of quantity .... [the] means ... of determining which is the acutest of two pains, or the intensest of two pleasurable sensations [is] the general suffrage of those who are familiar with both ..."

3. "... some kinds of pleasure are more desirable and more valuable than others."

4. "It would be absurd that, while in estimating all other things quality is considered as well as quantity, the estimation of pleasure should be supposed to depend on quantity alone."

5. "Of two pleasures, if there be one to which all or almost all who have experience of both give a decided preference, irrespective of any feeling of moral obligation to prefer it, that is the more desirable pleasure."

6. "If one of the two [pleasures] is, by those who are competently acquainted with both, placed so far above the other that they prefer it, even though knowing it to be attended with a greater amount of discontent, and would not resign it for any quantity of the other pleasure which their nature is capable of, we are justified in ascribing to the preferred enjoyment a superiority in quality so far outweighing quantity as to render it, in comparison, of small account."

Most simply put, the basic argument *is* the basic claim: "... some kinds of pleasure are more desirable and more valuable than others." The language of the claim, in the context of its utterance, is such that one is justified in distinguishing within the claim the specific claims that (a) there are *pleasures,* (b) there are *kinds* of pleasure, (c) some kinds of pleasure are *more desirable* than others, (d) some kinds of pleasure are *more valuable* than others.

The passages quoted under 1 exhibit Mill's use of the term "pleasures" in such a way that, in effect, we are given *examples* of what he calls "pleasures." (Such examples are sometimes called *paradigm cases.*) The pleasures are initially distinguished, not according to kind or "quality," but according to the faculties or animals involved. The nonlinguistical point of the passages under 1, then, is that *there are pleasures,* or (linguistically) *there are entities designated by the term "pleasures,"* as that term is used by Mill.

The quotations under 2 exhibit Mill's use of the term "quantity" (and also provide an account of the means for deciding which of two pleasures is the greater in quantity). We are shown that to consider the question of the *acuteness* or *intensity* of a pain or pleasure is to consider a "question of quantity."

The statement quoted as 4, considered in context, connects Mill's use of the term "quality" to his use of the term "kind" in such a way as to suggest that to consider the *quality* of one's pleasure and its *kind* is one and the same thing. We are also shown that to consider the *quality* of a pleasure is *different from* considering its *quantity*.

Sentence 5 may be taken as an operational definition of the term "desirable," as that term is used by Mill to describe pleasures. Sentence 6 explains, operationally, what "superiority in quality," as far as pleasures are concerned, consists in, and shows (by comparison with 5) that the expression "more desirable pleasure" (*as used* within a context in which consideration of quantitative differences is ruled out) has the same use as the expression "pleasure [having] superiority in quality." In other words, Mill's account shows that, *as he uses the terms,* a pleasure "more desirable" (than another pleasure) *because of quality* is "superior in quality" (to that other pleasure).

In appraising Mill's argument we are to be concerned, then, *not with the logic* of the argument but with the *advisability of Mill's descriptions.* We are to consider the *pragmatical question* as to whether what Mill calls "pleasures" are sometimes such that it is proper and illuminating to describe them as differing in "quality" and, sometimes because of qualitative differences, as differing in "desirability" or "value."

3. CRITICISM OF THE BASIC ARGUMENT

We must consider several *pragmatical* questions:

1. Are Mill's uses of the terms "pleasure," "pleasures," "quantity," "quality," "desirable," and "valuable" *ordinary* uses with which we are familiar? (This question is relevant in undertaking the appraisal of *this* argument, for Mill nowhere suggests that his uses of these terms are peculiar to himself.)

2. Insofar as Mill's uses of terms differ (if they do) from ordinary uses, are the differences justifiable because of a new emphasis or perspective afforded by the departure from ordinary use?
3. When Mill's use of the language of his claim has been made clear, have we been persuaded that his claim is (a) *true,* (b) *illuminating* in a novel way, and (c) *significant* (worth making)?

We begin by asking whether Mill is talking about *matters with which we are familiar* when he uses the term "pleasures" to mention the "pleasures" of the intellect, mental and bodily "pleasures," and the "pleasures" of the beast; and we also ask whether he talks about these matters in a *way* with which we are familiar.

It very quickly appears that unless we can understand Mill's way of talking about whatever turns out to be the subject of his discourse, we cannot hope to be able to decide whether, indeed, he is talking about matters with which we are familiar.

However, there is very little difficulty in understanding the subject of Mill's discourse. Mill's remarks about the pleasures of the imagination and the intellect, the pleasures of sensation, the mental and bodily pleasures, and the pleasures of the beast are all in accord with a conventional use of the term "pleasures," a use with which we are familiar. We are familiar also with the archaic expression "I wait upon your pleasure" and with that use of the term "pleasure" which makes reference to sensual pleasures exclusively and has a more limited range of reference than it does in Mill's argument; and it is clear that Mill's use of the term "pleasure" is to be distinguished from these latter two uses, even though certain relationships of usage may be made out.

What Mill calls a "pleasure," then, may alternatively be described as (under some circumstances) an "enjoyment" or an "agreeable experience." The pragmatist John Dewey has argued that experiences involve both "doing" and "undergoing," both action and response; and it is true that we sometimes use the term "pleasure" to call attention to an enjoyable activity without making a distinction between what a person does and what he undergoes: "Dining at your house was a pleasure." But Mill's use of the term "pleasures" is such that the emphasis is upon the *undergoing*—upon the "feelings" or "emotions" engendered by activity of a kind we describe as "agreeable." And since it is not critical to Mill's argument that the term "pleasures" be defined, as long as his use of the term is known to us and is fixed enough to provide a basis for consideration of the truth and worth of what he says about pleasures, we can proceed to a consideration of his use of the term "quality," with particular attention to the light such an investigation throws on Mill's use of the term "kind" in the claim being criticized: "some kinds of pleasure are more desirable and more valuable than others."

Mill remarks that "utilitarian writers in general" have emphasized "circumstantial advantages"—such as "permanency, safety, uncostliness"—rather than "intrinsic nature" in arguing that mental pleasures are superior to bodily pleasures. He identifies an appeal to the "intrinsic nature" of pleasures as an appeal on a "higher ground." He then uses the word "kinds" in making the pragmatical claim under consideration. Finally, in the following sentence, Mill introduces the word "quality" while restating the point that some kinds of pleasure are better than others. To talk about the "intrinsic nature" of a pleasure—it thus appears to us as readers—is to talk about whatever is also mentioned by the use of the terms "kind" and "quality." To consider the *quality* of a pleasure is to consider a feature distinct from quantity; the quality or *intrinsic nature* of a pleasure is something other than any circumstantial advantage that might come from being pleased in a certain way.

Mill then offers an account of the meaning of the term "quality" as he uses that word in mentioning the "difference of quality in pleasures." The implicit claim is that the operational definition offered is a true and useful account of the sign function of the term "quality" as that term is used by Mill. The definition is, then, what we would call a *semantical claim;* it purports to be an account of the meaning of the term "quality" relative to a use already exhibited.

In criticizing Mill's semantical claim we are primarily interested, as critics of his pragmatical claim that some kinds of pleasure are more desirable and valuable than others, in using the definition as a rule for the use of the term "quality" in the reading of Mill's argument. Were Mill's definition not in accord with his use, his account would be inconsistent. Since our first concern, however, is to understand Mill, we look for (but do not necessarily expect) consistency. We do not ask that the definition be absolutely invulnerable to the critical attack of one whose only concern is to appraise the definition as a clear and competent report on the meaning of the term "quality" as that term is used by Mill.

Examination of the instances of Mill's use of the term "quality" satisfies us that Mill's definition is in accord with his use and that it makes that use clear. "If I am asked what I mean by *difference of quality* in pleasures, or *what makes one pleasure more valuable than another,*" writes Mill (italics added)—indicating by the additional qualification "merely as a pleasure, except its being greater in amount" that the term "quality" is used to name the difference that can be made out even in cases where there is no quantitative difference—"there is but one possible answer." We are, of course, interested in that answer. But we first notice how the word "quality" functions in Mill's account: as a term to designate, not the quantity, but *the specific character* of an experience already identified as that which Mill calls a "pleasure." Were the term "pleasure" used as the name for the *specific character* of the experience, for the *particular kind* of feeling involved, it would be self-contradictory to speak of *different kinds of pleasure*; but, as we shall see, the term "pleasure" is used to designate a *desirable* feeling, while the term "quality" is used to designate the *specific kind* of desirable feeling. A question as to the "quality" of an experience, then, is a question as to what "specific kind" of experience it is; a question as to the "quality" of a *pleasure* is a question as to what "specific kind" of pleasure it is.

Mill's semantical claim concerning the meaning of the term "quality" is in accord with his pragmatical exhibition; that is, his definition fits his use of the term defined. Let us examine his definitive account:

Of two pleasures, if there be one to which all or almost all who have experience of both give a decided preference, irrespective of any feeling of moral obligation to prefer it, that is the more desirable pleasure. If one of the two is, by those who are competently acquainted with both, placed so far above the other that they prefer it, even though knowing it to be attended with a greater amount of dis-

content, and would not resign it for any quantity of the other pleasure which their nature is capable of, we are justified in ascribing to the preferred enjoyment a superiority in quality so far outweighing quantity as to render it, in comparison, of small account.

The first sentence of this passage is useful as offering a semantical clarification of the term "desirable." We are working within a context in which the concern is with what is *generally* the case. Mill's reference to "all or almost all" does not represent a covert attempt to give priority to the concerns of the majority; rather, the reference is needed in an account which attempts to explain what is meant by saying, without explicit qualification, that one pleasure is "more desirable" than another. The account is such that were one interested in an explanation of the meaning of the expression "more desirable" as used in a statement of the sort "Whatever the others may have preferred, he himself found the one pleasure to be more desirable than the other," one could easily adapt the definition to serve as a semantical explanation of "more desirable" as used in this particular instance; thus: to say that "he himself found the one pleasure to be more desirable than the other" is to suggest that "he himself found that the one pleasure, of which he had experience, was preferred by him to the other pleasure, of which he also had experience." To say that one kind of pleasure is more desirable than another is to suggest that the one kind is *generally* more desirable, that "all or almost all," upon having experience of both, would prefer the one to the other.

Again, in the second sentence of the passage quoted, Mill uses a conditional sentence to explain the meaning of "superiority in quality." The second account of quality considers an extreme case in order to emphasize the degree to which a particular pleasure might appeal to those who have had experience of it—irrespective of gross quantitative differences. *If* one of two pleasures with which persons were acquainted (that is, if one of two pleasant experiences) were preferred, even though having the preferred experience involved a considerable amount of discontent (a circumstantial disadvantage), and *if* the preference were so strong that no quantity of the other pleasure would change the order of preference, *then* (surely) such a preferred pleasure would deserve to be called "superior in quality." The case is extreme in order that the meaning of "quality" be made clear and the reader be won to assent to Mill's use of terms and to his pragmatical claim concerning the superiority, on qualitative grounds, of certain pleasures.

It may be maintained that Mill's use of the term "quality," if not different from *some* ordinary use, is at least different from any *common* ordinary use. Mill's use of the term is a technical, philosophical use. He is concerned to distinguish between "intrinsic," "felt" characteristics (what one might call "ways of feeling")—which he calls "qualities"—and attendant, circumstantial, utilitarian, causal properties (such as "permanency, safety, uncostliness, etc."). Yet as the term "quality" is commonly used, a thing "of quality" is a thing that can be said to be "superior in kind," "excellent in character." Mill seems to have reversed the common order in that, as he uses the terms "pleasure" and "quality," it is the term "pleasure," *not* the term "quality," which is the *value term;* it is the term "quality," not the term "pleasure," which refers to the *intrinsic character* of an experience.

Nevertheless, Mill's uses of the critical terms are clear. We know *from his uses* of the terms "pleasure" and "quality" *how he is using* the terms; and we find that his accounts of the meanings of the terms, relative to his uses of them, are illuminating and helpful. Furthermore, we must distinguish between the *common use* of a term and the *common opinion* (if any) concerning the meaning of the term in its use. No one denies that the term "pleasures" has a common use; in fact, the common use—or, at least, *a* common use—of the term is the one exhibited by Mill in his discourse. But the opinion held by many persons, including many philosophers, that the term "pleasure" names an *indefinable, intrinsic quality* (in Mill's sense of the term "quality") is, in my opinion as the critic, an erroneous opinion. We submit that the common practice, for users of English, is to report that a feeling (or emotional state) found to be agreeable (such that, upon having it, one is inclined to maintain it) is *said* to be "a pleasant feeling" or the "pleasure" secured by the activity that provoked it. An enduring emotional state that wins the approval of the person whose state it is can properly be described as "desirable," "good," or "happy"; and the noun "happiness" is used to call attention to a state that is intrinsically desirable (the kind of state one likes on its own account, *as* a feeling or emotion, quite apart from any moral or practical considerations).

The same point, made *nonlinguistically,* is that *pleasure is necessarily good in quality.* Such a claim, although grammatically "about" pleasure, has the *logical function* of suggesting that such a statement as "Some pleasures are not qualitatively (or intrinsically) good" is self-contradictory. The defense of this latter, *explicitly linguistical* claim consists in showing that, relative to an exhibited use of the term "pleasures" (the instances of use constituting what we call "pragmatical data"), the term "pleasures" *means* qualitatively good experiences. Thus, by an appeal to the use of a term, a semantical (definitional) claim is defended; by an appeal to the semantical claim, a logical claim is defended. Mill's case is made, we agree, on the pragmatical level: his description of pleasures as varying in quality and value is a meaningful, true, and illuminating description. But the basic case is supplemented by semantical claims to which we also give assent. Let us now consider, in particular, the claims Mill makes about the terms "desirable" and "pleasant."

We turn our attention to one of the most-discussed passages in Mill's *Utilitarianism:*

> *The only proof capable of being given that an object is visible is that people actually see it. The only proof that a sound is audible is that people hear it; and so of the other sources of our experience. In like manner, I apprehend, the sole evidence it is possible to produce that anything is desirable is that people do actually desire it.*

The British philosopher G. E. Moore, in his *Principia Ethica* (1903), makes what has come to be the common philosophical objection to Mill's account of the test of desirability:

> *Well, the fallacy in this step is so obvious, that it is quite wonderful how Mill failed to see it. The fact is that 'desirable' does not mean 'able to be desired' as 'visible' means 'able to be seen.' The desirable means simply what* ought *to be desired or* deserves *to be desired; just as the detestable means not what can be but what ought*

to be detested and the damnable what deserves to be damned. Mill has, then, smuggled in, under cover of the word 'desirable,' the very notion about which he ought to be quite clear. 'Desirable' does indeed mean 'what it is good to desire'; but when this is understood, it is no longer plausible to say that our only test of that, is what is actually desired. Is it merely a tautology when the Prayer Book talks of good desires?

Moore's criticism appears to be based on an incomplete reading of Mill, for no reference is made by Moore to the kind of qualification which appears over and over again in Mill's account of what is meant in talking about "quality" and "desirability." The qualification is explicit in such remarks as the following: "all or almost all *who have experience of both,*" "those who are *competently acquainted with both,*" "those who are *equally acquainted with and equally capable of appreciating and enjoying both,*" "And if the fool, or the pig, are of a different opinion, it is because *they only know their own side* of the question. The other party to the comparison *knows both sides,*" "It may be questioned whether anyone who has remained *equally susceptible to both* classes of pleasures ever *knowingly* and calmly preferred the lower," "the judgment of those who are *qualified by knowledge of both,*" "the general suffrage of those who are *familiar with both,*" and "the feelings and judgment *of the experienced*" (italics added in all above cases).

Mill's claim, then, is *not* that if something is desired, it is desirable—whether or not the person who desires is "qualified by knowledge" of the object of his desire—in the respect in which he desires it. Mill's claim, rather, is that if something is *desired by a person* "*competently acquainted*" with the object of his desire (and if his acquaintance encompasses all such features of the object as relate to his desire), then that thing is *desirable.*

We must remember that Mill defines the terms "quality" and "desirable" while working within the context of a discussion about *pleasures.* In order to have "experience of" a pleasure (considered simply *as* a pleasure, as a pleasant feeling), to be "competently acquainted" with a pleasure, to "know" a pleasure, and to be "familiar with" a pleasure—qualitatively, not circumstantially—nothing more is required than that one undergo that pleasure, that one have the feeling, that one be pleased in that way. To consider, under such circumstances—that is, while enjoying a state of pleasure—whether the experience is *desirable,* quite apart from any circumstantial advantages or disadvantages of being in that state, is only to consider whether one "desires" the experience; that is, whether one prefers the feeling to its absence and whether one likes the way one feels.

We grant that we do not ordinarily say that we "desire" *what we already possess.* We may *like* what we have, or we may *prefer* it to some alternative; but insofar as our desire has some bearing on what we already possess, it is the desire that our present state continue.

But Mill's use of the term "desire" is clearly such as to permit the term to function as the terms "like" and "approve" sometimes function. To "desire" one's own feeling or emotion, according to Mill's use of the term "desire," is to *like, approve,* be *drawn to,* be *positively disposed toward* that feeling or emotion. Thus, the sense of Mill's claim concerning the desirability of pleasure is made clear if we state that, according to Mill, a feeling state is desirable if and only if a person, upon having that feeling, would desire it—that is, would be positively disposed toward the feeling—*as a feeling.* It follows from the definition that if a person has a feeling and likes the feeling that he has, when he considers the feeling simply as a feeling, that feeling is, in Mill's sense of the term, "desirable." Mill is right in claiming that the only test of the desirable is that it be desired, *provided that* the person be acquainted with the object of his desire in the respect in which and for which it is desired. What is particularly significant about feelings and emotions considered simply as feelings and emotions is that a person having a feeling cannot fail to be acquainted with the feeling as a feeling. Thus, if a person "desires" the feeling that he has (and desires it *as* a feeling), the feeling cannot fail to be desirable.

Mill comes close to making this sort of point when he writes that "desiring a thing and finding it pleasant, aversion to it and thinking of it as painful, are phenomena entirely inseparable or, rather, two parts of the same phenomenon—in strictness of language, two different modes of naming the same psychological fact; that to think of an object as desirable (unless for the sake of its consequences) and to think of it as pleasant are one and the same thing; and that to desire anything except in proportion as the idea of it is pleasant is a physical and metaphysical impossibility."

However, insofar as Mill's generalization covers matters other than *pleasures,* the *psychological* claim he makes is open to challenge on the ground that, as a matter of fact, not all men find pleasant the idea of doing something desirable that entails suffering for themselves and others. It may be that, of all the courses of action open to a man, only acts probably productive of suffering can be chosen. Knowing this probability, the man may "desire" (approve) that act which, according to his evidence, will probably lead to the least amount of suffering; but, under such circumstances, it is unlikely that the man would find the idea of action pleasant, even though the action were morally desirable.

But considered as a linguistical comment on the terms "desirable" and "pleasant," and *limited in its scope to discourse on feelings,* Mill's remark is pertinent and revealing. To parallel Mill: desiring a *feeling* (as opposed to a "thing") and finding it pleasant, aversion to it and thinking of it as painful are phenomena entirely inseparable or, rather, two parts of the same phenomenon—in strictness of language, two different modes of naming the same psychological fact; that to think of a *feeling* (as opposed to "object") as desirable (unless for the sake of its consequences) and to think of it as pleasant are one and the same thing. We now have only to add that to think of a feeling as "pleasant" and to think of it as "a pleasure" is one and the same thing.

It now becomes clear why it is that, as far as pleasures are concerned, the only test of the desirable is that it is desired. If one has a feeling, one knows it as a feeling; if one desires the feeling, one desires it as a feeling. Such a feeling is consequently both "a pleasure" and something "desirable."

We are prepared also to grant that, whatever the object of desire, *provided that it is known* in the respect in which or for which it is desired, it follows from the fact that the object is desired that it is desirable. Pleasures are paradigm cases of entities which, by virtue of being desired, may justifiably be regarded as desirable. Objects of desire other than pleasures are desirable insofar as their status as "objects" is defined by the intention of the one who desires (so that the "girl of one's dreams," who is desired, can be nothing other than desirable, for as the object of desire she *is* as she is conceived to be); but insofar as the object of one's desire may, in fact, be *other* than it is conceived in desire to be, it may not be desirable: it may not be such that, *if known,* it would be desired.

Mill's claim, that the only test of the desirable is that it is desired, is granted, then, because the qualification "if known" is repeatedly appended to the claim. Moore's criticism ignores this critical qualification by the use of which Mill's claim turns out to be not only salvageable but positively illuminating.

Let us, now that we have examined the language of Mill's claim, appraise the claim itself.

Mill says, "some kinds of pleasures are more desirable and more valuable than others." Are we willing to grant that the expressions "more desirable" and "more valuable," as used by Mill, do indeed apply to some pleasures, not because of quantitative differences (differences of duration and intensity), and not because of circumstantial considerations (considerations of "permanency, safety, uncostliness, etc."), but because of qualitative differences?

We are in no position to compare the quality of Socrates' experience with the quality of a pig's experience. We cannot presume to compare our own experience with that of Socrates; and in any case, his experience is not available to us for comparison. Nor can we be so incautious as to speak with authority about the experiences of the pig. But we can compare a pleasant experience we have had—say, the experience of receiving pay for a job already accomplished—with another experience we have had—say, the experience of receiving a kiss from a young lady—and we conclude (perhaps because the amount of money was considerable, and because the kiss was slight) that the two pleasures were of, approximately, the same duration and intensity. Nevertheless, although the two pleasures, considered simply as pleasures, were alike in *quantity,* they were markedly different in *quality.* The *feeling* of receiving pay is obviously and significantly different from the *feeling* of receiving a kiss; one can never confuse the one feeling with the other, even when they are alike in quantity and are both pleasant. The feeling of having arrived at a destination longed for (a certain town, perhaps) is clearly different from the feeling of having arrived at a conclusion sought (the answer to a logical puzzle, perhaps). The pleasure of meeting an old friend is different, qualitatively, from the pleasure of coming across a familiar but forgotten poem. The pleasure of eating onion soup is qualitatively different from the pleasure of eating a Caesar salad—and both are qualitatively different from the experience of having a companion pick up the check.

It will not do to protest that, although the *causes* of pleasures differ, pleasures themselves, since they are pleasures, must be alike in the quality of being pleasurable, of having pleasantness. For we have seen that the term "pleasure" is used not to designate a *way* of feeling (a quality), but to designate a feeling that is intrinsically desirable (a feeling that, whatever its quality, provokes and sustains the approval of the person whose feeling it is). Our present problem is not so much that of defending the semantical conviction that "pleasure," as that term is used by Mill, *means* desirable feeling *qua* feeling, as it is that of showing the sorts of differences to which the use of the term "kinds" of pleasures calls attention. There is some sense in talking about "qualities" of pleasures, for we find that, under certain circumstances, we are inclined to say that pleasures differ in quality; and the circumstances are such that our claims as to "quality" are not vulnerable to criticism. The claim that one pleasure is qualitatively different from another may provoke a critic's dissent; but the claim cannot be refuted, and for the claimant it has already been verified.

We agree to say, with Mill, that pleasures vary in quality. Since we would not call an experience a "pleasure" unless we found it desirable (an experience of a kind we "go for"), all pleasures are desirable. Some pleasures are more desirable than others because they are qualitatively more appealing. And any pleasure more desirable than another can be said to be "more valuable" than the other. Hence, we grant Mill's claim that it is true and illuminating to say, in the manner he exhibits, that "some kinds of pleasure are more desirable and more valuable than others."

Expressed linguistically, Mill's pragmatical claim is that some of the entities we call "pleasures" (in speaking of such matters as "the pleasures of the intellect" and the "pleasures of mere sensation") are such as to be worthy of the description "more desirable and more valuable than others." In justification of this claim (which is, in effect, a suggestion that a distinction worth noticing is brought out by the description proposed), Mill calls attention to the experiences (and discourse) of those who have found what Mill calls "superiority in quality" in some of those experiences called "pleasures," and he underscores the point that the test of desirability (as shown by the use of the term "desirable") is provided by the desires provoked by the acquaintance with "objects."

COMMENTS ON THE ANALYSIS OF MILL'S ARGUMENT

A philosopher who decides that a certain matter ought to be described in a way that brings out features that are ordinarily missed by those whose attention to the world is limited by the perspectives afforded by ordinary, practical discourse is usually best able to make his point not by discussing the advisability of a new way of talking about the matter in question, but by actually exhibiting the endorsed way of describing. The *way* of describing the matter with which the philosopher is concerned is shown in the act of describing which the philosopher undertakes.

Thus, we know from Mill's discourse not only *what* he claims but *how* he claims it; and we know, further, that he endorses his manner of speaking as providing a new and revealing perspective on a matter of common experience. In granting Mill's claim, we assent to his evaluation of the language of his claim: not only do we grant that pleasures vary in quality and value, but we also agree with him in being positively disposed toward making the point in the way he does —through using, and calling attention to the use of, such terms as "quality," "kind," and "desirable."

In rejecting Moore's criticism, not only do we deny that he is right in claiming that Mill committed an obvious fallacy—for in our opinion Mill committed no fallacy at all—but also we reject the semantical claim that the term "desirable" as used in Mill's analogy (in which the uses of "visible" and "audible" are compared to the use of "desirable") means (or is claimed by Mill to mean) "able to be desired."

The linguistical fact (the truth about the language used) is that we might better say that the term "visible" means "ought to be seen" than say that it means "able to be seen." If something is normally visible, then anyone with normal (as specified by a standard) vision *ought*—under conditions suitable for visual observation and with the object present—to see it; that is, under such conditions, such an observer, were he observant, *would* see it. But having an experience (such as, for example, the experience of "seeing" pink elephants) on the basis of which a person *claims* that he sees something is not always sufficient to justify the conclusion that something visible is present.

Of course, if "able to be seen" means, as in certain contexts appears to be the case, "able to provoke a distinctive visual experience in a normal observer acquainted, under conditions suitable for visual observation, with the object," then there is no pragmatical difference between "able to be seen" and "ought to be seen." Analogously, if the expression "able to be desired" is used the same way as the expression "able to be seen" is used, insofar as both expressions make implicit reference to what *would* occur to an observer under certain conditions, then "able to be desired" is pragmatically equivalent to "ought to be desired" and, hence, equivalent to "desirable." If something is (normally) desirable, then anyone capable of normal (as specified by a standard) desire ought to desire it; that is, anyone capable of normal desire would, under circumstances suitable for attending to an object and responding to it in attitude, desire it. Either way, the analogy holds.

But, in any case, Mill's pragmatical claim does not depend on the analogy. If Mill is right in saying that "the sole evidence it is possible to produce that anything is desirable is that people do actually desire it," then Moore is wrong in denying it, even if Moore were right in finding fault with the analogy. And we have found good reasons for assenting to Mill's claim, which we understand to have been made secure by the critical qualification of the kind "among those acquainted with."

There may be other claims made by Mill—such as that "the general happiness [is] a good to the aggregate of all persons"—that are either nonsensical or indefensible. But the two claims with which we have been concerned—namely, that pleasures vary in quality and value, and that the evidence of desirability is the desire of an informed observer—deserve to be recognized (despite the plethora of criticism directed against them) as providing true, illuminating, and significant comments on matters of common experience and concern.

QUESTIONS FOR DISCUSSION

1. How is it possible to determine what the subject of discourse is when the term naming the subject is not defined?

2. If something would not ordinarily be described in a certain way suggested by a philosopher, does it follow that it ought not to be described in that way?

3. Since the term "pleasures" is a noun, does it follow from the fact that we are conscious of pleasures that there are things, or objects of some sort, with which the "consciousness" comes in contact?

4. Could Mill have been mistaken in using the term "quality" as something other than a value term?

5. Could anything other than a feeling or an emotion meaningfully be said to have an "intrinsic nature"?

6. Demonstrate the use (or a use) of the term "chair." Attempt to define the term according to its use. If the definition cannot be made perfectly precise, is it a useless definition? If some of the terms used in a definition are not entirely clear in meaning, does the definition itself lack clarity?

7. If the facts are known with regard to a certain matter, how can a problem arise as to how that matter ought to be described?

8. If a decision is made as to how a certain matter ought to be described, how can that decision be justified?

9. What is the difference, if any, between pleasure and happiness? What method can be used to determine whether there is a difference? Need the difference be specifically describable?

10. "Are some pains good in themselves?" Can the preceding question be used meaningfully?

HUME

Beyond the constant conjunction of
similar objects, and the consequent
inference from one to the other, we
have no notion of any necessity or
connexion—*a semantical claim*

HUME'S ARGUMENT

*Every one will readily allow, that there is a considerable differ-
ence between the perceptions of the mind, when a man feels the pain
of excessive heat, or the pleasure of moderate warmth, and when he
afterwards recalls to his memory this sensation, or anticipates it by
his imagination. These faculties may mimic or copy the perceptions
of the senses; but they never can entirely reach the force and vivacity
of the original sentiment. The utmost we say of them, even when they
operate with greatest vigour, is, that they represent their object in so
lively a manner, that we could almost say we feel or see it: But, except
the mind be disordered by disease or madness, they never can arrive
at such a pitch of vivacity, as to render these perceptions altogether
undistinguishable. All the colours of poetry, however splendid, can
never paint natural objects in such a manner as to make the descrip-*

tion be taken for a real landskip. The most lively thought is still inferior to the dullest sensation.

*　　*　　*　　*

Here therefore we may divide all the perceptions of the mind into two classes or species, which are distinguishable by their different degrees of force and vivacity. The less forcible and lively are commonly denominated Thoughts *or* Ideas. *The other species want a name in our language, and in most others; I suppose, because it was not requisite for any, but philosophical purposes, to rank them under a general term or appellation. Let us, therefore, use a little freedom, and call them* Impressions; *employing that word in a sense somewhat different from the usual. By the term* impression, *then, I mean all our more lively perceptions, when we hear, or see, or feel, or love, or hate, or desire, or will. And impressions are distinguished from ideas, which are the less lively perceptions, of which we are conscious, when we reflect on any of those sensations or movements above mentioned.*

*　　*　　*　　*

. . . all our ideas or more feeble perceptions are copies of our impressions or more lively ones.

*　　*　　*　　*

. . . When we entertain, therefore, any suspicion that a philosophical term is employed without any meaning or idea (as is but too frequent), we need but enquire, from what impression is that supposed idea derived? *And if it be impossible to assign any, this will serve to confirm our suspicion. By bringing ideas into so clear a light we may reasonably hope to remove all dispute, which may arise, concerning their nature and reality.*

[From *An Enquiry Concerning Human Understanding* (1777), Section II, by David Hume (1711–1776).*]

*Edition used: Open Court Publishing Co., 1949.

All reasonings concerning matter of fact seem to be founded on the relation of Cause *and* Effect. *By means of that relation alone we can go beyond the evidence of our memory and senses. If you were to ask a man, why he believes any matter of fact, which is absent; for instance, that his friend is in the country, or in France; he would give you a reason; and this reason would be some other fact; as a letter received from him, or the knowledge of his former resolutions and promises. A man finding a watch or any other machine in a desert island, would conclude that there had once been men in that island. All our reasonings concerning fact are of the same nature. And here it is constantly supposed that there is a connexion between the present fact and that which is inferred from it. Were there nothing to bind them together, the inference would be entirely precarious. The hearing of an articulate voice and rational discourse in the dark assures us of the presence of some person: Why? because these are the effects of the human make and fabric, and closely connected with it. If we anatomize all the other reasonings of this nature, we shall find that they are founded on the relation of cause and effect, and that this relation is either near or remote, direct or collateral. Heat and light are collateral effects of fire, and the one effect may justly be inferred from the other.*

If we would satisfy ourselves, therefore, concerning the nature of that evidence, which assures us of matters of fact, we must enquire how we arrive at the knowledge of cause and effect.

I shall venture to affirm, as a general proposition, which admits of no exception, that the knowledge of this relation is not, in any instance, attained by reasonings a priori; *but arises entirely from experience, when we find that any particular objects are constantly conjoined with each other. Let an object be presented to a man of ever so strong natural reason and abilities; if that object be entirely new to him, he will not be able, by the most accurate examination of its sensible qualities, to discover any of its causes or effects. Adam, though his rational faculties be supposed, at the very first, entirely perfect, could not have inferred from the fluidity and transparency of water that it would suffocate him, or from the light and warmth of fire that it would consume him. No object ever discovers, by the qualities which appear to the senses, either the causes which produced it, or the effects which will arise from it; nor can our reason, unassisted by experience, ever draw any inference concerning real existence and matter of fact.*

* * * *

It is certain that the most ignorant and stupid peasants—nay infants, nay even brute beasts—improve by experience, and learn the qualities of natural objects, by observing the effects which result from them. When a child has felt the sensation of pain from touching the flame of a candle, he will be careful not to put his hand near any candle; but will expect a similar effect from a cause which is similar in its sensible qualities and appearance. If you assert, therefore, that the understanding of the child is led into this conclusion by any process of argument or ratiocination, I may justly require you to produce that argument; nor have you any pretense to refuse so equitable a demand. You cannot say that the argument is abstruse, and may possibly escape your enquiry; since you confess that it is obvious to the capacity of a mere infant. If you hesitate, therefore, a moment, or if, after reflection, you produce any intricate or profound argument, you, in a manner, give up the question, and confess that it is not reasoning which engages us to suppose the past resembling the future, and to expect similar effects from causes which are, to appearance, similar. This is the proposition which I intended to enforce in the present section. If I be right, I pretend not to have made any mighty discovery. And if I be wrong, I must acknowledge myself to be indeed a very backward scholar; since I cannot now discover an argument which, it seems, was perfectly familiar to me long before I was out of my cradle.

[From *An Enquiry Concerning Human Understanding,* Section IV.]

. . . When any natural object or event is presented, it is impossible for us, by any sagacity or penetration, to discover, or even conjecture, without experience, what event will result from it, or to carry our foresight beyond that object which is immediately present to the memory and senses. Even after one instance or experiment where we have observed a particular event to follow upon another, we are not

entitled to form a general rule, or foretell what will happen in like cases; it being justly esteemed an unpardonable temerity to judge of the whole course of nature from one single experiment, however accurate or certain. But when one particular species of event has always, in all instances, been conjoined with another, we make no longer any scruple of foretelling one upon the appearance of the other, and of employing that reasoning which can alone assure us of any matter of fact or existence. We then call the one object, Cause; *the other,* Effect. *We suppose that there is some connexion between them; some power in the one, by which it infallibly produces the other, and operates with the greatest certainty and strongest necessity.*

It appears, then, that this idea of a necessary connexion among events arises from a number of similar instances which occur of the constant conjunction of these events; nor can that idea ever be suggested by any one of these instances, surveyed in all possible lights and positions. But there is nothing in a number of instances, different from every single instance, which is supposed to be exactly similar; except only, that after a repetition of similar instances, the mind is carried by habit, upon the appearance of one event, to expect its usual attendant, and to believe that it will exist. This connexion, therefore, which we feel *in the mind, this customary transition of the imagination from one object to its usual attendant, is the sentiment or impression from which we form the idea of power or necessary connexion. Nothing farther is in the case. Contemplate the subject on all sides; you will never find any other origin of that idea. This is the sole difference between one instance, from which we can never receive the idea of connexion, and a number of similar instances, by which it is suggested. The first time a man saw the communication of motion by impulse, as by the shock of two billiard balls, he could not pronounce that the one event was* connected: *but only that it was* conjoined with *the other. After he has observed several instances of this nature, he then pronounces them to be* connected. *What alteration has happened to give rise to this new idea of* connexion? *Nothing but that he now* feels *these events to be* connected *in his imagination, and can readily foretell the existence of one from the appearance of the other. When we say, therefore, that one object is connected with another, we mean only that they have acquired a connexion in our thought,*

*and give rise to this inference, by which they become proofs of each
other's existence: A conclusion which is somewhat extraordinary, but
which seems founded on sufficient evidence.*

* * * *

*. . . Similar objects are always conjoined with similar. Of this we have
experience.* Suitably to this experience, therefore, we may define a
cause to be an object, followed by another, and where all the objects
similar to the first are followed by objects similar to the second. *Or
in other words* where, if the first object had not been, the second never
had existed. *The appearance of a cause always conveys the mind, by
a customary transition, to the idea of the effect. Of this also we have
experience.* We may, therefore, suitably to this experience, form another definition of cause, and call it, an object followed by another
and whose appearance always conveys the thought to that other. *But
though both these definitions be drawn from circumstances foreign to
the cause, we cannot remedy this inconvenience, or attain any more
perfect definition, which may point out that circumstance in the
cause, which gives it a connexion with its effect. We have no idea of
this connexion, nor even any distinct notion what it is we desire to
know, when we endeavour at a conception of it. We say, for instance,
that the vibration of this string is the cause of this particular sound.
But what do we mean by that affirmation? We either mean that this*
vibration is followed by this sound, and that all similar vibrations
have been followed by similar sounds: *Or,* that this vibration is followed by this sound, and that upon the appearance of one the mind
anticipates the senses, and forms immediately an idea of the other.
*We may consider the relation of cause and effect in either of these two
lights; but beyond these, we have no idea of it.*
   [From *An Enquiry Concerning Human Understanding,* Section
VII.]

   *It seems evident that, if all the scenes of nature were continually
shifted in such a manner that no two events bore any resemblance to
each other, but every object was entirely new, without any similitude
to whatever had been seen before, we should never, in that case, have
attained the least idea of necessity, or of a connexion among these*

objects. We might say, upon such a supposition, that one object or event has followed another; not that one was produced by the other. The relation of cause and effect must be utterly unknown to mankind. Inference and reasoning concerning the operations of nature would, from that moment, be at an end; and the memory and senses remain the only canals, by which the knowledge of any real existence could possibly have access to the mind. Our idea, therefore, of necessity and causation arises entirely from the uniformity observable in the operations of nature, where similar objects are constantly conjoined together, and the mind is determined by custom to infer the one from the appearance of the other. These two circumstances form the whole of that necessity, which we ascribe to matter. Beyond the constant conjunction *of similar objects, and the consequent* inference *from one to the other, we have no notion of any necessity or connexion.*

[From *An Enquiry Concerning Human Understanding*, Section VIII, Part I.]

AN ANALYSIS OF HUME'S ARGUMENT

1. THE BASIC CLAIM

Hume describes the circumstances under which we call one "object" a "cause" and another an "effect": "But when one particular species of event has always, in all instances, been conjoined with another, we make no longer any scruple of foretelling one upon the appearance of the other, and of employing that reasoning which can alone assure us of any matter of fact or existence. We then call the one object, *Cause*; the other, *Effect*." Later, in discussing the "idea of *connexion*," Hume writes, "When we say . . . that one object is connected with another, we mean only that they have acquired a connexion in our thought . . . ." Finally, he ventures to "define a cause," and he offers alternative definitions: ". . . we may define a cause to be *an object, followed by another, and where all the objects similar to the first are followed by objects similar to the second. Or in other* words *where, if the first object had not been, the second never had existed,"* and "We may . . . form another definition of cause, and call it, *an object followed by another and whose appearance always conveys the thought to that other."*

Hume's basic claim, then, is a *semantical* claim; it is a claim to the effect that a certain *term* "cause," the *use* of which is *exhibited* in the text, *has a specifiable meaning* which is stated in the *definitions*.

Having discussed how the terms "cause," "effect," and "connected" are used, Hume summarizes his finding, with regard to the meaning of the term "cause," in the definitions cited above; and he also concerns himself with what we "might say" were "the scenes of nature . . . continually shifted in such a manner that no two events bore any resemblance to each other," and he concludes: "Beyond the constant *conjunction* of similar objects, and the consequent *inference* from one to the other, we have no notion of any necessity or connexion." His basic claim may be broadened, then, to include his *semantical claims* concerning the terms "necessity" and "connexion."

2. THE BASIC ARGUMENT

Hume's definition of "cause" is what we have called a semantical *claim,* not a semantical *stipulation;* Hume sets out to *report* the meaning of the term "cause," a meaning that the term has acquired in its use. Hume's intention is not to create an arbitrary or verbal definition by reference to which he would discipline his use of the term for certain technical purposes; his intention is to relate the use of the term "cause" to the circumstances disclosed by experience as having been designated by the term in its use. He does not define the term in order to use it according to his definition; he begins with the use of the term and attempts to fashion his definition so as to call attention to the actual sign function of the term.

In order to appraise Hume's semantical claim, then, we must consider whether his definition does report, within reasonable limits of clarity and accuracy, the sign function of the term "cause" in the use to which the philosophical account alludes. Our first task is to attend to the relevant *use* of the term "cause"; we call this phase of our inquiry *pragmatical investigation*. We ask, with regard to the use of the term "cause," whether the term in that use has a *descriptive, emotive,* or *syntactical* function: Is the term used to call attention to some matter to be understood in relation to experience, or is it used to express or communicate experience itself, or is it used to relate parts of a sentence to one another in such a way as to make the sentence, as used, an effective piece of discourse? (More refined accounts of linguistical functioning can be devised, and have been; but we are here interested in extending the uses of the terms "descriptive," "emotive," and "syntactical" in such a way as to allow a rough-and-ready, but nonetheless useful, division of functions, in order to provide an initial limitation of the pragmatical problem of getting at the specific function of the term in question.)

We cannot discover Hume's use of the term "cause" by referring to his definition of the term, for the whole point at issue here is whether the definition is in accordance with the use. Of course, if the author-philosopher, in this case Hume, neither *exhibits* the use he attempts to clarify semantically, nor *indicates* the use (through identifying it as the use exhibited in a certain text or in a certain body of discourse), we presume that it is the opinion of the writer that there is an obvious body of public discourse which is revelatory of common and ordinary usage. If pragmatical investigation fails to disclose an obvious body of "common usage," in a case in which the use in question is neither exhibited nor indicated, criticism of the semantical claim is made impossible.

Fortunately, Hume's account is such as to indicate that a common use of the term "cause" is the use in question, and examples of that use provide pragmatical data on the basis of which criticism can proceed. Hume claims that reasoning concerning factual matters is based on the relation of "Cause and Effect," and he offers, as examples of causal "connexion," the relation between a letter and the absence of a friend; the relation between a watch found on a desert island and the presence of men there. A voice in the darkness is causally related to a person there; heat and light are the effects of fire, which is the cause. He mentions also the experience of the child who finds that a sensation of pain is caused by touching a flame, and he speaks of "the communication of motion" resulting from "the shock of two billiard balls." It is apparent, then, that Hume's use of the term "cause" is a common use with which we are familiar.

Hume wrote in the eighteenth century; we read and criticize him in the twentieth century—but the eighteenth-century use of the term "cause" has persisted. We attend not only to Hume's examples, but also to the linguistical practice exemplified by them, for the practice has persisted, and we, too, may talk of the child's blister as having been caused by the flame, or of a watch on a desert island as one of the effects of man's presence there.

3. CRITICISM OF THE BASIC ARGUMENT

In appraising Hume's proposed definition of "cause," we ask not only whether the definition fits the particular examples given of the use of the term "cause," but also whether the definition fits other examples which may be found by attending further to the specified conventional use of the term "cause." The decision as to whether the definition "fits" is determined by the answer to the question as to whether the term "cause," as used in the manner Hume indicates, calls our attention to the matters described in the definition and does so in the manner described or suggested by the definition.

Thus, we ask specifically with regard to Hume's definition whether the term "cause," as used in the manner exhibited, calls our attention to "an object, followed by another, and where all the objects similar to the first are followed by objects similar to the second." We ask (a) whether, in using the term "cause," we *designate an object;* (b) if so, whether we designate the object *as followed by another;* and (c) if so, whether we designate the object *as of a kind constantly conjoined with, through being followed by, another kind of object.* Finally, since Hume offers, as an alternative definition, the claim that a cause is "an object followed by another and whose appearance always conveys the thought to that other," we ask whether, in attending to an object as being what we call a "cause," *we are forced, by habit, to think of the kind of object we presume to be constantly conjoined with the object we regard as the "cause."*

To complete our critical appraisal of the definition, we ask not only whether whatever we would call a "cause" would be what Hume describes it as being (were we not mistaken in our designation of something as a "cause"), but also whether anything we would, without error, describe according to Hume's definition is also what we would—were we informed concerning the truth of our description, and were we using the term "cause" in the ordinary way exemplified by Hume's examples—call a "cause." Briefly, we ask whether (a) *every* cause is an object, followed by another (and so on), and whether (b) *every* object followed by another (and so on) is a cause (what we would correctly call a "cause").

Perhaps we shall find—almost surely we shall find—that some of the terms used by Hume in his definition are somewhat ambiguous or vague; almost surely we shall find that some instances of what we would call a "cause" can only with charity and ingenuity be said to be in accord with Hume's definitive account; and almost surely we shall find that some matters that seem to be of the sort described in Hume's definitive account are not what we would ordinarily call "causes." But if the definitive description can be used in much the same manner, descriptively, as we use the term "cause," even though there are instances in which the resemblance of function is forced, and if Hume's definitive description to some extent illuminates the meaning of the term "cause" by reporting the sorts of factors to which the term in its use calls attention, it is acceptable to that extent and on that account. Perhaps a competing definition might prove to be more illuminating by virtue of more accurately defining, through description, the character of "causes"; but Hume's definition can fail, as a semantical claim, only if it misses some feature common to the majority of instances or includes, as a common feature, some feature not common to the majority of instances.

By a "common feature" is meant some feature that *could, in some way, be said* to be "common," when the reasons that might be given for saying that it is common would be generally acceptable. For example, it might be argued that all games are "amusing," even though it is acknowledged (as prompted by Wittgenstein) that what leads one to call chess "amusing" is a feature different from that which leads one to call ring-a-ring-a-roses "amusing" (the difference perhaps being that chess sets one a-musing; ring-a-ring-a-roses sets one a-laughing)—and one *could say* that all games that are amusing have, "in common," that feature of being what (in one way or another) we call "amusing."

It is clear from a reading of Hume that the philosopher is not aiming at the isolation of the "essence" of cause; he nowhere suggests that he seeks a "universal," nor does he anywhere proceed as if it were possible to find a constant, static, and absolutely common character designated by the term "cause." His central concern, the work shows, is to rid others of the belief that the causal relations we uncover through experience involve an element of what we call "necessity"; he argues that "when one particular species of event has always, in all instances, been conjoined with another" (that is, in all instances falling within the range of our experience), we "suppose that there is some connexion between them; some power in the one, by which it infallibly produces the other, and operates with the greatest certainty and strongest necessity." But he then goes on to argue that it is a connection "we *feel* in the mind," a "customary transition of the imagination from one object to its usual attendant," which provides "the sentiment or impression from which we form the idea of power or necessary connexion." Hume explicitly denies that there is some absolutely common feature open to observation: ". . . there is nothing in a number of instances . . . which is supposed to be exactly similar; except only, that after a repetition of similar instances, the mind is carried by habit, upon the appearance of one event, to expect its usual attendant, and to believe that it will exist."

Thus, in criticizing Hume's semantical claim (his definition), we cannot argue that in proposing a definition Hume shows himself committed to the naive and ancient view that descriptive terms name essences or universals. Hume's entire effort is simply that of making clear the sense of saying that one event is the "cause" of another. He asks us to consider the experiences on the basis of which we make causal claims; and he suggests that we are led, through observing that one kind of event constantly follows another, to expect—when we encounter an event of the one kind—to be able to observe an event of the other kind conjoined with the former in the way with which we have become familiar.

Hence, we ask whether, in fact, we do use the term "cause" to call attention to events we have found to be *constantly conjoined* with others; and we ask also whether, while using the term "cause," we are in the habit of *ascribing the impression we have*—an impression occasioned by the habit of expecting events to be conjoined in a certain way—*to the events themselves.* We do *not* ask whether Hume has succeeded in isolating the *essence of cause,* for nothing in the text suggests that that was his intention. Of course, we *could say* that Hume attempts to spell out the essence of cause, in that he attempts to describe the conditions which obtain when we are correct in saying, relative to ordinary usage, that one event is the "cause" of another— but our claim would then be distinguishable from the claim that some *absolutely common* feature, a "universal," must provide the ground for the use of a descriptive term.

Hume defines the term "cause" to mean "an object . . . ." Do we, then, in using the term "cause," designate *objects?*

When a question as to the "cause" of something is asked, we *sometimes* answer by referring to what we might very well call an "object"; for example, if someone asks, "What caused this window to break?" the answer might be, "The baseball." We *sometimes* answer by referring to what we might very well call an "event"; for example, in response to the same question we might say, "The ball glanced off Johnny's bat." Sometimes Hume uses the word "object" and sometimes he uses the word "event"; the latter term is preferable, in that, in discoursing about what we call "causes and effects," we are obviously not talking about static and isolated physical objects but about relations between events, about actions and reactions, or actions and consequent actions: it is the "shock of two billiard balls," their *meeting,* that results in "the communication of motion." Since Hume's examples and, on occasion, Hume's use of the term "event" suggest that in using the term "object" Hume was talking about the subject of discourse and not about static, inactive physical objects—and since Hume's account makes it clear that discourse about "causes" is discourse about *events*—we are *willing to say* that what we call a "cause" is, in this sense of the term "object," an object.

Do we correctly call an event a "cause" only when we have observed that it is similar to events we have observed to be constantly conjoined with events of a second kind, in that the events of the second kind follow the events of the first kind? Is it the case that every event we correctly call a "cause" is "an object, followed by another, and where all the objects similar to the first are followed by objects similar to the second"?

Hume offers a definition of the term "cause," but he does more than this: he also makes certain claims concerning the use of the term "cause." His semantical claim is accompanied by, and presumably supported by, certain pragmatical claims. He repeatedly asserts that the observation of a single instance will never give rise to the idea of causation or of connection; he claims that if events never resembled one another and we were to observe that an event was followed by another, we might say "that one object or event has followed another; not that one was produced by the other."

It does seem likely that in a world of pure novelty we would not think of events as causally related. Nothing we might observe in such a world would prompt us to use the term "cause" as we do use it in our world, *provided that* we did not come to the world of novelty from the world of causal relations. But having learned, in this world, the use of the term "cause" in describing what we encounter through experience, we might very well, upon arriving in a world of novelty, describe every event as a "cause" in relation to events contiguous to and succeeding it.

We now recognize the necessity, if clarity of meaning is to be achieved, of distinguishing between the *meaning* a term acquires in its habitual use and the *habit* which makes that use possible. In fact, it helps in distinguishing between the *meaning* and the *habit* (the linguistical habit) to recognize the degree to which it is advisable, because illuminating, to say that *the habit is the use:* the way a term is used, the habitual way, is what someone is after who, instead of asking for the meaning, asks for the use. And, often, the only way to satisfy a person who asks for the use of a term is to show him the use of it—to exercise the linguistical habit oneself—in order that he might acquire that habit and, hence, the use of the term.

Hume claims that the linguistical habit which establishes the use of the term "cause," that habit the practice of which constitutes the use of the term, is acquired, in part, through the observation of repeated instances of conjoined events, so related that events of one kind regularly follow events of another kind. When observation of conjoined events is accompanied by recognition of the linguistic propriety of calling events so related "causes" and "effects," the habit of so using the terms is established.

We can now understand what would prompt a person, coming from a world in which the use of the term "cause" was developed habitually through the observation of conjoined events, to use the term "cause" to designate the earlier in any pair of conjoined events, even though every pair were novel. Observing that an event of a certain novel kind was immediately succeeded by an event of another novel kind, the observer would be inclined to call the former the "cause" of the latter event. Only the observation of subsequent pairs of conjoined events such that in each case the first of the pair was similar in kind to the first of the original pair, but the second, in each case, was different in kind from the second of the original pair would disturb the observer and discourage the continued use of the term "cause" to designate the earlier event in every pair.

We conclude that insofar as Hume's account suggests that the term "cause" is never used to designate the earlier of two conjoined events unless the observer has found through experience that events similar in kind to the earlier have repeatedly been conjoined with events similar in kind to the subsequent event, Hume's account is mistaken. The linguistic habit which observation establishes is *not* the habit of calling events "causes" *only* when repeated observations of similar cases have led the observer to expect an event of the second kind whenever he observes an event of the first kind; the habit is established through the observation of events regularly conjoined, but the habit which is established is that of calling the earlier of *any* pair of conjoined events the "cause," whether or not the pair is of a kind formerly observed. However, insofar as Hume's account suggests how the habit of using the word "cause" in a certain way is established, through recognizing the propriety (relative to ordinary use) of calling the earlier of regularly conjoined events the "cause," his account is true and illuminating, even though the linguistic habit so established may be exercised in novel situations.

Is it true that every event we could describe correctly as "an object, followed by another, and where all the objects similar to the first are followed by objects similar to the second" is an event we could describe correctly as a "cause"?

If we use the term "object" as we use the term "event," and if we add "and conjoined with" to the expression "followed by," and if we append to the phrase "the objects similar to the first" the qualification "if any," we can answer that it is true that every such event is one that could correctly be described as a "cause." That is, if and only if an event is followed by and conjoined with another, and all the events similar to the first, if any, are followed by and conjoined with events similar to the second, can the earlier event correctly be described as a "cause." We can accept Hume's definition, as so amended.

But we have not sufficiently clarified the use and meaning of the critical term "conjoined." When can an event properly be said to be "conjoined" with another? We must explore the "idea" of what Hume calls "connexion."

We gather from Hume's use of the term "conjoined" that an event is conjoined with another when the one occurs and then the other "follows." But Hume seems to assume that we understand what it is for one event to "follow" another, and it may be that we are prepared to use the terms "conjoined" and "follow" in much the same way Hume does—but until we are offered an account which lays bare the procedure involved in using these terms, his semantical account is incomplete.

There is a fallacy called *post hoc, ergo propter hoc,* which is the mistake of supposing that simply because one event *follows* another, the former is the cause of the latter. Hume argues that it is the observation of the constant *conjunction* of events that gives rise to the habit of expecting events of a second kind (effects) to follow events of a first kind (causes). He assumes that we all know the difference between a case of "conjunction" and a case of "following" accidentally. But, it might be maintained, whenever we speak of the "conjunction" of events, we distinguish, if we do, between what we call "conjunction" and an accidental coincidence only when we mean by "conjunction" *causal* conjunction. And when we go on to suppose that events which are conjoined are in some invariable way "connected," it is because we have already supposed them to be *causally* conjoined; and we so use the term "causally" that if events are "causally" conjoined, they are what we might appropriately call "connected," *causally* connected.

Hence, the term "causal" remains to perplex us; it qualifies the terms used to explicate its own meaning. The definition of "cause" appears to fit the cases given because the *definiens,* the defining description, implicitly utilizes the *definiendum*, the term to be defined.

However, Hume is correct in maintaining that we do not, by sense experience alone, observe any "necessity." And he is right in suggesting that some persons ascribe to events the invariable urgency they feel upon witnessing causal connections of a kind previously observed. But he appears to be mistaken in supposing that the only justification one has for ascribing necessity to a causal connection is that one is driven, by habit, to expect effects upon observing causes. If, under carefully controlled conditions, we have observed that a single change we have introduced into a situation is followed by other changes we did not introduce, we quite properly regard the latter changes as "effects" of the change we introduced, the "cause." We may be confident enough of our control of the situation to claim that the connection is a causal one, that there is, indeed, a causal *necessity* exhibited by the developing situation. We can draw this conclusion, and be justified in doing so, even though we have had no opportunity to develop the habit of expecting the results we got, and even though we may never repeat the experiment.

Of course, a person claiming, through experimental observation, to have uncovered a causal connection may be mistaken in what he claims; the necessity he presumes may not hold between the events he witnessed. But when that is so, it is so because what the observer took to be the cause and the effect were not so related, perhaps because the situation was not controlled (and an unintended change or condition affected the result), or perhaps because the observer was not carefully observant.

We conclude that to say two events are "necessarily connected" is to say that they are causally related, and we so use the expression "causally related" that whenever two events are causally related, there cannot be an event of the type we identify as the "cause" that is not followed by an event of the type we identify as the "effect." Our use of these terms allows no departure from the script by which we read the course of nature. The necessity is logical, but it enhances our descriptions, which may sometimes be mistaken, of the relations between events.

Hume's semantic analysis of the meaning of the term "cause"

is deficient, then, in that it does not adequately clarify the meaning of the term "conjoined," and it does not distinguish between the *meaning* a term acquires in its habitual use and the *habit* which makes that use possible. It may be that the observation of constant conjunction provides cases of what can habitually be called "causes" and "effects," but it does not follow that the discourse which is used to report the results of this observation is such as to provide the terms "cause" and "effect" with meanings involving reference to constant conjunction. Furthermore, pragmatical observation of the uses of the terms "cause" and "effect" reveals that these terms can be employed properly even in novel cases (relative to the experience of the observer), when there is no temptation whatsoever to ascribe a felt necessity to events, for in such cases no necessity is *felt*.

COMMENTS ON THE ANALYSIS OF HUME'S ARGUMENT

We have contended that the problem of discovering the *nature* or *essence* of something—the task of isolating a feature "common" to a multiplicity of cases—is a *semantical* problem. But such a problem is not resolved by an appeal to a dictionary, for the lexicographer himself must engage in pragmatical and semantical investigation and construction if he is to frame definitive accounts that will satisfy those who want to clarify their thinking with regard to matters to which ordinary discourse calls attention. The philosopher does not assume that the lexicographer's data and concerns were those which provoke the philosopher, nor does the philosopher assume that the lexicographer is so skilled in the pragmatical and semantical arts as to need no critical appraisal of his work. Consequently, although works by other philosophers and dictionaries produced by lexicographers may provide helpful and, occasionally, entirely satisfactory resolutions to particular semantical problems that engage the interest of the philosopher, any seeker after the "nature" or "essence" of something, if he is to be philosophically responsible, must fix the data for analysis by independent pragmatical investigation: he must begin with a set of instances of the use of the term which designates the "things" whose nature is in question. He must "look and see" whether, in fact, the things designated by a term do share a feature which, without qualification or pragmatic shifting (changes in the uses of terms), can be said to be "common" to them all. If there is no such feature, the philosopher—if he is not so naive as to expect language to be nothing more than the pasting of verbal labels on things identical in kind—goes on to consider the possibility of so using descriptive phrases (which may, to some extent and in various ways, be ambiguous or vague) as to be able to claim (although, now, with at least implicit qualification) that the things designated are alike in kind, that is, are in some respect "common." If it may be plausibly argued, on the basis of pragmatical evidence, that the term used to designate the things whose nature is in question designates them *qua* being of this "common" nature, the account of the "common" feature, as uncovered by pragmatical analysis and as fixed by semantical decision, is the philosopher's account of "essence."

We have found, in reading Hume, that the philosopher was very much aware of language and of the degree to which the use of language is philosophically pertinent. He speaks of what "are commonly denominated *Thoughts* or *Ideas*," of perceptions which "want a name in our language," and of ranking some of them "under a general term" for "philosophical purposes"; furthermore, he makes a pragmatical stipulation: "Let us . . . use a little freedom, and call them *Impressions;* employing that word in a sense somewhat different from the usual." He describes what he considers to be the circumstances under which we "call the one object, Cause; the other, Effect."

Hume is a refreshing philosopher because he attempts to relate systematically the uses of the terms "cause" and "effect" to matters that fall within the range of ordinary experience. He has no patience with those who suppose that there are mysterious "necessities" that operate in nature but cannot be recognized by any observer, and he attempts to account for the general belief in causal necessity by suggesting that most persons, having observed events of certain kinds to be constantly conjoined, develop a habit of expectation the force of which is attributed (naively) to the events observed. The method is modern, and the philosophical artistry displayed is of a high order; and even though we have found some reasons for objecting to Hume's semantical account, we acknowledge the incisive integrity with which this philosopher disposed of traditional, metaphysical conceptions of whatever it is we call attention to when we use the terms "cause" and "effect" in ordinary discourse.

QUESTIONS FOR DISCUSSION

1. Criticize the claim "When we say . . . that one object is connected with another, we mean only that they have acquired a connexion in our thought . . . ." *Could* we mean this and not know that we mean it? *Do* we mean it? (Consider the force of the use of the word "only.")

2. What is the difference between two events' *seeming to be similar* and *actually being similar*? Suppose that two events are actually similar: can they then be known to appear to be similar without being known actually to be similar?

3. Criticize the claim that a cause and its effect are but the earlier and immediately subsequent phases of a single complex event.

4. What sorts of objections can be made to a proposed definition? What are the appropriate rejoinders for each of these sorts of objections?

5. How is one to distinguish (if at all) between an emotive use of a descriptive term and a descriptive use of an emotive term? How can a term, considered apart from a particular use of that term, meaningfully be said to be a descriptive term (or an emotive term)?

6. Are there terms which have uses but cannot be defined?

7. Could there be a difference between using a term in its broad sense strictly and using the same term in its narrow sense loosely? Must there be a difference? Consider: Person *A* says, "The earth is spherical," meaning, "Strictly speaking, the earth is (roughly) spherical," and person B says, "The earth is spherical," meaning, "Loosely speaking, the earth is (geometrically) spherical."

8. Could there be a world without causes?

9. Why might it not be better to fashion an entirely new vocabulary by devising stipulative definitions than to undertake the attempt to define terms already in use? Would not such an approach (that of fashioning precise definitions for specific purposes) be superior to the philosophical approach?

10. George Santayana claimed that when the uncritical person says, "It is beautiful," he supposes that his pleasure is a quality of the object said to be beautiful. Criticize this claim; compare it to Hume's claim that in describing events as necessarily connected, we attribute to the events something we feel in our minds.

IV

ZENO

THE SLOWEST WILL NEVER BE OVERTAKEN IN
ITS COURSE BY THE SWIFTEST—a *logical claim*

ZENO'S ARGUMENT (AS REPORTED BY ARISTOTLE)

*The second [of Zeno's arguments about motion] is what is known
as 'the Achilles,' which purports to show that the slowest will never
be overtaken in its course by the swiftest, inasmuch as, reckoning from
any given instant, the pursuer, before he can catch the pursued, must
reach the point from which the pursued started at that instant, and so
the slower will always be some distance in advance of the swifter.*

[From *The Physics,* Book VI, Chapter 9, by Aristotle (384–
322 B.C.); translated by Philip H. Wicksteed and Francis M.
Cornford.*]

AN ANALYSIS OF ZENO'S ARGUMENT

1. THE BASIC CLAIM

    The argument we are considering is the argument we find in
the *translation* of Aristotle's *Physics.* If, as we have been claiming,

**Edition used: Harvard University Press and William Heinemann Ltd.,
1952.*

the criticism of a philosophical argument is a responsible one only if it proceeds on the basis of a careful examination of the uses, meanings, and forms of the statements used in the argument, how can our criticism of Zeno's argument be responsible if the version we are considering here is two times removed from the original (which is not available for examination)?

The answer is that we are concerned with the argument as here expressed; the language we examine is the language here used. Aristotle's version of Zeno's argument is generally regarded as authoritative; but, relative to our purposes, it is only of historical interest whether the argument we consider is the argument, or close to the argument, that Zeno presented. Our interest is not historical, but critical. We consider the argument before us as an attempt to establish a logical point logically, and we presume—although it matters only historically—that the kind of argument we consider bears some resemblance to the kind of argument Zeno used.

The conclusion of the argument being considered is here expressed as follows: "the slowest will never be overtaken in its course by the swiftest . . . ." The context and character of the argument, as one of a series of logical paradoxes attributed to Zeno, is such as to make it evident that the conclusion is *logical*; that is, the conclusion, although supported by reasons (premises), has a logical point, a point perhaps better expressed by saying (nonlinguistically) that the slowest *can* never be overtaken in its course by the swiftest, or by saying (linguistically) that it would be a *contradiction* in terms to state, "The slowest is overtaken in its course by the swiftest."

Our task is to consider whether, relative to the use of language here exhibited, it would indeed be contradictory to state that the slowest is overtaken in its course by the swiftest.

In our examination of the argument we shall visualize the scene in the traditional manner; that is, as having to do with a race between a tortoise, the slower, which has a head start, and Achilles, the swifter, who, having fallen behind, can win the race only by overtaking and passing the tortoise.

2. THE BASIC ARGUMENT

Zeno (for we shall regard him as the author of the argument

here translated from Aristotle) argues that his conclusion follows from the premise that "reckoning from any given instant, the pursuer, before he can catch the pursued, must reach the point from which the pursued started at that instant," for Zeno suggests (with the expression "and so") that from this basic premise another premise, itself an intermediate conclusion, follows; namely, that "the slower will always be some distance in advance of the swifter." The conclusion, that the slowest will (can) never be overtaken in its course by the swiftest, is presumed to follow.

The basic premise is a logical claim, to which we are alerted by the use of the term "must." Considered nonlinguistically and grammatically (that is, with regard to syntax alone), the statement is about "the pursuer," and the claim is that the pursuer, Achilles, *if* he is to catch the pursued, the tortoise, *must* reach the point at which the tortoise was when the pursuit, or any particular phase of the pursuit, began. Put linguistically, the claim is concerned with the logical form of a statement. The claim is that the statement "Achilles catches up with the tortoise and has not reached the point from which the tortoise started at the beginning of the pursuit" is *self-contradictory*; or we could say that the claim is that the statement "Achilles catches up with the tortoise after having reached the point at which the tortoise was when the pursuit began" is tautological.

Let us, then, take as an expression of the first premise of Zeno's argument the following:

1. *The statement "If Achilles overtakes the tortoise, he first reaches the points at which the tortoise was as each phase of the pursuit began" is tautological.*

Zeno then adds (according to Aristotle), "and so the slower will always be some distance in advance of the swifter." This logical transition is understandable only on the assumption that if to overtake the tortoise Achilles must first reach the points at which the tortoise was as each phase of the pursuit began, then by the time Achilles reaches the point at which the tortoise was when the pursuit *first* began (let us call that point "p_1"), the tortoise has advanced *some* distance farther to another point (call it "p_2"); but by the time Achilles reaches *that* point, p_2, the tortoise, which is, presumably,

continually moving, has had time to reach another point (call it "p_3");
but by the time Achilles reaches p_3, the tortoise has reached p_4, and
so on, *ad infinitum*. It is on the basis of some such consideration, we
presume, that Zeno adds, "and so the slower will always be *some
distance in advance* of the swifter" (italics added).

Let us, then, as a statement of the second, implicit premise,
use the following:

> 2. *The statement "If Achilles reaches a point at which the
> tortoise was as a particular phase of the pursuit began, the
> tortoise has moved some distance ahead" is tautological.*

Since the suggestion of the argument (as considered logically)
is that—if at the termination of every phase of the pursuit (as limited
by Achilles' reaching the point at which the tortoise was as any given
phase of the pursuit began), the tortoise is still some distance ahead—
Achilles *cannot* overtake the tortoise, we provide a third premise:

> 3. *The statement "The tortoise has moved some distance ahead
> and Achilles has overtaken the tortoise" is contradictory.*

Or we could write:

> 3. *The statement "If the tortoise has moved some distance
> ahead, Achilles has not overtaken the tortoise" is tauto-
> logical.*

The conclusion, then, may be stated:

> ∴ *The statement "Achilles overtakes the tortoise" is self-
> contradictory.*

3. CRITICISM OF THE BASIC ARGUMENT

Let us begin the criticism of Zeno's basic argument by considering the argument nonlinguistically. Perhaps in this way we shall come
to appreciate the reasons that led to Zeno's logical claims:

> 1. *If Achilles overtakes the tortoise, he must first have reached
> the points at which the tortoise was as each phase of the
> pursuit began.*
> 2. *Whatever such point Achilles has reached, the tortoise must
> have moved some distance ahead.*

3. *If the tortoise has moved some distance ahead, Achilles must not have overtaken the tortoise.*

∴. *If Achilles overtakes the tortoise, he must not have overtaken the tortoise.* Or, in other words, *Achilles cannot overtake the tortoise.*

The conclusion *appears* to follow logically from the premises, and by a simple symbolism (adequate for our present purposes) we can *show* the structure of the argument. An examination of the logical diagram that can be constructed by reference to the premises as symbolized may then provide evidence on the basis of which we can justify our impression that Zeno's argument, in its present form, is valid.

Let us symbolize the first premise by simply indicating (with "→") the "if . . . then . . ." relation between the propositions that *Achilles overtakes the tortoise* (which we shall symbolize by "*O*") and *Achilles has reached the points at which the tortoise was as each phase of the pursuit began* ("*R*"):

$$O \rightarrow R$$

Now, although the second premise considers the aforementioned points distributively, not collectively, we shall represent the logical transition needed by using the following symbolization:

$$R \rightarrow M$$

—where "*M*" represents the proposition that *the tortoise has moved some distance ahead*.

The third premise may now be symbolized as follows:

$$M \rightarrow \sim O$$

—where "$\sim O$" is used to mean that it is *not* true that *Achilles has overtaken the tortoise*.

Now we can construct a logical diagram of the argument, a kind of picture or map of the logical route taken by Zeno:

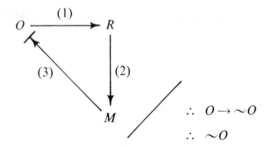

$$\therefore \ O \rightarrow \sim O$$

$$\therefore \ \sim O$$

The argument is designed to show (as the representations of the conclusion indicate) that if one begins with *O*, one ends with non-*O*. Or, if *O* is true, *O* is false. Since *O* is either true or false but cannot be both (since, that is, either Achilles overtakes the tortoise or he does not); and since *if O is true*, then (as the diagram shows) *O* is *false*; and since if *O* is *false*, *O* is *false*, then (since either alternative leads to the conclusion that *O* is *false*) *O* is *false*. The diagram shows that, given the premises, the conclusion logically follows.

But our logical diagram is *tentative* in that it is subject to revision on the basis of pragmatical and semantical considerations that might lead to logical revisions of the premises. If we are led to change the symbolization of the premises, we shall have to reconsider the logical character of the argument; but if examination of the premises does not lead to revision of their logical symbolization, our judgment of the validity of the argument stands.

However, even if we decide that the argument is valid, we are not bound to accept the conclusion. For we may deny one or more of the premises of the argument; and if we do, we may interrupt the logical progression on which the force of the argument depends. In this case, denying one of the premises would break the logical chain and destroy the force of the argument.

Thus, we now consider each of the premises in turn. We have interpreted the premises as *logical* claims; hence, our appraisal of their acceptability will depend on our decisions as to the *meanings* of the statements with which the three claims are concerned; and our decisions with regard to meanings will be determined by discoveries and decisions with regard to the *uses* of the terms involved. (We are now logically appraising the logical *claims;* we are *not now* considering the logical character of the *argument* as a whole.)

PREMISE 1

Are we willing to grant that *if Achilles overtakes the tortoise, he must first have reached the points at which the tortoise was as each phase of the pursuit began?* The logical claim involved here is that it *follows* (logically) from the proposition that *Achilles overtakes the tortoise,* that *Achilles first reaches the points . . . ,* and so on. And the only apparent ground for such a claim would be that the *meaning* of the term "overtakes" is such that overtaking the tortoise *involves* reaching all the points at which the tortoise was as each phase of the pursuit began.

To decide whether the implicit semantical claim is acceptable, we consider the use of the term "overtake" as used in Zeno's argument. The term is used in the *description* of a race between the tortoise, which has a head start, and Achilles, the swifter runner, who has somehow been left behind. The argument suggests that to "overtake" the tortoise, Achilles must "catch the pursued," and the logic of the argument suggests that to "catch the pursued" Achilles must *come even* with the tortoise: the tortoise cannot "be some distance in advance." There is nothing odd about this description; we should all be inclined to accept this way of talking and, consequently, to agree that to "overtake" something, the pursuer must reach a point at which he has come even with the pursued. And we agree, also, that prior to coming to that point, the pursuer must reach the various points at which the pursued was as each phase of the pursuit began. To fail to reach the points at which the pursued *was* would make impossible the task of overtaking the pursued.

In making this semantical concession, however, we do not commit ourselves to any such absurd view as that Achilles can meaningfully be said to "occupy" each of a series of "points," infinite in number, previously "occupied" by the tortoise. Nothing, in any ordinary sense of the term "occupies," occupies a *point* (although something can meaningfully be said to occupy a "place"), if by "point" is meant what could be defined as the intersection of two one-dimensional line segments. But Zeno does not claim that Achilles successively occupies an infinite number of points; Zeno's claim is simply that to overtake something, the pursuer must reach the places in the course through which the tortoise has already passed. The word "point" is used in the translation; but the use of the term is clearly not geometrical, but rather nontechnically conventional.

Let us, then, grant premise 1. We agree that it is trivially and tautologically true to say that if Achilles *overtakes* the tortoise, he first reaches the points reached by the tortoise. Reaching the points the tortoise *has* formerly reached *necessarily comes before* reaching the point at which the tortoise *is*. The necessity here is a logical necessity insured by our use of tenses. We have not exhausted the semantical and pragmatical analysis of the statements logically related in premise 1, but our consideration of the terms used is such as to lead us to concede the point.

PREMISE 2

Are we also willing to concede that *whatever* "point" or place in the course Achilles reaches, the tortoise *must* have moved some distance ahead? Would it be contradictory to state that Achilles has reached the place where he has come even with the tortoise? Would it be contradictory to say that Achilles has reached that point in the race at which he passes the tortoise?

Relative to ordinary usage, it would surely not be contradictory to say, "Achilles is passing the tortoise"; and yet, if Achilles is now passing the tortoise, he must already have passed through all those places the tortoise has passed through. That is, Achilles can satisfy the requirement of premise 1—that he reach, or pass through, every place reached by the tortoise—and nevertheless, for an instant, be as far advanced as the tortoise, immediately prior to drawing away from the tortoise and taking the lead.

We notice, however, that premise 2 has to do with reaching "points" the tortoise *was* at, points "from which the pursued started," and it is true with regard to all such points that upon reaching any one of them, Achilles would still be some distance behind the tortoise. So long as Achilles is the "pursuer," engaged in closing the distance between himself and the tortoise, the tortoise is maintaining the lead, because in the interval between the time Achilles starts to close a given gap and the time when he reaches the point reached by the tortoise as Achilles began to close the gap, the tortoise has moved ahead. Every time Achilles reaches a point at which the tortoise *was,* the tortoise has moved on. But when Achilles finally reaches the point at which the tortoise *is,* he reaches a point of which it cannot truly be said that, as of that instant, it is the point at which the tortoise *was.* Hence, although we may concede that whenever Achilles reaches a point at which the tortoise *was,* the tortoise is some distance ahead, we need not concede—and, in fact, we would deny—that when Achilles reaches the point at which the tortoise *is,* the tortoise has moved some distance ahead. (And there is no gainsaying the observable fact that Achilles, the faster runner, as representative of the swifter, sometimes overtakes and passes the tortoise, the image of the slower runner. The argument with Zeno is not an argument as to whether, *in experience,* we find swifter runners overtaking slower runners and going on to win races; the argument is as to whether there is anything wrong in Zeno's *description* of what happens; for according to Zeno's description of what happens, Achilles—the swifter runner—could never overtake the slower runner, and this is a conclusion we are reluctant to accept.)

Since in the original (translated) version of the argument the claim here expressed as premise 2 is concerned with the "pursuer" and with the advancement of the "pursued" during the time the pursuer closes the gap between the point at which the pursuer was and the point at which the pursued was when the pursuit began, let us regard premise 2 as making reference to points at which the tortoise "was," excluding any point at which the tortoise "is." We then concede that whenever Achilles reaches a point at which the tortoise *was,* the tortoise is no longer there, but some distance ahead. Thus, premise 2, to be made clear, needs a *time* reference. We rephrase it as follows: *Whenever* Achilles reaches a point at which the tortoise *was,* the tortoise, by the time Achilles reaches that point, has moved some distance ahead.

We can now accept premise 2 without being committed to the proposition that whenever Achilles reaches the point at which the tortoise *is,* the tortoise *at that instant* is some distance ahead. This latter proposition is contradictory, for the statement of it describes the tortoise as being both *at* and *not at* the point Achilles has reached, in that if the tortoise can be said to be "some distance ahead" of a point, it cannot (relative to the meaning of "some distance ahead") be said *then* (at the same time) to be *at* that point; yet the earlier part of the description says that the tortoise is *at* the point Achilles reaches.

Let us now consider the progress of the argument to this point. Let us emphasize the claim expressed in premise 1 by adding the term "all" and underscoring the term "was":

1. If Achilles overtakes the tortoise, he must first have reached *all* the points at which the tortoise *was* as each phase of the pursuit began.

And we rewrite premise 2 in order to tie it into premise 1:

2. If Achilles has reached *all* the points at which the tortoise *was*, the tortoise must have moved some distance ahead.

Now we *reject* premise 2, for in this statement we find the contradiction we were at pains to avoid. Far from conceding that if Achilles has reached *all* the points at which the tortoise *was,* the tortoise has (or, even worse, *must* have) moved some distance ahead, we deny that the tortoise could then be ahead at all. Achilles, having covered all the points at which the tortoise *was*, is, at any given instant, either even with the tortoise or ahead of the tortoise; and in either case, the tortoise is *not* some distance ahead.

We must rewrite premise 2 to tie it (logically) into premise 1, if we are to retain the logical structure on which the validity of the argument depends. Yet premise 2, as tied into premise 1, is unacceptable because it is self-contradictory.

If, on the other hand, we retain a formulation to be designated as premise 2 which sets forth a proposition we find to be acceptable —namely, that at the instant Achilles reaches a point at which the tortoise *was*, the tortoise is some distance ahead—we break the logical chain. Premise 1 has to do with the proposition that Achilles has reached *all* the points at which the tortoise *was,* while premise 2, in the form in which it is acceptable, has to do with the situation that obtains at the time Achilles reaches any *one* such point.

Perhaps it might appear as if Achilles could satisfy the requirement of covering *all* the points at which the tortoise *was* and yet *not* be up to, or past, the point at which the tortoise *is*. This could happen, it might be supposed, if Achilles has arrived at the *last* of the points at which the tortoise *has been*, but has *not yet* made the transition to the point at which the tortoise *is*; it might be maintained that it would be the case, at that instant, that Achilles has reached *each and every* point at which the tortoise *has been* and yet, since he is *one point short* of the tortoise's present position, *not* be at the point at which the tortoise *is*.

The fallacy in this argument resides in the assumption that it makes sense to speak of being "one point short" of coming even with the tortoise. In the description of the race, the term "point" is not used to designate a determinable physical entity or a physically definable place. To say that Achilles has reached a point formerly reached by the tortoise does not mean that he has reached one in a series of self-contained and geographically definable places. Alternatively, we might say, with regard to Achilles' reaching a point the tortoise has passed, that "Achilles is now where the tortoise was"; or even, "Achilles still has not caught up with the tortoise." In our analysis of a distance or of a given period of time we may, through the use of the language of mathematics, name any one of an infinite number of "points" between the beginning and the end of a spatial or temporal segment; we can speak of the "point" half-way between the beginning and the end of a line segment, and of the "point" half-way between the beginning and the point that is half-way between the beginning and the end of the line segment, and so forth, *ad infinitum*. Since between any "point" so identified and named and the "point" which marks the precise end of the line segment (that is, the *end*) any number of points may be identified and named, there is no sense in talking about a "next-to-last" point. When the practice of a method of analysis is interminable, there is no "last" or "next-to-last" product of the analysis.

But the fallacy exhibited in the argument of our hypothetical critic is not Zeno's fallacy. Zeno nowhere maintains that there is any such entity as a next-to-last point. Zeno's fallacy is either that of limiting his analysis to the *pursuit* of the tortoise—thereby, in effect, *defining* Achilles as "the pursuer" and leaving out of the account those latter phases of the race during which Achilles comes even with the tortoise and draws ahead—or that of attributing to the race, or to a phase of the race, a feature of the mode of analysis adopted by Zeno; namely, the *interminability* of considering successive moves by which Achilles comes to points beyond which the tortoise has had time to move.

Thus, although we are inclined to agree that the terms "overtake" and "catch" are so used in Zeno's argument that one could reasonably claim that to "overtake" the tortoise Achilles must cover the distance between himself and the tortoise so as to close the gap between them—and, hence, must reach every point from which the tortoise moves as various phases of the pursuit begin—we do *not* agree that the tortoise will always be some distance ahead, for we do not agree that there is no end to the process of covering the points the tortoise first covers. Achilles can cover all the points previously covered by the tortoise, and the tortoise would not then be in the lead but, on the contrary, it would be, at a given instant, either even with Achilles or some distance behind. Consequently, we do not agree that it is self-contradictory to state, "Achilles overtakes the tortoise."

Our critical conclusion is that premises 1 and 3 can be so phrased as to be acceptable; but premise 2, if made acceptable, does not connect logically with the other two premises, and if it is in the form which makes it logically useful for Zeno—in that it provides the link that makes the argument valid—it is not acceptable.

COMMENTS ON THE ANALYSIS OF ZENO'S ARGUMENT

The analysis of Zeno's argument makes evident the truth of the claim that *a logical truth depends upon the meaning* of the statement of the truth, and *the meaning depends upon the use* of the language of the statement. We have found that, in certain cases, even the *tense* of the verb is critical in determining the logical character of a claim. In Zeno's argument, the claim that *if Achilles has reached a point at which the tortoise* was, *the tortoise has moved some distance ahead* can be accepted as logically true (given the context in which the tortoise is moving continually toward the goal), but the claim that *if Achilles has reached the point at which the tortoise is, the tortoise has moved some distance ahead* is rejected as being logically false.

The fallacy in Zeno's argument can most readily be uncovered if we first of all designate the swifter runner as "Achilles" or as the "swifter runner" rather than as "the pursuer." The claim that *the pursuer is in the lead* appears to be contradictory, although if by "the pursuer" is meant "he who initiated the pursuit by pursuing" rather than "he who is now pursuing," then it is not self-contradictory to speak of a "pursuer" as enjoying the consequences of having taken the lead or of having captured the maiden (or the tortoise, or whatever). Consideration of this point leads us to recognize the logical consequences of using a descriptive term which may be applicable to something at one time, *definitively,* as a term applicable at any time. Thus, whether or not the sentence "The fat boy is now thin" is self-contradictory depends on the use of the term "fat"; if the term is used *definitively*, the statement is contradictory; if, on the other hand, the descriptive adjective "fat" at one time applied to a certain boy but need not be applicable to him (for he is identified in some way other than as being "essentially" fat), it is not contradictory to speak of a boy, who was at one time fat, as now being thin.

We have seen, also, how such a term as "point," which in certain contexts (mathematical) has one use, in other contexts has uses which yield quite different logical consequences. "I'll meet you in the same old place, at the point where the three roads meet" refers to a possibility, even though I am a person of three (at least) dimensions, and even though a point, relative to the mathematical use of that term, has no dimensions.

In the analysis of an argument used to support a logical claim, then, we must pay close attention to the use of the language of the argument, not only to the uses of terms considered as calling attention to various properties or things, but also to the uses of entire expressions, for it is sometimes central in the appraisal of an argument to decide whether an expression is being used in a *contingently descriptive* way or in a *definitive* (necessarily descriptive) way. And, of course, it is first of all necessary to determine, if one is to get at the logical structure of an argument or claim, whether the use of language is such as to provide a logical structure of the kind to which the claim (whether explicitly or implicitly) alludes. It sometimes happens that a statement is primarily *expressive* in its function, even though the grammatical structure of the statement suggests that the statement is propositional and has a logical form. The lover's cry "This *must* be Venus!" should not be subjected to logical analysis. Such a statement is more to be acted upon than thought about.

QUESTIONS FOR DISCUSSION

1. The translation of Aristotle's account of Zeno's argument reads, ". . . the slowest *will* never be overtaken in its course by the swiftest . . ." (italics added). How can the critic be justified in claiming that the term "will" means what "can" means?

2. If there is no finite number of "points" to be covered by Achilles in overtaking the tortoise, does it make sense to speak of "every" point reached by the tortoise before it is overtaken? If so, *how* does it make sense?

3. Can there be a point which is the point before the point at which Achilles comes even with the tortoise? Can there be a point which is a point before the point at which Achilles comes even with the tortoise? Can there be a point at which it looks as though Achilles might not catch up with the tortoise? If so, could this point be the point just before the point at which Achilles does catch up with the tortoise?

4. Zeno also argued that the swifter runner cannot overtake the slower because the swifter always has half the distance remaining between himself and the slower. (When Achilles has covered half the distance between himself and the tortoise, he still has half the distance remaining to cover before he can close the gap. But when he has covered *that* half, he has half of the remainder to cover. And so on, *ad infinitum*.) Criticize this argument.

5. In the paradox of the flying arrow, Zeno argues that ". . . if everything when it occupies an equal space is at rest, and if that which is in locomotion is always occupying such a space at any moment, the flying arrow is therefore motionless." (That is, at any moment of its flight the arrow is somewhere, occupying a space defined by its dimensions; but to be somewhere is to be at rest, and motion cannot be a series of rests. Hence, the arrow cannot be moving.) Criticize this argument.

6. Locate or construct five paradoxes made possible by pragmatical switches (going from one use of a term to another). Are such statements merely verbal curiosities, or do they sometimes make a point that could not be made as effectively in any other way? Why are paradoxes useful?

7. The Socratic method is often explained as the method of bringing out, through questions and responses, contradictions implicit in a claim. Analyze some instances of the use of the Socratic method (as provided by Plato's *Dialogues*) and test the claim that the Socratic method is often the method of using pragmatical switches so as to make a covert change in the meaning of a claim being challenged.

8. Is it paradoxical that two judges could agree on the facts secured by evidence and yet disagree in their "findings," the one judge finding the accused to be guilty and the other judge finding him innocent? Must one judge be mistaken?

9. Is there any difference between a contradiction and a paradox? Is a paradox contradictory until it is resolved?

10. Consider the merits of the claim that Zeno devised his paradoxes in the effort to argue against certain modes of analysis and that he did not intend to deny the reality of motion. (The evidence of intention must be found in the argument.)

V

KANT

THE THINGS WHICH WE INTUIT ARE NOT IN
THEMSELVES WHAT WE INTUIT THEM AS
BEING—*a metaphysical claim*

KANT'S ARGUMENT

... That space and time are only forms of sensible intuition, and so only conditions of the existence of things as appearances; that, moreover, we have no concepts of understanding, and consequently no elements for the knowledge of things, save in so far as intuition can be given corresponding to these concepts; and that we can therefore have no knowledge of any object as thing in itself, but only in so far as it is an object of sensible intuition, that is, an appearance—all this is proved in the analytical part of the Critique. Thus it does indeed follow that all possible speculative knowledge of reason is limited to mere objects of experience. *But our further contention must also be duly borne in mind, namely, that though we cannot* know *these objects as things in themselves, we must yet be in position at least to*

think *them as things in themselves;** otherwise we should be landed in the absurd conclusion that there can be appearance without anything that appears. Now let us suppose that the distinction, which our Critique has shown to be necessary, between things as objects of experience and those same things as things in themselves, had not been made. In that case all things in general, as far as they are efficient causes, would be determined by the principle of causality, and consequently by the mechanism of nature. I could not, therefore, without palpable contradiction, say of one and the same being, for instance the human soul, that its will is free and yet is subject to natural necessity, that is, is not free. For I have taken the soul in both propositions* in one and the same sense, *namely as a thing in general, that is, as a thing in itself; and save by means of a preceding critique, could not have done otherwise. But if our Critique is not in error in teaching that the object is to be taken* in a twofold sense, *namely as appearance and as thing in itself; if the deduction of the concepts of understanding is valid, and the principle of causality therefore applies only to things taken in the former sense, namely, in so far as they are objects of experience—these same objects, taken in the other sense, not being subject to the principle—then there is no contradiction in supposing that one and the same will is, in the appearance, that is, in its visible acts, necessarily subject to the law of nature, and so far* not *free, while yet, as belonging to a thing in itself, it is not subject to that law, and is therefore* free. *My soul, viewed from the latter standpoint, cannot indeed be known by means of speculative reason (and still less through empirical observation); and freedom as a property of a being to which I attribute effects in the sensible world, is therefore also not knowable in any such fash-*

---

*To know *an object I must be able to prove its possibility, either from its actuality as attested by experience, or* a priori *by means of reason. But I can* think *whatever I please, provided only that I do not contradict myself, that is, provided my concept is a possible thought. This suffices for the possibility of the concept, even though I may not be able to answer for there being, in the sum of all possibilities, an object corresponding to it. But something more is required before I can ascribe to such a concept objective validity, that is, real possibility; the former possibility is merely logical. This something more need not, however, be sought in the theoretical sources of knowledge; it may lie in those that are practical.*

ion. For I should then have to know such a being as determined in its existence, and yet as not determined in time—which is impossible, since I cannot support my concept by any intuition. But though I cannot know, I can yet think freedom; that is to say, the representation of it is at least not self-contradictory, provided due account be taken of our critical distinction between the two modes of representation, the sensible and the intellectual, and of the resulting limitation of the pure concepts of understanding and of the principles which flow from them.

If we grant that morality necessarily presupposes freedom (in the strictest sense) as a property of our will; if, that is to say, we grant that it yields practical principles—original principles, proper to our reason—as a priori data of reason, and that this would be absolutely impossible save on the assumption of freedom; and if at the same time we grant that speculative reason has proved that such freedom does not allow of being thought, then the former supposition—that made on behalf of morality—would have to give way to this other contention, the opposite of which involves a palpable contradiction. For since it is only on the assumption of freedom that the negation of morality contains any contradiction, freedom, and with it morality, would have to yield to the mechanism of nature.

Morality does not, indeed, require that freedom should be understood, but only that it should not contradict itself, and so should at least allow of being thought, and that as thus thought it should place no obstacle in the way of a free act (viewed in another relation) likewise conforming to the mechanism of nature. The doctrine of morality and the doctrine of nature may each, therefore, make good its position. This, however, is only possible in so far as criticism has previously established our unavoidable ignorance of things in themselves, and has limited all that we can theoretically know to mere appearances.

This discussion as to the positive advantage of critical principles of pure reason can be similarly developed in regard to the concept of God and of the simple nature of our soul; but for the sake of brevity such further discussion may be omitted. [From what has already been said, it is evident that] even the assumption—as made on behalf of the necessary practical employment of my reason—of

God, freedom, *and* immortality *is not permissible unless at the same time speculative reason be deprived of its pretensions to transcendent insight. For in order to arrive at such insight it must make use of principles which, in fact, extend only to objects of possible experience, and which, if also applied to what cannot be an object of experience, always really change this into an appearance, thus rendering all* practical extension *of pure reason impossible. I have therefore found it necessary to deny* knowledge, *in order to make room for* faith. . . .

[From *The Critique of Pure Reason*, Preface to Second Edition (1787), by Immanuel Kant (1724–1804); translated by Norman Kemp Smith.*]

There can be no doubt that all our knowledge begins with experience. For how should our faculty of knowledge be awakened into action did not objects affecting our senses partly of themselves produce representations, partly arouse the activity of our understanding to compare these representations, and, by combining or separating them, work up the raw material of the sensible impressions into that knowledge of objects which is entitled experience? In the order of time, therefore, we have no knowledge antecedent to experience, and with experience all our knowledge begins.

But though all our knowledge begins with experience, it does not follow that it all arises out of experience. For it may well be that even our empirical knowledge is made up of what we receive through impressions and of what our own faculty of knowledge (sensible impressions serving merely as the occasion) supplies from itself. If our faculty of knowledge makes any such addition, it may be that we are not in a position to distinguish it from the raw material, until with long practice of attention we have become skilled in separating it.

This, then, is a question which at least calls for closer examination, and does not allow of any off-hand answer:—whether there is any knowledge that is thus independent of experience and even of all impressions of the senses. Such knowledge is entitled a priori, *and distinguished from the* empirical, *which has its sources* a posteriori, *that is, in experience.*

Edition used: Macmillan & Co. Ltd., 1950.

The expression 'a priori' *does not, however, indicate with sufficient precision the full meaning of our question. For it has been customary to say, even of much knowledge that is derived from empirical sources, that we have it or are capable of having it* a priori, *meaning thereby that we do not derive it immediately from experience, but from a universal rule—a rule which is itself, however, borrowed by us from experience. Thus we would say of a man who undermined the foundations of his house, that he might have known* a priori *that it would fall, that is, that he need not have waited for the experience of its actual falling. But still he could not know this completely* a priori. *For he had first to learn through experience that bodies are heavy, and therefore fall when their supports are withdrawn.*

In what follows, therefore, we shall understand by a priori *knowledge, not knowledge independent of this or that experience, but knowledge absolutely independent of all experience. Opposed to it is empirical knowledge, which is knowledge possible only* a posteriori, *that is, through experience.* A priori *modes of knowledge are entitled pure when there is no admixture of anything empirical. Thus, for instance, the proposition, 'every alteration has its cause', while an* a priori *proposition, is not a pure proposition, because alteration is a concept which can be derived only from experience.*

[From *The Critique of Pure Reason*, Introduction, I.]

In all judgments in which the relation of a subject to the predicate is thought (I take into consideration affirmative judgments only, the subsequent application to negative judgments being easily made), this relation is possible in two different ways. Either the predicate B belongs to the subject A, as something which is (covertly) contained in this concept A; or B lies outside the concept A, although it does indeed stand in connection with it. In the one case I entitle the judgment analytic, in the other synthetic. Analytic judgments (affirmative) are therefore those in which the connection of the predicate with the subject is thought through identity; those in which this connection is thought without identity should be entitled synthetic. The former, as adding nothing through the predicate to the concept of the subject, but merely breaking it up into those constituent con-

cepts that have all along been thought in it, although confusedly, can also be entitled explicative. *The latter, on the other hand, add to the concept of the subject a predicate which has not been in any wise thought in it, and which no analysis could possibly extract from it; and they may therefore be entitled ampliative. If I say, for instance, 'All bodies are extended', this is an analytic judgment. For I do not require to go beyond the concept which I connect with 'body' in order to find extension as bound up with it. To meet with this predicate, I have merely to analyse the concept, that is, to become conscious to myself of the manifold which I always think in that concept. The judgment is therefore analytic. But when I say, 'All bodies are heavy', the predicate is something quite different from anything that I think in the mere concept of body in general; and the addition of such a predicate therefore yields a synthetic judgment.*

Judgments of experience, as such, are one and all synthetic. For it would be absurd to found an analytic judgment on experience. Since, in framing the judgment, I must not go outside my concept, there is no need to appeal to the testimony of experience in its support. That a body is extended is a proposition that holds a priori *and is not empirical. For, before appealing to experience, I have already in the concept of body all the conditions required for my judgment. I have only to extract from it, in accordance with the principle of contradiction, the required predicate, and in so doing can at the same time become conscious of the necessity of the judgment—and that is what experience could never have taught me. On the other hand, though I do not include in the concept of a body in general the predicate 'weight', none the less this concept indicates an object of experience through one of its parts, and I can add to that part other parts of this same experience, as in this way belonging together with the concept. From the start I can apprehend the concept of body analytically through the characters of extension, impenetrability, figure, etc., all of which are thought in the concept. Now, however, looking back on the experience from which I have derived this concept of body, and finding weight to be invariably connected with the above characters, I attach it as a predicate to the concept; and in doing so I attach it synthetically, and am therefore extending my knowledge. The possibility of the synthesis of the predicate 'weight'* with the concept of 'body' thus rests upon experience. While the one concept is not contained in the other, they yet belong to one another, though only contingently, as parts of a whole, namely, of an experience which is itself a synthetic combination of intuitions. But in a priori synthetic judgments this help is entirely lacking. [I do not here have the advantage of looking around in the field of experience.] Upon what, then, am I to rely, when I seek to go beyond the concept A, and to know that another concept B is connected with it? Through what is the synthesis made possible? Let us take the proposition, 'Everything which happens has its cause'. In the concept of 'something which happens', I do indeed think an existence which is preceded by a time, etc., and from this concept analytic judgments may be obtained. But the concept of a 'cause' lies entirely outside the other concept, and signifies something different from 'that which happens', and is not therefore in any way contained in this latter representation. How come I then to predicate of that which happens something quite different, and to apprehend that the concept of cause, though not contained in it, yet belongs, and indeed necessarily belongs, to it? What is here the unknown $= X$ which gives support to the understanding when it believes that it can discover outside the concept A a predicate B foreign to this concept, which it yet at the same time considers to be connected with it? It cannot be experience, because the suggested principle has connected the second representation with the first, not only with greater universality, but also with the character of necessity, and therefore completely a priori and on the basis of mere concepts. Upon such synthetic, that is, ampliative principles, all our a priori speculative knowledge must ultimately rest; analytic judgments are very important, and indeed necessary, but only for obtaining that clearness in the concepts which is requisite for such a sure and wide synthesis as will lead to a genuinely new addition to all previous knowledge.

[From *The Critique of Pure Reason*, Introduction, IV.]

In whatever manner and by whatever means a mode of knowledge may relate to objects, intuition *is that through which it is in immediate relation to them, and to which all thought as a means is directed. But intuition takes place only in so far as the object is given to us. This again is only possible, to man at least, in so far as the mind is affected in a certain way. The capacity (receptivity) for receiving representations through the mode in which we are affected by objects, is entitled* sensibility. *Objects are* given *to us by means of sensibility, and it alone yields us* intuitions; *they are* thought *through the understanding, and from the understanding arise* concepts. *But all thought must, directly or indirectly, by way of certain characters, relate ultimately to intuitions, and therefore, with us, to sensibility, because in no other way can an object be given to us.*

The effect of an object upon the faculty of representation, so far as we are affected by it, is sensation. *That intuition which is in relation to the object through sensation, is entitled* empirical. *The undetermined object of an empirical intuition is entitled* appearance.

That in the appearance which corresponds to sensation I term its matter; *but that which so determines the manifold of appearance that it allows of being ordered in certain relations, I term the* form *of appearance. That in which alone the sensations can be posited and ordered in a certain form, cannot itself be sensation; and therefore, while the matter of all appearance is given to us* a posteriori *only, its form must lie ready for the sensations* a priori *in the mind, and so must allow of being considered apart from all sensation.*

I term all representations pure *(in the transcendental sense) in which there is nothing that belongs to sensation. The pure form of sensible intuitions in general, in which all the manifold of intuition is intuited in certain relations, must be found in the mind* a priori. *This pure form of sensibility may also itself be called* pure *intuition. Thus, if I take away from the representation of a body that which the understanding thinks in regard to it, substance, force, divisibility, etc., and likewise what belongs to sensation, impenetrability, hardness, colour, etc., something still remains over from this empirical intuition, namely, extension and figure. These belong to pure intuition, which, even without any actual object of the senses or of sensation, exists in the mind* a priori *as a mere form of sensibility.*

The science of all principles of a priori *sensibility I call* transcendental aesthetic. *There must be such a science, forming the first part of the transcendental doctrine of elements, in distinction from that part which deals with the principles of pure thought, and which is called transcendental logic.*

In the transcendental aesthetic we shall, therefore, first isolate *sensibility, by taking away from it everything which the understanding thinks through its concepts, so that nothing may be left save empirical intuition. Secondly, we shall also separate off from it everything which belongs to sensation, so that nothing may remain save pure intuition and the mere form of appearances, which is all that sensibility can supply* a priori. *In the course of this investigation it will be found that there are two pure forms of sensible intuition, serving as principles of* a priori *knowledge, namely, space and time.* . . .

[From *The Critique of Pure Reason,* Transcendental Doctrine of Elements, First Part, Transcendental Aesthetic.]

What we have meant to say is that all our intuition is nothing but the representation of appearance; that the things which we intuit are not in themselves what we intuit them as being, nor their relations so constituted in themselves as they appear to us, and that if the subject, or even only the subjective constitution of the senses in general, be removed, the whole constitution and all the relations of objects in space and time, nay space and time themselves, would vanish. As appearances, they cannot exist in themselves, but only in us. What objects may be in themselves, and apart from all this receptivity of our sensibility, remains completely unknown to us. We know nothing but our mode of perceiving them—a mode which is peculiar to us, and not necessarily shared in by every being, though, certainly, by every human being. With this alone have we any concern. Space and time are its pure forms, and sensation in general its matter. The former alone can we know a priori, *that is, prior to all actual perception; and such knowledge is therefore called pure intuition. The latter is that in our knowledge which leads to its being called* a posteriori *knowledge, that is, empirical intuition. The former inhere in our sensibility with absolute necessity, no matter of what kind our sensations may be; the latter can exist in varying modes. Even if we could bring our intuition to the highest degree of clearness, we should not thereby come any nearer to the constitution of objects in themselves. We should still know only our mode of intuition, that is, our sensibility. We should, indeed, know it completely, but always only under the conditions of space and time—conditions which are originally inherent in the subject. What the objects may be in themselves would never become known to us even through the most enlightened knowledge of that which is alone given us, namely, their appearance.*

*   *   *   *

We commonly distinguish in appearances that which is essentially inherent in their intuition and holds for sense in all human beings, from that which belongs to their intuition accidentally only, and is valid not in relation to sensibility in general but only in relation to a particular standpoint or to a peculiarity of structure in this or that sense. The former kind of knowledge is then declared to represent the object in itself, the latter its appearance only. But this distinction is merely empirical. If, as generally happens, we stop short at this point, and do not proceed, as we ought, to treat the empirical intuition as itself mere appearance, in which nothing that belongs to a thing in itself can be found, our transcendental distinction is lost. We then believe that we know things in themselves, and this in spite of the fact that in the world of sense, however deeply we enquire into its objects, we have to do with nothing but appearances. The rainbow in a sunny shower may be called a mere appearance, and the rain the thing in itself. This is correct, if the latter concept be taken in a merely physical sense. Rain will then be viewed only as that which, in all experience and in all its various positions relative to the senses, is determined thus, and not otherwise, in our intuition. But if we take this empirical object in its general character, and ask, without considering whether or not it is the same for all human sense, whether it represents an object in itself (and by that we cannot mean the drops of rain, for these are already, as appearances, empirical objects), the question as to the relation of the representation to the object at once becomes transcendental. We then realise that not only are the drops of rain mere appearances, but that even their round shape, nay even the space in which they fall, are nothing in themselves, but merely modifications or fundamental forms of our sensible intuition, and that the transcendental object remains unknown to us.

[From *The Critique of Pure Reason,* Transcendental Aesthetic, General Observations on the Transcendental Aesthetic.]

AN ANALYSIS OF KANT'S ARGUMENT

1. THE BASIC CLAIM

Kant's *Critique of Pure Reason* is a work designed to show that synthetic *a priori* knowledge is possible. Kant argues that our knowledge of what he called "the forms of intuition" and "the concepts of the understanding" provides the ground for knowledge that is *a priori* in that it is "knowledge absolutely independent of all experience" and *synthetic* in that it is knowledge that could not be secured through analysis of subject terms. But we shall not attempt to consider whether Kant was justified in making this *logical* claim, for to do so would involve us in an examination and appraisal of the entire work, a task that would be fascinating but practically inexpedient as a philosophical demonstration.

We choose, rather, to consider whether Kant was justified in claiming that "the things which we intuit are not in themselves what we intuit them as being, nor their relations so constituted in themselves as they appear to us, and that if the subject, or even only the subjective constitution of these senses in general, be removed, the whole constitution and all the relations of objects in space and time, nay space and time themselves, would vanish."

The claim, considered nonlinguistically, is about what Kant calls "things in themselves"; and, considered in context, the claim appears to be twofold:

1. *There are things in themselves;* and
2. *Things in themselves are not what we intuit them as being.*

In the Preface to the Second Edition of the *Critique of Pure Reason,* Kant claims that "we can . . . have no knowledge of any object as thing in itself, but only in so far as it is an object of sensible intuition, that is, an appearance . . . ." The distinction is drawn between "objects of experience," or *appearances,* and "things in themselves," or *that which appears.* He describes the distinction as "between things as objects of experience and *those same things* as things in themselves" (italics added); and he speaks of the *Critique* as "teaching that the object is to be taken *in a twofold sense,* namely as appearance and as thing in itself . . . ." These passages, among others, lead us to understand the distinction as one which *logically* distinguishes things *as* the "objects of experience" from things *as* "things in themselves"; there is no suggestion here that there are two kinds of *things.* (We shall consider this problem of interpretation at greater length in the criticism that follows.)

We now restate the twofold claim so as to incorporate the distinctions which Kant's account provides:

1. *There are things that are not objects of experience.*
2. *Things that are not objects of experience are not as they appear to be.*

Whatever is paradoxical in the expression of this claim shall receive examination in the critical appraisal that follows.

2. THE BASIC ARGUMENT

Central to Kant's argument is the distinction between things considered as objects of experience and things *not* considered as objects of experience. We regard this distinction as the one marked by the use of the terms "objects of experience" and " things in themselves." We are encouraged in this interpretation by Kant's remark that it would be absurd to conclude "that there can be appearance without anything that appears." If the distinction can be clarified and maintained in the context of the basic argument to be abstracted from Kant's account, the probability of the correctness of the interpretation will be increased. Let us, then, examine the basic argument.

According to Kant, space and time are "only forms of sensible intuition, and so only conditions of the existence of things as appearances . . . ." Whenever we perceive a thing by the use of the senses, we perceive the thing as spatially and temporally related. It could not be otherwise, Kant suggests, for we so *form* the "appearances" of things as to *give* the appearances spatial and temporal relations; by our way of sensing, things appear to be in space and time: *as* objects of experience, things *are* in space and time.

The word "only" is very important in Kant's account; for if space and time are "only" forms of sensible intuition, there is no possibility of their being *also* forms of things in themselves. Kant draws the logical conclusion that "we can . . . have no knowledge of any object as thing in itself" from the proposition that "space and time are only forms of sensible intuition" and the proposition that "we have no concepts of understanding, and consequently no elements for the knowledge of things, save in so far as intuition can be given corresponding to these concepts . . . ." Space and time are *forms* of sensible *intuition;* the concepts of the understanding are *forms* of the *thoughts* of objects in general. Kant calls the study of the "principles of *a priori* sensibility"—that is, the study of the forms of objects as given in sense experience, the study of the *forms of "intuition"*—"transcendental aesthetic"; and he calls the study of the "principles of pure thought"—that is, the study of the forms of thought or the *concepts* by which objects of experience are thought —"transcendental logic." Kant's claim is that there is a great deal that can be said, prior to the experience of particular things, about objects of experience in general. *A priori* knowledge—"knowledge absolutely independent of all experience" but nevertheless *not* analytic, *not* logically derivable by the analysis of the meanings of terms, and, hence, *synthetic*—is possible because the human being, in experiencing things, *forms* them according to his modes of *sensing* and *thinking* them.

Let us, then, mark the features of Kant's argument by constructing a summary account:

1. *Space and time are only forms of sensible intuition.*
(∴ Space and time *cannot* be forms of things in themselves, for by "things in themselves" is meant things *qua* not objects of experience; hence, things as *not* given in intuition.)

2. *The concepts of our understanding are applicable only to objects of sensible intuition.*

(∴ The concepts of our understanding *cannot* be applicable to things in themselves.)

3. *Only the concepts of the understanding provide elements for the knowledge of things.*

(∴ Things in themselves *cannot* be known.) But,

4. *We can think of something if and only if it is not contradictory to do so,* and

5. *It would be contradictory to think that there are appearances without that which appears.*

(∴ We *can* think of objects as things in themselves.) Furthermore,

6. *There are good practical reasons for assuming (by faith) that there are things in themselves and that they have certain properties we cannot know them to have.* (For example, we cannot know that the will in itself is free, but morality presupposes freedom; hence, without making pretensions to transcendent insight, we assume the freedom of the will.)

∴ *There are things in themselves, and they cannot be what we intuit and understand them as being.*

3. CRITICISM OF THE BASIC ARGUMENT

We note, as previously suggested, that the conclusion of Kant's argument involves two claims; namely, the claim that *there are things in themselves,* and the claim that *things in themselves cannot be what we intuit and understand them as being.*

Let us consider, first of all, the claim that things in themselves *cannot* be what we intuit and understand them as being. We classify the claim as *logical,* for the argument in support of the claim is directed toward showing that it would be *contradictory to speak* of "knowing," "intuiting," or "understanding" *things in themselves.* To appraise the logical claim we must clarify the meanings—through an examination of the uses—of such terms as "things in themselves," "intuit," and "understand."

The use of the term "thing in itself" (in German, *Ding-an-sich*) is central to the argument. We have noted that Kant so uses the term as to make a clear distinction (because of a logical dichotomy) between a thing *as object of experience*—a thing *as it appears to be* —and a thing *in itself.* The problem that occupies the critic at this point is the problem of determining the use of the expression "in itself."

To consider a thing "in itself" is *not* to consider it as it appears to be; but is it possible, if one does not consider a thing as it appears to be, to consider the thing at all? Kant claims that although we *cannot intuit or understand* a thing in itself, we can nevertheless *think* of objects as things in themselves. Our initial critical question is whether Kant is justified in the making of this claim: are there reasons which he gives that might lead us to assent to his claim?

Suppose that we meet someone who appears to be honest and generous. Is it possible that the man himself is neither honest nor generous?

It is obviously possible that a person we meet is not what he appears to be. The man *as we understand him* may be different from the man *as he really is.*

But what method may be used to determine whether a man who *appears* to be honest *really* is honest? Is it not the method of determining what, after an exhaustive investigation, an objective observer —one without prejudice and with the ability to decide—would find the man to appear to be? If for all practical purposes everything that bears on the question of the man's honesty has appeared in the course of the investigation, then what the man appears to be is what he is. (We are attempting to show the relevance of the pragmatical observation that when an investigator after a thorough investigation says, with regard to a suspect, "Well, it now *definitely appears* that he is the murderer," he might as well have said, and on similar occasions does say, "Well, now we *know* he is the murderer.")

It might be claimed, then, that it is pragmatically empty to talk of "things in themselves" if by "things in themselves" is meant things considered apart from any reference to any possible appearance. It might be claimed that to consider a thing without considering how, under some set of circumstances, it would appear to someone is not to consider the thing at all.

ANALYSIS: CRITICISM · 107

But Kant's use of the term "thing in itself" involves no commitment on his part to the claim that something positive can be said about things in themselves. It is surely meaningful, whether before or after the investigation of things, to talk about things as they appear to be. But is it meaningful to talk about things without considering how they appear, or might appear, to be?

The answer that occurs to us is that it is meaningful to talk about things without considering how they appear provided that what we call "talking about things in themselves" is what we might more discerningly describe as "talking about the logic of the use of the term 'thing in itself.' " To say that things in themselves cannot appear to us at all is to point out nonlinguistically that the term "things in themselves" is used to mention things considered in abstraction from any appearance. The term "thing in itself" is not a descriptive term; that is, it does not tell us what, under certain circumstances, we would find the thing appearing to be. The term is used to designate, without describing, that which would be describable relative to experience. The term "thing in itself," like a proper name, is used to *mention without describing;* but the difference between the use of the term "thing in itself" and the use of a proper name is that although ordinarily it is possible to describe a thing that a name names, it is not possible, because of a logical restriction, to describe a thing that the term "thing in itself" mentions, for the term "thing in itself" is used to refer to a thing apart from its being described, experienced, or understood.

The following passage from Chapter III, Book II, the First Division (Transcendental Analytic) of the Transcendental Logic of Kant's *Critique of Pure Reason* appears to make much the same point:

> *If the objective reality of a concept cannot be in any way known, while yet the concept contains no contradiction and also at the same time is connected with other modes of knowledge that involve given concepts which it serves to limit, I entitle that concept problematic. The concept of a* noumenon—*that is, of a thing which is not to be thought as object of the senses but as a thing in itself, solely through a pure understanding—is not in any way contradic-*

tory. For we cannot assert of sensibility that it is the sole possible kind of intuition. Further, the concept of a noumenon is necessary, to prevent sensible intuition from being extended to things in themselves, and thus to limit the objective validity of sensible knowledge. The remaining things, to which it does not apply, are entitled noumena, in order to show that this knowledge cannot extend its domain over everything which the understanding thinks. But none the less we are unable to comprehend how such noumena can be possible, and the domain that lies out beyond the sphere of appearances is for us empty. That is to say, we have an understanding which problematically *extends further, but we have no intuition, indeed not even the concept of a possible intuition, through which objects outside the field of sensibility can be given, and through which the understanding can be employed* assertorically *beyond that field. The concept of a noumenon is thus a merely* limiting concept, *the function of which is to curb the pretensions of sensibility; and it is therefore only of negative employment. At the same time it is no arbitrary invention; it is bound up with the limitation of sensibility, though it cannot affirm anything positive beyond the field of sensibility.*

Let us, then, grant the second part of Kant's claim; namely, the proposition that things in themselves are not what we intuit them as being; for surely if by "things in themselves" is meant things *qua not* objects of experience, and if only objects of experience can be given in intuition, then things in themselves are not comparable in character to objects of experience, even though in mentioning things *as* things in themselves we may be mentioning things that may also be considered *as* objects of experience.

Kant writes of the "pretensions of sensibility" and of the "limitation of sensibility," and we are inclined to agree that sensibility has its limits and that speculation would be pretentious and illegitimate were it to seek to proceed beyond those limits in the search for knowledge. But our concession is not a metaphysical concession; it is the result of the discovery of the *logical* ground for Kant's claim: the terms "things in themselves" and "intuit" are so used that it would be *contradictory* to speak of "intuiting things in themselves." We grant, however, that it is not contradictory to speak of things in themselves, for it is possible to mention things considered in abstraction from their being known.

Let us now consider the claim that *there are things in themselves*.

In reviewing the reasons Kant gives for supposing that there are things in themselves, we find that the preparation of the argument for the claim contains all the elements we have suggested be present in the context of a claim that is to be described as "metaphysical." Kant argues that it is *meaningful* to speak of "things in themselves" and that to do so *does not involve a contradiction;* he maintains that "we cannot *know* . . . objects as things in themselves" (and we have discovered that there is indeed a *logical barrier* in the way of knowing such objects); finally, he offers an account of the *practical advantages* of exercising a "speculative reason" which affirms by *faith* what it cannot legitimately claim to know.

There remains, however, the logical possibility that the appearances we call "objects of experience" are *nothing but* objects of experience; that is, it may be that the thing that appears *is* the appearance; it may be that the appearance is not the appearance *of something*. Perhaps it would, under such circumstances, be "absurd" to speak of an "appearance without anything that appears"; but that absurdity would disappear with the abandonment of the use of the term "appearance": one could call the objects of experience "the given" or the "data," using the terms in such a way so as not to presuppose anything more than what is given.

But a reading of Kant leads one to the conclusion that Kant does more than distinguish logically between the object of experience *qua* experienced and the object of experience *qua* mentionable as object without reference to experience. In arguing that morality presupposes freedom and that a "free act" may conform to "the mechanism of nature," Kant suggests that features such as freedom from causal determination may belong to the world of "things in themselves" that do not, and cannot, belong to the world of experienced objects. Kant further argues that a person as object of experience is subject to the mechanism of nature; as thing in itself, the person may be free—morality demands that he be free, and faith affirms that he is.

Thus, whether or not Kant's use of the term "thing in itself" is such as to allow for the possibility that, in fact, there is no distinction between the appearance and that which appears, Kant clearly shows his concern to "make room for *faith*" by arguing that things in themselves may have features we cannot know them to have. His claim that things in themselves are not as they appear to be is not merely negative; it is not merely the logical point that we cannot consistently talk of the empirical character of things in themselves. The claim that things in themselves are not as they appear to be prepares the way for the claim that things in themselves *are* as they *appear not* to be. We must now consider whether the claim, as interpreted positively, is meaningful.

Kant argues that it is not necessary "that freedom should be understood, but only that it should not contradict itself, and so should at least allow of being thought . . . ." To be free, presumably, is *not* to be subject to the kind of causal determination to which the self, as object of experience, is subject. But the difficulty here is that we are not talking about *two* selves, the self in the world of experience and the self in the free world; we are talking about the self *qua* experienced and the self *qua* that which is experienced (or may be experienced) considered in abstraction from any experience. We are unable to understand how it can make sense to say that the self "in itself" is "free" although, as experienced, it is not free. Kant's claim that the freedom of the thing in itself is *not* to be *understood* but simply *thought* does not provide any positive meaning for the term "free" as used in the characterization of things in themselves. Thus, the claim that things in themselves (human beings as things in themselves) are free is either absurd (since we cannot use, in the characterization of things considered without reference to experience, terms that acquire their meaning empirically) or meaningless.

But although we are inclined to deny that Kant can consistently and meaningfully, even by faith, declare that things in themselves have certain features denied them in the world of experience, we are prepared to grant that he can consistently and meaningfully declare, by faith, that there are things that are not mere appearances or phenomena. (In fact, this claim is nothing more than the fundamental proposition of the realist: that there is something other than "idea," "phenomenon," "appearance.")

The only question remaining for the critic is the question as to whether he shares Kant's faith. Here we come to matters of attitude that are beyond further discussion. "Practical reasons" may be advanced in support of a metaphysical claim, but such reasons are persuasive factors relating to our concerns; they have no logical or empirical utility in the building of proofs.

Our interest in Kant's argument is confined to the argument as an expression and defense of a metaphysical claim. We follow Kant as he attempts to show that what he claims is meaningful, contingent, logically beyond empirical inquiry, and nevertheless worthy of belief as answering to certain human concerns that cannot be satisfied by speculative confinement to the world as experienced.

COMMENTS ON THE ANALYSIS OF KANT'S ARGUMENT

The criticism of a metaphysical claim is a complex but fascinating enterprise. When a philosopher speaks as a metaphysician, he speaks not only as one whose faith must find expression but also as a responsible intellectual prepared to defend the meaningfulness, the cogency, and the urgency of what he claims. Everyone who lives must act on faith, for there is neither the time nor the opportunity to be assured of everything: we assume that buildings will not collapse, that some men mean what they say, that life is not only a dream. Those who count on the support of some god or gods may act on the basis of an assurance they can neither explain nor justify. But the metaphysician, who may share the faith of the common man or of the uncommon mystic, is a philosopher, and as a philosopher he works to make his ideas clear and to uncover the logical barriers which only faith can leap. Thus, it is a complex task to analyze an argument by which a metaphysician seeks to make the content of his faith clear, the necessity for faith obvious, and the demand for faith persuasive; for to analyze a metaphysical argument is to follow a line of thought through all four levels of the philosophic art. The task is also fascinating, for a metaphysical argument is an expression of the whole philosopher, of the man who, through the pragmatical, semantical, and logical dimensions of language, emerges at last into the "world beyond," the transcendental world that faith describes and affirms.

Our criticism of Kant has been concerned with but one of the many challenging metaphysical claims which the philosopher made and defended in his revolutionary and monumental *Critique of Pure Reason*. Even the limited attention we have paid to Kant's argument shows that Kant was a painstaking philosophical craftsman: not only is the work itself architecturally eloquent, but also each definition, each logical claim, each metaphysical expression is so expressed and qualified as to provide the reader with as complete an expression of the defense of faith as any critic could reasonably demand.

Is it possible, then, that such a man could be mistaken? Would it not be better, out of respect for Kant's genius, to read and appreciate his work but leave the frightening job of criticism to those who presume themselves to be capable of operating at Kant's level?

Again, we must suggest that *really* to read, *actually* to appreciate (pragmatical emphasis and claim) the work of Kant or any other philosopher, one *must* (logical consequence) read him *critically;* one must seek to grasp the *use of language* (a use that may be somewhat bizarre, perhaps technical, possibly inconsistent), the *meanings of terms* (meanings that may not be in accord with the definitions advanced to clarify the terms), the *logical consequences* (which may not suit the author's plans), and the *declarations of faith* (which may be superfluous or indefensible).

Having grasped the linguistical factors and having uncovered the faith being expressed, the reader (who, as one who must appreciate, must criticize) *passes judgment* on the argument: he accepts or rejects the claim, either because the defense is not adequate or is not necessary, or because the faith runs counter to the reader's own.

The philosopher sets out—pragmatically, semantically, logically, or metaphysically—to *describe* the "world," to *justify* his description, to make his description persuasive and appealing, and to convince others of the importance of what he says. He does not uncover new facts, but he recovers old ones by describing them in novel and illuminating ways; and he suggests, when he is metaphysical in an original way, that there is more between heaven and earth than is dreamed of in other men's philosophies or can be dreamed of in anyone's science.

QUESTIONS FOR DISCUSSION

1. Kant claims that *synthetic a priori* knowledge is possible because of the factors contributed to empirical knowledge by our faculty of knowledge. Is knowledge of the contributions made by our faculty of knowledge *a priori* or *a posteriori?* If *a priori,* is knowledge of the faculty of knowledge analytic or synthetic? If analytic, can such knowledge provide the basis for synthetic *a priori* knowledge? If the knowledge of the faculty of knowledge is *a posteriori,* can such knowledge provide the basis for synthetic *a priori* knowledge? On the basis of your consideration of these questions, suggest the lines that a criticism of Kant's claim might follow.

2. If by *"a priori"* knowledge is meant "knowledge absolutely independent of all experience" (that is, knowledge which, although beginning with experience, does not arise out of experience), and if by "synthetic" knowledge is meant knowledge in which the connection of the predicate with the subject is "thought without identity" (that is, knowledge in which the predicate *cannot* be derived from the subject by logical analysis), is synthetic *a priori* knowledge possible? If this question is not clear, consider the following: If by *"a priori"* knowledge is meant knowledge the statement of which is universally and necessarily true, and if by "synthetic" knowledge is meant knowledge that cannot be acquired by logical analysis, is synthetic *a priori* knowledge possible?

3. Can a kind of utterance (a declarative sentence) be used in one context in such a way that the sentence expresses a synthetic *a posteriori* proposition, and be used in another context in such a way that it expresses an analytic *a priori* proposition? Give examples.

4. Are analytic *a posteriori* propositions possible?

5. Is the statement "All bodies are heavy" analytic or synthetic? Compare your claim with Kant's.

6. Kant talks about the "concept" of body. What is a concept, and how does it acquire content? Can philosophy be concerned with concepts and thereby avoid linguistical issues?

7. We find the following sentence in Kant: "The rainbow in a sunny shower may be called a mere appearance, and the rain the thing in itself." Does Kant, then, regard the rain as a thing in itself?

8. In the sentence "The dog bit the postman," the word "dog" is *used;* in the sentence " 'Dog' has three letters," the word "dog" is *mentioned*. Construct a sentence about a sentence illustrating the use of a word to mention a word used to mention another word.

9. Could the sentence "The soul survives the death of the body" be used as the expression of a metaphysical claim? If so, exhibit and explain the use of the word "soul" and specify the logical barriers which prohibit empirical investigation of the claim.

10. Classify and criticize the claim that space and time are "only forms of sensible intuition."

VI

BERKELEY

To be is to be perceived

BERKELEY'S ARGUMENT

It is evident to anyone who takes a survey of the objects *of human knowledge that they are either ideas actually imprinted on the senses, or else such as are perceived by attending to the passions and operations of the mind, or lastly, ideas formed by help of memory and imagination—either compounding, dividing, or barely representing those originally perceived in the aforesaid ways. By sight I have the ideas of light and colors, with their several degrees and variations. By touch I perceive, for example, hard and soft, heat and cold, motion and resistance, and of all these more and less either as to quantity or degree. Smelling furnishes me with odors, the palate with tastes, and hearing conveys sounds to the mind in all their variety of tone and composition. And as several of these are observed to accompany each other, they come to be marked by one name, and so to be reputed as one thing. Thus, for example, a certain color, taste, smell, figure, and consistence having been observed to go together, are accounted one distinct thing signified by the name "apple"; other collections of ideas constitute a stone, a tree, a book, and the like sensible things—which as they are pleasing or disagreeable excite the passions of love, hatred, joy, grief, and so forth.*

2. *But, besides all that endless variety of ideas or objects of knowledge, there is likewise something which knows or perceives them and exercises divers operations, as willing, imagining, remembering, about them. This perceiving, active being is what I call "mind," "spirit," "soul," or "myself." By which words I do not denote any one of my ideas, but a thing entirely distinct from them, wherein they exist or, which is the same thing, whereby they are perceived—for the existence of an idea consists in being perceived.*

3. *That neither our thoughts, nor passions, nor ideas formed by the imagination exist without the mind is what everybody will allow. And it seems no less evident that the various sensations or ideas imprinted on the sense, however blended or combined together (that is, whatever objects they compose), cannot exist otherwise than in a mind perceiving them.—I think an intuitive knowledge may be obtained of this by anyone that shall attend to what is meant by the term "exist" when applied to sensible things. The table I write on I say exists, that is, I see and feel it; and if I were out of my study I should say it existed—meaning thereby that if I was in my study I might perceive it, or that some other spirit actually does perceive it. There was an odor, that is, it was smelled, there was a sound, that is to say, it was heard; a color or figure, and it was perceived by sight or touch. This is all that I can understand by these and the like expressions. For as to what is said of the absolute existence of unthinking things without any relation to their being perceived, that seems perfectly unintelligible. Their* esse *is* percipi, *nor is it possible they should have any existence out of the minds or thinking things which perceive them.*

4. *It is indeed an opinion strangely prevailing amongst men that houses, mountains, rivers, and, in a word, all sensible objects have an existence, natural or real, distinct from their being perceived by the understanding. But with how great an assurance and acquiescence soever this principle may be entertained in the world, yet whoever shall find in his heart to call it in question may, if I mistake not, perceive it to involve a manifest contradiction. For what are the forementioned objects but the things we perceive by sense? And what do we perceive besides our own ideas or sensations? And*

*is it not plainly repugnant that any one of these, or any combination
of them, should exist unperceived?*

*5. If we thoroughly examine this tenet it will, perhaps, be
found at bottom to depend on the doctrine of* abstract ideas. *For can
there be a nicer strain of abstraction than to distinguish the existence
of sensible objects from their being perceived, so as to conceive them
existing unperceived? Light and colors, heat and cold, extension and
figures— in a word, the things we see and feel—what are they but so
many sensations, notions, ideas, or impressions on the sense? And
is it possible to separate, even in thought, any of these from perception? For my part, I might as easily divide a thing from itself. I may,
indeed, divide in my thoughts, or conceive apart from each other,
those things which, perhaps, I never perceived by sense so divided.
Thus I imagine the trunk of a human body without the limbs, or conceive the smell of a rose without thinking on the rose itself. So far, I
will not deny, I can abstract—if that may properly be called "abstraction" which extends only to the conceiving separately such objects as it is possible may really exist or be actually perceived asun-
der. But my conceiving or imagining power does not extend beyond
the possibility of real existence or perception. Hence, as it is impossible for me to see or feel anything without an actual sensation of
that thing, so it is impossible for me to conceive in my thoughts any
sensible thing or object distinct from the sensation or perception of
it.*

*6. Some truths there are so near and obvious to the mind that
a man need only open his eyes to see them. Such I take this important
one to be, to wit, that all the choir of heaven and furniture of the
earth, in a word, all those bodies which compose the mighty frame
of the world, have not any subsistence without a mind—that their
being is to be perceived or known, that, consequently, so long as
they are not actually perceived by me or do not exist in my mind or
that of any other created spirit, they must either have no existence at
all or else subsist in the mind of some eternal spirit—it being perfectly unintelligible, and involving all the absurdity of abstraction, to
attribute to any single part of them an existence independent of a
spirit. To be convinced of which, the reader need only reflect, and*

try to separate in his own thoughts, the being *of a sensible thing from its* being perceived.

[From *A Treatise Concerning the Principles of Human Knowledge* (1710; second edition, 1734; present quotation is from the second edition) by George Berkeley (1685–1753).*]

[Philonous.] *What mean you by "sensible things"?*
[Hylas.] *Those things which are perceived by the senses. Can you imagine that I mean anything else?*

Phil. *Pardon me, Hylas, if I am desirous clearly to apprehend your notions, since this may much shorten our inquiry. Suffer me then to ask you this further question. Are those things only perceived by the senses which are preceived immediately? Or may those things properly be said to be "sensible" which are perceived mediately, or not without the intervention of others?*

Hyl. *I do not sufficiently understand you.*

Phil. *In reading a book, what I immediately perceive are the letters, but mediately, or by means of these, are suggested to my mind the notions of God, virtue, truth, etc. Now, that the letters are truly sensible things, or perceived by sense, there is no doubt; but I would know whether you take the things suggested by them to be so too.*

Hyl. *No, certainly; it were absurd to think God or virtue sensible things, though they may be signified and suggested to the mind by sensible marks with which they have an arbitrary connection.*

Phil. *It seems then, that by "sensible things" you mean those only which can be perceived immediately by sense.*

Hyl. *Right.*

Phil. *Does it not follow from this that, though I see one part of the sky red, and another blue, and that my reason does thence evidently conclude there must be some cause of that diversity of colors, yet that cause cannot be said to be a sensible thing or perceived by the sense of seeing?*

Hyl. *It does.*

Phil. *In like manner, though I hear variety of sounds, yet I*

**Edition used: Library of Liberal Arts, Bobbs-Merrill Co., Inc., 1965.*

cannot be said to hear the causes of those sounds.

Hyl. *You cannot.*

Phil. *And when by my touch I perceive a thing to be hot and heavy, I cannot say, with any truth or propriety, that I feel the cause of its heat or weight.*

Hyl. *To prevent any more questions of this kind, I tell you once for all that by "sensible things" I mean those only which are perceived by sense, and that in truth the senses perceive nothing which they do not perceive immediately, for they make no inferences. The deducing therefore of causes or occasions from effects and appearances, which alone are perceived by sense, entirely relates to reason.*

Phil. *This point then is agreed between us—that* sensible things are those which are immediately perceived by sense. *You will further inform me whether we immediately perceive by sight anything besides light and colors and figures; or by hearing, anything but sounds; by the palate, anything besides tastes; by the smell, besides odors; or by the touch, more than tangible qualities.*

Hyl. *We do not.*

Phil. *It seems, therefore, that if you take away all sensible qualities, there remains nothing sensible?*

Hyl. *I grant it.*

Phil. *Sensible things therefore are nothing else but so many sensible qualities or combinations of sensible qualities?*

Hyl. *Nothing else.*

Phil. *Heat is then a sensible thing?*

Hyl. *Certainly.*

Phil. *Does the reality of sensible things consist in being perceived, or is it something distinct from their being perceived, and that bears no relation to the mind?*

Hyl. *To* exist *is one thing, and to be* perceived *is another.*

Phil. *I speak with regard to sensible things only; and of these I ask, whether by their real existence you mean a subsistence exterior to the mind and distinct from their being perceived?*

Hyl. *I mean a real absolute being, distinct from and without any relation to their being perceived.*

* * * *

Phil. *But is not the most vehement and intense degree of heat a very great pain?*

Hyl. *No one can deny it.*

Phil. *And is any unperceiving thing capable of pain or pleasure?*

Hyl. *No, certainly.*

Phil. *Is your material substance a senseless being or a being endowed with sense and perception?* [Philonous has previously maintained that "there is no such thing as what philosophers call 'material substance,' " while Hylas has contended that there is nothing "more fantastical, more repugnant to common sense or a more manifest piece of skepticism than to believe there is no such thing as matter . . . ."]

Hyl. *It is senseless, without doubt.*

Phil. *It cannot, therefore, be the subject of pain?*

Hyl. *By no means.*

Phil. *Nor, consequently, of the greatest heat perceived by sense, since you acknowledge this to be no small pain?*

Hyl. *I grant it.*

Phil. *What shall we say then of your external object: is it a material substance, or no?*

Hyl. *It is a material substance with the sensible qualities inhering in it.*

Phil. *How then can a great heat exist in it, since you own it cannot in a material substance? I desire you would clear this point.*

Hyl. *Hold, Philonous, I fear I was out in yielding intense heat to be a pain. It should seem rather that pain is something distinct from heat, and the consequence or effect of it.*

Phil. *Upon putting your hand near the fire, do you perceive one simple uniform sensation or two distinct sensations?*

Hyl. *But one simple sensation.*

Phil. *Is not the heat immediately perceived?*

Hyl. *It is.*

Phil. *And the pain?*

Hyl. *True.*

Phil. *Seeing therefore they are both immediately perceived at the same time, and the fire affects you only with one simple or un-*

compounded idea, it follows that this same simple idea is both the intense heat immediately perceived and the pain; and, consequently, that the intense heat immediately perceived is nothing distinct from a particular sort of pain.

Hyl. *It seems so.*

Phil. *Again, try in your thoughts, Hylas, if you can conceive a vehement sensation to be without pain or pleasure.*

Hyl. *I cannot.*

Phil. *Or can you frame to yourself an idea of sensible pain or pleasure, in general, abstracted from every particular idea of heat, cold, tastes, smells, etc.?*

Hyl. *I do not find that I can.*

Phil. *Does it not therefore follow that sensible pain is nothing distinct from those sensations or ideas—in an intense degree?*

Hyl. *It is undeniable; and, to speak the truth, I begin to suspect a very great heat cannot exist but in a mind perceiving it.*

Phil. *What! are you then in that* skeptical *state of suspense, between affirming and denying?*

Hyl. *I think I may be positive in the point. A very violent and painful heat cannot exist without the mind.*

*   *   *   *

Phil. *Can any doctrine be true that necessarily leads a man into an absurdity?* [Hylas has suggested that *intense* heat and intense cold cannot exist outside the mind, but he argues that bodies perceived to be *moderately* warm or cold must have warmth or cold in them and that, therefore, such qualities can exist outside the mind, in unthinking substances.]

Hyl. *Without doubt it cannot.*

Phil. *Is it not an absurdity to think that the same thing should be at the same time both cold and warm?*

Hyl. *It is.*

Phil. *Suppose now one of your hands hot, and the other cold, and that they are both at once put into the same vessel of water, in an intermediate state, will not the water seem cold to one hand, and warm to the other?*

Hyl. *It will.*

Phil. *Ought we not therefore, by your principles, to conclude it is really both cold and warm at the same time, that is, according to your own concession, to believe an absurdity?*

Hyl. *I confess it seems so.*

Phil. *Consequently, the principles themselves are false, since you have granted that no true principle leads to an absurdity.*

Hyl. *But, after all, can anything be more absurd than to say, "there is no heat in the fire"?*

Phil. *To make the point still clearer; tell me whether, in two cases exactly alike, we ought not to make the same judgment?*

Hyl. *We ought.*

Phil. *When a pin pricks your finger, does it not rend and divide the fibers of your flesh?*

Hyl. *It does.*

Phil. *And when a coal burns your finger, does it any more?*

Hyl. *It does not.*

Phil. *Since, therefore, you neither judge the sensation itself occasioned by the pin, nor anything like it to be in the pin, you should not, conformably to what you have now granted, judge the sensation occasioned by the fire, or anything like it, to be in the fire.*

Hyl. *Well, since it must be so, I am content to yield this point and acknowledge that heat and cold are only sensations existing in our minds. But there still remain qualities enough to secure the reality of external things.*

*   *   *   *

Hyl. *I frankly own, Philonous, that it is in vain to stand out any longer. Colors, sounds, tastes, in a word, all those termed "secondary qualities," have certainly no existence without the mind. But by this acknowledgment I must not be supposed to derogate anything from the reality of matter or external objects; seeing it is no more than several philosophers maintain, who nevertheless are the farthest imaginable from denying matter. For the clearer understanding of this you must know sensible qualities are by philosophers divided into* primary *and* secondary. *The former are extension, figure, solidity, gravity, motion, and rest. And these they hold exist really in bodies. . . .*

Phil. *But what if the same arguments which are brought against secondary qualities will hold good against these also?*

Hyl. *Why then I shall be obliged to think they too exist only in the mind.*

* * * *

Phil. *Since . . . it is impossible even for the mind to disunite the ideas of extension and motion from all other sensible qualities, does it not follow that where the one exist there necessarily the other exist likewise?*

Hyl. *It should seem so.*

Phil. *Consequently, the very same arguments, which you admitted as conclusive against the secondary qualities are, without any further application of force, against the primary, too. Besides, if you will trust your senses, is it not plain all sensible qualities coexist, or to them appear as being in the same place? Do they ever represent a motion or figure as being divested of all other visible and tangible qualities?*

Hyl. *You need say no more on this head. I am free to own, if there be no secret error or oversight in our proceedings hitherto, that all sensible qualities are alike to be denied existence without the mind. . . .*

* * * *

Hyl. *I agree with you.* Material substance *was no more than a hypothesis, and a false and groundless one, too. I will no longer spend my breath in defense of it. But whatever hypothesis you advance or whatsoever scheme of things you introduce in its stead, I doubt not it will appear every whit as false . . .*

Phil. *I assure you, Hylas, I do not pretend to frame any hypothesis at all. I am of a vulgar cast, simple enough to believe my senses and leave things as I find them. To be plain, it is my opinion that the real things are those very things I see and feel, and perceive by my senses. These I know and, finding they answer all the necessities and purposes of life, have no reason to be solicitous about any other unknown beings. A piece of sensible bread, for instance, would stay my stomach better than ten thousand times as much of that in-*

sensible, unintelligible real bread you speak of. It is likewise my opinion that colors and other sensible qualities are on the objects. I cannot for my life help thinking that snow is white, and fire hot. You, indeed, who by "snow" and "fire" mean certain external, unperceived, unperceiving substances are in the right to deny whiteness or heat to be affections inherent in them. But I who understand by those words the things I see and feel am obliged to think like other folks. And as I am no skeptic with regard to the nature of things, so neither am I as to their existence. That a thing should be really perceived by my senses and at the same time not really exist is to me a plain contradiction, since I cannot prescind or abstract, even in thought, the existence of a sensible thing from its being perceived. Wood, stones, fire, water, flesh, iron, and the like things which I name and discourse of are things that I know. And I should not have known them but that I perceived them by my senses; and things perceived by the senses are immediately perceived; and things immediately perceived are ideas; and ideas cannot exist without the mind; their existence therefore consists in being perceived; when, therefore, they are actually perceived, there can be no doubt of their existence. Away then with all that skepticism, all those ridiculous philosophical doubts. What a jest is it for a philosopher to question the existence of sensible things till he has it proved to him from the veracity of God or to pretend our knowledge in this point falls short of intuition or demonstration! I might as well doubt of my own being as of the being of those things I actually see and feel.

*   *   *   *

Hyl. Yes, Philonous, I grant the existence of a sensible thing consists in being perceivable, but not in being actually perceived.

Phil. And what is perceivable but an idea? And can an idea exist without being actually perceived? These are points long since agreed between us.

*   *   *   *

Hyl. I must needs own, Philonous, nothing seems to have kept me from agreeing with you more than this . . . mistaking the question. In denying matter, at first glimpse I am tempted to imagine you deny the things we see and feel, but, upon reflection, find there is no ground for it. What think you, therefore, of retaining the name "matter" and applying it to sensible things? This may be done without any change in your sentiments; and, believe me, it would be a means of reconciling them to some persons who may be more shocked at an innovation in words than in opinion.

Phil. With all my heart; retain the word "matter" and apply it to the objects of sense, if you please, provided you do not attribute to them any substance distinct from their being perceived. I shall never quarrel with you for an expression. . . .

Hyl. . . . I have been so long accustomed to the term "matter" that I know not how to part with it. To say there is no matter in the world is still shocking to me. Whereas to say there is no matter if by that term be meant an unthinking substance existing without the mind, but if by matter is meant some sensible thing whose existence consists in being perceived, then there is matter—this distinction gives it quite another turn; and men will come into your notions with small difficulty when they are proposed in that manner. . . .

Phil. I do not pretend to be a setter-up of new notions. My endeavors tend only to unite and place in a clearer light that truth which was before shared between the vulgar and the philosophers, the former being of opinion that those things they immediately perceive are the real things, and the latter, that the things immediately perceived are ideas which exist only in the mind. Which two notions put together do, in effect, constitute the substance of what I advance.

[From *Three Dialogues Between Hylas and Philonous* (1713).*]

AN ANALYSIS OF BERKELEY'S ARGUMENT

1. THE BASIC CLAIM

We must first determine the point of Berkeley's argument if we are to analyze and appraise the argument itself. What claim did

*Edition used: Library of Liberal Arts, Bobbs-Merrill Co., Inc., 1965.

Berkeley hope to support by the argument he devised? Fortunately, there is very little difficulty in isolating statements which may be taken correctly as expressions of the thesis Berkeley attempted to establish on the basis of the reasons he gave in his argument. We may take the argument presented by Philonous (whose name in Greek means, literally, "lover of mind" or "lover of reason") as a statement of Berkeley's argument, for it is substantially the same as the argument presented in Berkeley's *Treatise Concerning the Principles of Human Knowledge;* furthermore, Hylas (whose name appears to be built upon the prefix *hylo,* also of Greek derivation, meaning "matter" or "material," as in *hylozoism,* which is the name for the view that all matter is animated) represents, as capably as might reasonably be expected of an imaginary character who serves as the foil for the more incisive wit of Philonous, the advocate of the philosophical view that there are external, unthinking causes of sensations.

Berkeley's argument is directed against the view of the metaphysicians who claim that there are "external, unperceived, unperceiving substances," unthinking substances which exist outside the mind and are presumed to be the causes of sensations. Berkeley's basic claim is positive insofar as it states that the existence of sensible things consists in their being perceived; his claim is negative insofar as it denies the metaphysical assumption that there are unthinking objects the existence of which cannot be demonstrated.

Speaking of sensible objects, those things we know through sense experience, Berkeley claims that, for them, *"esse* is *percipi"* (to be is to be perceived), and he adds, "nor is it possible they should have any existence out of the minds or thinking things which perceive them." He maintains, with reference to "houses, mountains, rivers, and in a word all sensible objects," that they are things perceived by sense, and he concludes that since only ideas or sensations are perceived, such sensible objects cannot exist unperceived. Berkeley writes that "all those bodies which compose the mighty frame of the world . . . have not any subsistence without a mind" and that "their *being* is to be perceived or known . . . ." Again, having given as examples of sensible things "wood, stones, fire, water, flesh, iron, and the like things," Berkeley contends that such things are ideas; and that since ideas cannot exist without the mind, sensible objects are such that "their existence . . . consists in being perceived . . . ."

Let us, then, use the following as a statement of Berkeley's basic claim:

For all sensible objects, to be is to be perceived.

But the problem of determining Berkeley's basic claim is not resolved simply by isolating expressions which appear from the context to be statements of the conclusion of his argument. To know *what* Berkeley claimed one must know the *meaning* of the statements he used to express his claim.

The initial semantical problem for us, then, is to determine the meaning of the term "sensible objects" and that of the term "perceived" as those terms are used in the various statements of Berkeley's basic claim. (We shall not initially assume that these expressions, as used by Berkeley, are *in fact* meaningful, nor that they are always used by Berkeley in the same way; the investigation is intended to provide evidence, on the basis of which decisions can be made, as to whether the terms in question are used consistently and, if so, in what way and with what consequent meanings, if any.)

Confining ourselves to statements included in the above-quoted passages from Berkeley, let us abstract some of the statements in which the terms "sensible objects," "sensible things," and "perceived" (or their variants) are used:

1. "It is evident to anyone who takes a survey of the *objects* of human knowledge that they are either ideas actually imprinted on the senses, or else such as are perceived by attending to the passions and operations of the mind, or lastly, ideas formed by help of memory and imagination . . . ."
2. "By sight I have the ideas of light and colors . . . . By touch I perceive . . . hard and soft, heat and cold, motion and resistance . . . ."
3. "And as several of these [ideas imprinted on the senses] are observed to accompany each other, they come to be marked by one name, and so to be reputed as one thing.

Thus, for example, a certain color, taste, smell, figure, and consistence having been observed to go together, are accounted one distinct thing signified by the name 'apple'; other collections of ideas constitute a stone, a tree, a book, and the like sensible things . . . ."

4. "This perceiving, active being is what I call 'mind,' 'spirit,' 'soul,' or 'myself.' By which words I do not denote any one of my ideas, but a thing entirely distinct from them, wherein they exist or, which is the same thing, whereby they are perceived—for the existence of an idea consists in being perceived."

5. "And it seems no less evident that the various sensations, or ideas imprinted on the sense . . . cannot exist otherwise than in a mind perceiving them.—I think an intuitive knowledge may be obtained of this by anyone that shall attend to what is meant by the term 'exist' when applied to sensible things. The table I write on I say exists, that is, I see and feel it; and if I were out of my study I should say it existed—meaning thereby that if I was in my study I might perceive it, or that some other spirit actually does perceive it."

6. ". . . houses, mountains, rivers, and, in a word, all sensible objects . . . ."—". . . what are the forementioned objects but the things we perceive by sense? And what do we perceive besides our own ideas or sensations?"

7. "Light and colors, heat and cold, extension and figures—in a word, the things we see and feel—what are they but so many sensations, notions, ideas, or impressions on the sense?"

8. "*Phil.* What mean you by 'sensible things'?
"*Hyl.* Those things which are perceived by the senses."

9. "*Hyl.* . . . by 'sensible things' I mean those only which are perceived by sense, and . . . in truth the senses perceive nothing which they do not perceive immediately, for they make no inferences."

10. "*Phil.* This point then is agreed between us—that *sensible things are those only which are immediately perceived by*

sense. You will further inform me whether we immediately perceive by sight anything besides light and colors and figures; or by hearing, anything but sounds; by the palate, anything besides tastes; by the smell, besides odors; or by the touch, more than tangible qualities."

11. *"Phil.* Wood, stones, fire, water, flesh, iron, and the like things which I name and discourse of are things that I know. And I should not have known them but that I perceived them by my senses . . . ."

Let us call these statements *pragmatical data statements,* for it is such statements, given in the writings of Berkeley, which provide us, as analysts and critics, with *exhibitions* of Berkeley's *use of terms.*

Such a pragmatical datum statement as number 11 exhibits a use of the term "things" such that the term "things" may properly be taken as synonymous with the terms "sensible things" and "sensible objects." As examples of "things" we are referred to wood, stones, fire, water, flesh, iron, and the like. As Berkeley says, through Philonous, these are things, or kinds of things, we "name and discourse of." We are justified, on the basis of data statements 11, the first part of 6, and the very last part of 3 (beginning with the words "a stone"), in deciding that Berkeley—at least in the initial phase of his argument, while that argument was being developed or summarized—so used the term "sensible object," or a variant of it, as to denote (designate by naming) objects of the sort we would be inclined to describe as physical or material objects, objects of the sort which constitute the subject matter of the physical sciences.

But to *define* "sensible objects" as *meaning* "objects of the sort which constitute the subject matter of the physical sciences" or, even more radically, as "objects existing independently of observers, nonmental objects" would be to assume, by definition, what Berkeley was concerned explicitly to deny for the reasons given in his argument.

If, now, we consider data statements 1, 3, and 7, we are inclined to define "sensible object" as meaning "any collection of ideas imprinted on the senses, any collection of sensations observed to accompany each other." But to resolve the semantical problem of determining the meaning of "sensible object" by defining the term according to Berkeley's conclusion about the nature of whatever is designated by the term would be to interpret his argument as circular: if by definition we permit Berkeley to *mean* by "sensible object" any collection of sensations observed to go together, there would be *no possibility* of meaningfully claiming that perhaps sensible objects can exist independently of all perception.

To be fair to both Philonous and Hylas—to both Berkeley and to his philosophical opponents—we must begin the interpretation of the meaning of Berkeley's conclusion, as well as the construction of his basic argument, with an *ostensive* or *denotative* or, as we shall call it henceforth, a *pragmatical definition* of the key term "sensible object." Such a procedure is in accordance with the practice Berkeley himself exhibits in his argument.

Let us, then, by "sensible object" mean wood (wooden objects), stones, fire, water, flesh, iron, houses, mountains, rivers, apples, trees, books, and things like that. Put *pragmatically* (as indicating the *use* of the term), let us so use the term "sensible object" (or "sensible thing") as to refer to wood, stones, fire . . . and things like that.

We *leave open the question* as to what sort of things we are referring to when we refer to the things named above. We shall regard Berkeley's effort as that of showing that the things so designated are collections of sensations and, consequently, such that, in some sense, their existence consists in their being perceived. On the other hand, we interpret Hylas's effort as that of denying Berkeley's explanation (which is semantical) in favor of Hylas's own conviction that sensible things (of the sort referred to) are material or physical things, exterior to the mind, "distinct from, and without any relation to their being perceived."

We may now revise the statement of Berkeley's conclusion so as to remind ourselves that the subject of his claim is whatever belongs to the class partially designated by Berkeley's use of the term "sensible objects" in referring to apples, stones, and the like:

For all such objects as wood, stones, fire, and the like, to be is to be perceived.

How, now, is the expression "to be perceived" to be understood? Is a definition possible that would be agreeable both to Berkeley and his philosophical opponents, or must we, as with the term "sensible objects," make the meaning clear through a pragmatical definition?

In datum statement 1, Berkeley speaks of those objects of human knowledge which "are perceived by attending to the passions and operations of the mind . . . ." Apparently, to be aware of one's own anger or fear or to realize that one is thinking would be to perceive: perceiving, in this case, would be what we might alternatively call "introspecting."

In 2 and 3 Berkeley uses the term "perceive" in such a way that one may be said to "perceive" ideas, where the term "ideas" is so used as to be synonymous with the term "sensations." Thus, the word "perceive" is synonymous with the term "have," whenever the latter term is used as it is in the following excerpt from datum statement 2: "By sight I have the ideas of light and colors . . . ." Perceiving, in cases of this sort, is what we might alternatively call "having," as in the expression "having a pain" or "having a sensation of heat."

In 5 Berkeley speaks of perceiving a table, an object of the kind designated by his use of the term "sensible object": "The table I write on I say exists, that is, I see and feel it; and if I were out of my study I should say it existed—meaning thereby that if I was in my study I might perceive it, or that some other spirit actually does perceive it." This statement is particularly interesting in that it exhibits a use of the term "perceive" such that—if Berkeley is to be credited here with having said precisely what he intended to say—for a table to *be,* it is *not* necessary that it be perceived: it would be sufficient to its existence if, *were* an observer present, he *would* perceive it. Unfortunately, this particular datum statement does not allow us, without begging the question, to decide whether, in this case, to *perceive* is to be affected, through stimulation of the senses, by an object exterior to the mind; or whether to perceive is to "have" a collection of sensations which is itself one distinct thing, namely, a table. We cannot, then, conclude whether the use of "perceive" in 5 is or is not the same use as that exhibited in 2 and 3.

Datum statement 6 exhibits a familiar use of the term "perceive," for in 6 Berkeley speaks of perceiving "by sense" such commonplace objects of sense perception as "houses, mountains, rivers." But he then goes on to speak of perceiving "our own ideas or sensations"; in fact, he claims, through the use of a rhetorical question, that *only* ideas and sensations are perceived. Of course, it is apparent here, as elsewhere in his argument, that Berkeley *seeks* to identify the perception of such objects as houses, mountains, and rivers with the perception of such "objects" as ideas and sensations; but the present question, for the analyst, is not whether Berkeley *hoped* to identify the two by maintaining that such objects as houses, mountains, and rivers are really collections of sensations; the question is, rather, whether the *use* of the term "perceive" exhibited in talking about the sense perception of houses, mountains, and rivers is the *same use* as that exhibited in talking about the perception of sensations.

There is a way of using the term "perceive" in ordinary discourse such that to perceive such an object as a house or a mountain is to become aware of the object through the use of the senses; that is, through the use of such sense organs as the eyes or the ears. We could say, in talking about this use of the term "perceive," that to perceive a thing one must *see* it or *hear* it or in some way attend to it through the use of the sense organs, through the use of the *eyes* or *ears* or some other sense organ. The above generalization concerning one conventional use of the term "perceive" could function as a rule for the use of the term; relative to that rule, it would not be correct to say that one "perceived" an idea or the point of an argument or, even, something "in one's mind's eye" or in the imagination, or through the use of memory—for in all these latter kinds of cases, the act in question does not involve the use of the sense organs: one does not need one's eyes or ears or any other sense organ to have or comprehend an idea, to "see" the point of an argument, to "hear, as if it were only yesterday," the ringing of a bell that has long since rusted away.

As shown in the discussion of that use of the term "perceive" by which the term "perceive" comes to mean "to apprehend through the use of the sense organs," there is another use, or, in any case, something that could, by virtue of a difference, be *called* "another use," of the term "perceive" such that to perceive something it is not necessary that one use one's sense organs; and, in fact, the use of the sense organs, when they are used, is never sufficient to the act. This second conventional use of the term "perceive" is exhibited by such data statements, from ordinary discourse, as "I perceive another possibility," "I finally perceive the point of the argument," and "I perceive that she is uneasy, worried about her mother." When Sherlock Holmes commented on his companion's inability to make sense out of his sense experience, he often said something like, "My dear Watson, you *see* but you do not *perceive!*"

It is possible, then, even likely, that Berkeley, in writing about *perceiving* houses, rivers, and mountains, was taking advantage of that ordinary way of using the term "perceive" such that to perceive something one *must* use one's sense organs: one must see with the eyes, or hear with the ears, or taste with the tongue, and so forth; while, in writing about *perceiving* ideas or sensations, he was exhibiting that conventional use of "perceive" by which it is *no longer necessary* that to perceive something, say an idea, one need use one's sense organs. Thus, when Philonous agrees with Hylas in describing (definitively) sensible things as "those only which are immediately perceived by sense," the description (which functions as a semantical claim, that is, as a statement of the meaning of the term "sensible thing" relative to the use—or what is presumed to be *the* use—in question) is agreeable to Hylas because Hylas tends to use the term "perceived" as one uses it in talking about becoming aware of things through the use of the sense organs, while the description is agreeable to Philonous because Philonous tends to use the term "perceived" as one uses it in talking about becoming aware of one's own ideas or sensations.

The effort on Berkeley's part, with regard to the term "perceive," was to persuade the reader that the use preferred by Hylas, although superficially different from that preferred by Philonous, in that Hylas tends to identify as objects of perception such objects as houses, mountains, and rivers, while Philonous insists that *only* ideas or sensations are perceived, is in fact *identical* with Philonous's use, in that Philonous is perfectly willing to speak of "perceiving" such objects as houses, mountains, and rivers, even though he insists that only ideas or sensations can be "perceived."

What, then, are we to say about Berkeley's use of the term "perceive" in his conclusion that for the class of sensible things, that is, for all such objects as houses, mountains, rivers, wood, stones, fire, and the like, "to be is to be perceived"? We do not have to beg the question for the realist by insisting, with Hylas, that to perceive is to be aware, through the use of the sense organs, of objects exterior to the mind which are the causes of our sensations, nor do we have to agree with Philonous when he claims that to be aware of sensations is precisely the same thing as to be aware of such objects as stones, mountains, rivers, and the like; it is enough if we maintain, in the conclusion, a use of a term by which it can be suggested that there is what might be called a "common factor" revealed by the various statements, whether or not pragmatically identical, in which the term "perceive" is used. A term by the use of which the tension of possible differences in usage, and consequently of meaning, can be maintained is the term "aware."

Thus, again, *we leave open the question* in our interpretation of the conclusion by using a term which can serve in clarifying the meaning of the conclusion without, at the same time, so limiting the meaning of the conclusion as to give advantage either to Philonous (Berkeley) or to Hylas.

We understand Berkeley's conclusion, then, to be the following:

> For all such objects as wood, stones, fire, and the like, to be is to be the object of someone's awareness; that is, if there is any such object as a stone or a fire, then there is someone who is aware of that object.

In the reconstruction of Berkeley's argument, however, we shall, as far as possible, retain the language of the argument. But when the time comes for the logical appraisal of the argument and for consideration of the acceptability of Berkeley's premises, matters of interpretation will again become critical.

2. THE BASIC ARGUMENT

We are assisted in the construction of Berkeley's basic argument, that is, in the logical summary of his argument, by a summary statement to be found in the *Third Dialogue Between Hylas and Philonous:*

> Phil. . . . . *I cannot prescind or abstract, even in thought, the existence of a sensible thing from its being perceived. Wood, stones, fire, water, flesh, iron, and the like things which I name and discourse of are things that I know. And I should not have known them but that I perceived them by my senses; and things perceived by the senses are immediately perceived; and things immediately perceived are ideas; and ideas cannot exist without the mind; their existence therefore consists in being perceived . . . .*

Let us begin by symbolizing (in a readily understandable way and in the language of Berkeley's argument) the *conclusion* of the argument. We shall write the conclusion—that *to be is to be perceived,* or that *all sensible things are perceived*—as follows:

$$\therefore \ (x) \ [Sx \rightarrow Px]$$

The symbol "$\therefore$" may be read "therefore"; it signifies that what follows is the *conclusion* of the argument. The symbol "(x)" is called the *universal quantifier;* the symbol is a *quantifier* in that it indicates the *quantity* being described (in this case, the *entire* class of sensible things); and the symbol is a *universal* quantifier in that it signifies that *all* members of the subject class are included within the range of the generalization. The symbol "$\rightarrow$" signifies an "if . . . then . . ." relation.

Thus, in this case, we may read the logical expression of the conclusion as follows: *Whatever* may be considered, that is, *whatever* may be referred to by substituting a name or descriptive term for the variable symbol "x", *if* it is a sensible thing, *then* it is a perceived thing.

The symbol "$\rightarrow$" may alternatively be read "implies"; thus, the logical expression of the conclusion may alternatively be read: *What-*

ever one talks about, its being a sensible thing *implies* that it is a perceived thing.

In other words, for *every* member of the class of sensible things, to *be* (that is, to be a sensible thing) is to *be perceived.*

The symbol "→", the symbol of implication, may also be read through the use of *negatives,* as illustrated by the following reading of our logical expression of Berkeley's conclusion: Whatever may be considered, it is *not* true that it is a sensible thing and also *not* a perceived thing. This reading of the statement can be symbolized as follows:

$$(x) \ [\sim (Sx \cdot \sim Px)]$$

The symbol "$\sim$", then, is the symbol of *negation*; the symbol "$\cdot$" (read "and") is the symbol of *conjunction.* The universal quantifier governs the entire expression within the brackets. In this particular expression we find that the first negation sign within the brackets, to the left of the expression within parentheses, signifies the negation of the expression enclosed by parentheses. The second negation sign covers only that part of the expression which involves the use of the predicate symbol "P" and the variable symbol "x".

Since the subject term of the conclusion is the entire class of sensible things, and since Berkeley uses, in expressing one of the premises of his argument, a statement in which the entire class of sensible things is referred to and by which, through examples, he attempts to make clear what it is he is talking about throughout the argument, let us use the following statement as an expression of what we shall take to be Berkeley's first premise:

1. *Sensible things are things like wood, stones, fire, water, flesh, iron, apples, trees, books, houses, mountains, and rivers.*

We shall justify this statement as representing one of the basic premises in Berkeley's argument by referring to data statements 11, 3, and 6. Where Berkeley does not explicitly state that the kinds of objects he refers to are sensible things, the context is such as to make it evident to us that Berkeley's attempt in these cases is to give examples of what he calls "sensible objects" or "sensible things."

Since premise 1 is a premise in which Berkeley *shows how he is using the term* "sensible things," namely, to refer to objects of the kind illustrated, let us call premise 1 a *pragmatical statement,* for we shall mean by "pragmatical statement" *any statement the point of which is to exhibit, or show, the use of a term.* In such a statement as datum statement 6, in which houses, mountains, and rivers are mentioned and referred to as sensible objects, the point of the statement (to the extent that it makes such a reference through the use of examples) is *not* to *explain* what sensible things are; the point is *not* to describe, or to define through description, the class of sensible things; the point is, simply, to *show,* through examples in this case, *how the term "sensible things" is being used by the writer.* It may be that we are not satisfied with the demonstration; we may not regard it as sufficient; but, in any case, whenever we can recognize the point of a statement to be a pragmatical one, in our sense of "pragmatical," we are prepared, as critics, to consider whether the statement successfully serves its function.

Let us symbolize premise 1 as follows:

$$(x) \; [S_1 x \longleftrightarrow (Wx \lor Fx \lor Ax \lor \ldots)] \qquad (1)$$

This symbolization is to be read: *Whatever we might consider, if it is a sensible thing, then it is either a wooden thing or a fire or an apple or something like that, and vice versa.* (There is no need to mention every one of Berkeley's examples of sensible things, for Berkeley himself does not attempt to exhaust the list of sensible things, and we have here limited ourselves to some representative cases.)

Let us take as the second premise of Berkeley's basic argument a proposition which ties in with the first: "Wood, stones, fire, water, flesh, iron, and the like things, which I name and discourse of, are things that I know." (See datum statement 11.) We now have to decide whether Berkeley here meant to claim that the things mentioned are *things he knew as individual things,* or *things of the sort he knew,* or *things of the sort that are known* (that is, things known to be members of classes of things some members of which are known, or have been known, by someone). Surely he meant to assert the third, although he would not have denied the second. There is certainly no reason to believe that Berkeley meant to claim that he knew *every* wooden thing, *every* stone, *every* fire, *every* apple; he meant only to claim that the things mentioned are the sorts of things that are known. The point of the statement, then, is that the various kinds of sensible things mentioned are *knowable*: such things *can* be known; and it is apparent that they can be known because *some* things of each kind *have been known.*

Although Berkeley does finally come to the conclusion that every sensible thing is perceived and, consequently, known by some-one, we need not suppose that Berkeley intended, *at the outset of his argument,* to limit the class of sensible things to those known individ-ually. Such a procedure would have left him open to the charge of being circular, and although philosophers have on occasion assumed at the outset of an argument what they purported to prove, there is as yet no justification for claiming that Berkeley is here guilty of such circularity.

We shall understand the second premise, then, to be the prop-osition that *wooden things, fires, apples, and things like that are things that can be known; such things are knowable:*

$$(x) \; [(Wx \vee Fx \vee Ax \vee \ldots) \rightarrow Kx] \qquad (2)$$

Premise 2 is to be read: *Whatever we might consider* (or, for all values of the variable symbol "x"; that is, no matter what indi-vidual "thing" of any sort is named throughout the expression wherever "x" marks the place for the name), *if it* (the individual named) *is a wooden thing or a fire or an apple or something like that, then it is something that can be known.*

Having maintained that "Wood, stones, fire . . . and the like things . . . are things that I know," Philonous (in datum statement 11) continues: "And I should not have known them but that I per-ceived them by my senses." In other words, to know such things is to perceive them; if such things are knowable, they are perceivable. Thus, we symbolize premise 3 as follows:

$$(x) \; [(Wx \vee Fx \vee Ax \vee \ldots) \rightarrow (Kx \longleftrightarrow P_1x)] \qquad (3)$$

Premise 3 is to be read: *Whatever we might consider, if it is a wooden thing or a fire or an apple or something like that, then, if it is knowable, it is perceivable by the senses; and if it is perceivable by the senses, it is knowable.* To be knowable and to be perceivable by the senses is one and the same thing; consequently, for such things, to be known is to be perceived by the senses. (We are using "P_1" to symbolize the property of *being perceivable,* and we shall later use "P_2" to symbolize the condition of *being perceived.*)

In premise 2 we are told that things of the sort mentioned, sensible things, are knowable; in 3 we are told that such things, if knowable, are perceivable; consequently, we may deduce that such things are perceivable. We use as an expression of this intermediate conclusion (which we need not have stated, but which we include because it emphasizes a point which Berkeley makes repeatedly) the following:

$$(x) \ [(Wx \lor Fx \lor Ax \lor \ldots) \rightarrow P_1x] \qquad (4)$$

Hylas, having stated in agreement with Philonous that "by *sensible things* I mean those only which are perceived by sense" (datum statement 9), goes on to assert that "in truth the senses perceive nothing which they do not perceive immediately, for they make no inferences"; and Philonous agrees that "sensible things are those only which are immediately perceived by sense" (10). Thus, we shall take as the next premise the proposition that *things perceivable by sense are things immediately perceivable by sense.* (We continue to assume that Berkeley is not begging the question by assuming that sensible things are *perceived*—only that they are the sorts of things that are perceived, that they are *perceivable.*)

Thus, as premise 5 we have:

$$(x) \ [P_1x \rightarrow \sim Mx] \qquad (5)$$

Premise 5 is to be read: *Whatever we might consider, if it is a thing perceivable by sense, then it is a thing immediately perceivable.* (We have used "$\sim M$", meaning *immediately perceivable,* because such an expression emphasizes Berkeley's use of the term "immediately" to mean *not by means of inferences;* furthermore, the symbolism allows us to reserve the convenient symbol "*I*" for the critical Berkeleian predicate *being an idea.*)

The next critical link in Berkeley's argument is the claim that things immediately perceived are *sense qualities* (see datum statement 10):

$$(x) \ [\sim Mx \rightarrow Qx] \tag{6}$$

—And sense qualities are *sensations* (datum statement 6):

$$(x) \ [Qx \rightarrow S_2x] \tag{7}$$

(We have used "S_1" to mean the property of being a *sensible thing*; here "S_2" means the property of being a *sensation*.)

—And sensations are *ideas* ("imprinted on the senses"), as indicated by data statements 1, 2, 3, 6, and 7:

$$(x) \ [S_2x \rightarrow Ix] \tag{8}$$

—And ideas are *within the mind (not external to the mind):*

$$(x) \ [Ix \rightarrow \sim Ex] \tag{9}$$

(This claim, premise 9, is made in several places in Berkeley's writings; among them, in datum statement 5: "ideas . . . cannot exist otherwise than in a mind perceiving them"; in Section 6 of the *Principles:* "all those bodies . . . have not any subsistence without a mind"; and in the grand summary statement made by Philonous in the *Dialogues,* in which he does some of the work of analysis for us: "and ideas cannot exist without the mind . . . .")

—And things within the mind are *perceived:*

$$(x) \ [\sim Ex \rightarrow P_2x] \tag{10}$$

(We have used "P_1" to mean the property of being *perceivable;* "P_2" is here used to mean the property of being *perceived.*)

We may now restate the conclusion:

$$\therefore \ (x) \ [S_1x \rightarrow P_2x]$$

(We recall that in the *Principles,* Section 3, Berkeley, in speaking of sensible things, argues that their "*esse* is *percipi.*" Again, in Section 5, he maintains that it is "impossible for me to conceive in my thoughts any sensible thing or object distinct from the sensation or perception of it." In Section 6 he again claims, in regard to "all those bodies which compose the mighty frame of the world," that "their *being* is to be perceived or known," and he invites the reader to attempt "to separate in his own thoughts the *being* of a sensible thing from its *being perceived*.")

Berkeley's argument against the philosophical materialist who argues that material or sensible things are external to the mind and are unknown and unknowable causes of our sensations is complete: if sensible things are necessarily known and, as known, are sensations within the mind which perceives them, then it could not be the case that possibly some sensible things are not known, not perceived, and different from what, as sensed, they appear to be.

Let us now draw the premises together in a symbolic restatement of Berkeley's basic argument. We shall consider the *validity* of the argument *as so symbolized:* we ask whether *if* the premises were true, the conclusion would then necessarily be true. Finally, we shall consider whether the premises are *acceptable*. If we grant that Berkeley's argument is valid and that his premises are true, we cannot consistently deny his conclusion.

The basic argument, as we have symbolized it, is as follows:

1. $(x) [S_1x \longleftrightarrow (Wx \vee Fx \vee Ax \vee \ldots)]$
2. $(x) [(Wx \vee Fx \vee Ax \vee \ldots) \to Kx]$
3. $(x) [(Wx \vee Fx \vee Ax \vee \ldots) \to (Kx \longleftrightarrow P_1x)]$
∴ 4. $(x) [(Wx \vee Fx \vee Ax \vee \ldots) \to P_1x]$ (from 2 and 3)
5. $(x) [P_1x \to \sim Mx]$
6. $(x) [\sim Mx \to Qx]$
7. $(x) [Qx \to S_2x]$
8. $(x) [S_2x \to Ix]$
9. $(x) [Ix \to \sim Ex]$
10. $(x) [\sim Ex \to P_2x]$ /   ∴ $(x) [S_1x \to P_2x]$

If in our appraisal of the logical structure of this argument we first of all review the manner by which Berkeley moved to what we have called premise 4 by way of premises 2 and 3, we can then appreciate the economy with which the author of this argument fashioned the logical chain which leads from the reference to sensible things to the connection with the predicate *being perceived*. According to Berkeley, no matter what we consider, if it is a sensible thing, then it is wood, fire, apple, or something like that; if something like that, then knowable; if something like that and knowable, then perceivable; if perceivable, then immediately perceivable; if immediately perceivable, then possessing sensible qualities; if sensible qualities, then sensations; if sensations, then ideas; if ideas, then existing within the mind; if within the mind, then perceived; consequently, all sensible objects are perceived. The argument as stated is obviously valid, but the question remains as to whether the premises are all acceptable to us.

By constructing a diagram which shows the logical connections which the argument makes, we can actually trace out the logical progression from the antecedent "sensible things" of the first premise to the consequent "perceived" of the last. A person who understands the use, through the ordering of premises, of the logical symbolism involved in our summary of Berkeley's argument can in a sense be said to "see" that the argument is valid; however, through the use of the chain diagram one can *literally* "see" the integrity of the logical chain which Berkeley has fashioned.

Since this particular argument, as we have summarized it, involves the universal quantifier throughout, we can show the logical structure of the argument without using the variable "x" or any other symbol which could represent a hypothetical individual. We shall, of course, understand the diagram to represent the logical relations reputed to hold among the various properties to which Berkeley refers, and we may then suppose that the structure represented applies to any particular case we might consider. (In graphically representing other arguments to be considered in this series of demonstrations of the analysis of philosophical arguments, we shall sometimes find it necessary to use constant symbols, such as "a", "b", "c", to represent values of the variable symbol "x".)

Let us, then, by the use of predicate symbols and various natural symbols for logical relationships show that, *for anything we might consider, its being a sensible thing implies* (indicates, leads to the conclusion) *that it is either wood, or a fire, or an apple, or something like that—and vice versa* (premise 1):

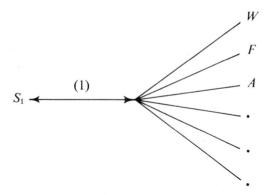

Premise 2 is *about* the things given in premise 1 as examples of sensible things. To show that *if something is either wood or a fire or an apple or something like that, then it is knowable,* we begin another implication arrow at the juncture of the alternatives (one such arrow already runs to "S_1") and draw it so that it points to "K":

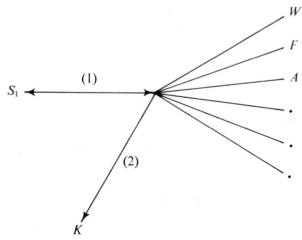

Premise 3 is also about the alternatives; consequently, to show that *if a thing is either wood or a fire or an apple or something like that, then, if it is knowable, it is perceivable,* we must run an arrow from the juncture of the alternatives to the center of the shaft of the implication arrows pointing at "K" and "P_1":

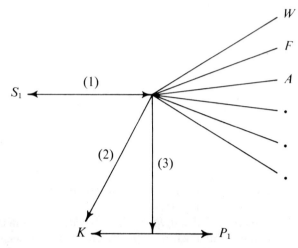

From the diagram we may conclude that premise 4 follows from premises 2 and 3, and thus we shall not include 4 in the diagram. The diagram shows that if anything is either wood or fire or an apple or something like that, it is perceivable *if* it is knowable, but the diagram shows that any such thing is knowable; hence, such a thing is perceivable.

Premise 5 states that if anything has the property P_1, then it has the property $\sim M$ (that is, if anything is perceivable, it is immediately perceivable, *not* mediately perceivable). To show this premise on the diagram in such a way as to relate it to the previous premises, we draw an arrow from "P_1" to "$\sim M$". The change of direction of the arrow indicates that "$P_1 \rightarrow \sim M$" is a separate premise, not part of any other premise shown, although it is tied into, logically linked with, the premises which have as a consequent "P_1" or a consequent involving reference to "P_1". (Diagram, facing page.)

We may now complete the diagram of the argument by tying in premises 6, 7, 8, 9, and 10. The "tying in" or "linking" of the premises is in accordance with the argument *as Berkeley probably wished to have it understood*. Berkeley's argument *suggests* a logical chain, which we here represent. This initial diagram, then, is intended

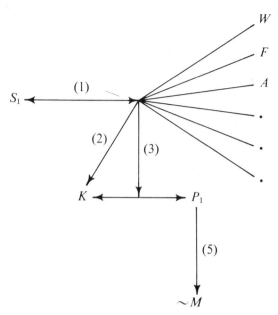

to do no more than to show the structure of the argument that Berkeley probably attempted to build. The premises serve as the expressions of *reasons* advanced for accepting the conclusion as true. If the diagram shows a valid argument, we should be able to move from the symbol representing the *antecedent* of the conclusion, "S_1", to the *consequent* of the conclusion, "P_2". The diagram *does* permit that logical journey; hence, the *diagram* represents a *valid* argument. (Diagram, top of next page.)

At the bottom of the diagram we have indicated, to the right of the diagonal line, the conclusion of Berkeley's argument; namely, *if anything is a sensible thing, then it is perceived.* The argument is valid if its structure is that of the diagram, for the diagram shows that if anything is a *sensible thing,* then (following the logical course) it is knowable; perceivable; immediately perceivable; a collection of sense qualities, of sensations, of ideas; not external to the mind; *perceived.*

However, although Berkeley's argument encourages the construction of the logical chain represented by the diagram, we cannot

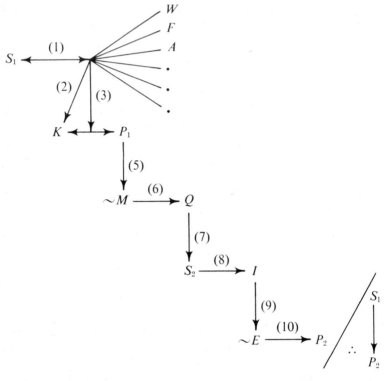

conclude that Berkeley's argument itself is valid and corresponds in logical form to the argument type symbolized unless we first of all make certain that at every point of connection, that is, wherever a symbol represents both a consequent and an antecedent—the consequent of one premise, the antecedent of another—the symbol represents the *same term*. We have shown the logic, the structure, of the argument Berkeley constructed; provided that by "the argument Berkeley constructed" we mean the *verbal* chain as he presented it, the chain uncritically accepted and fashioned as he would have it fashioned. We *could* have demanded, prior to the symbolization of any premise, justification for the use of our symbols; we *could* have refused, prior to a careful examination of the use of terms (pragmatical investigation), to use a symbol twice if the use of terms did not justify the repetition. But we have reserved our criticism until now to make possible a representation of the argument as Berkeley meant to have it envisaged (we presume from knowledge of the context). We can now understand why Berkeley supposed his argument to be persuasive. Our task, as critics, becomes the task of attending to the use of terms in order to determine whether the present symbolization can stand and, if it cannot, what the consequences are as concerns both the validity and the soundness of the argument.

3. CRITICISM OF THE BASIC ARGUMENT

We are interested in determining whether Berkeley's argument is *valid* and whether his premises are *true;* if the argument is valid and the premises true, we shall accept the argument as sound.

To determine whether the argument is valid, we must first of all determine whether the structure of the argument, *relative to the actual use of terms,* corresponds to that of the diagram, which represents the structure of the argument *as Berkeley wished it to be understood.* Thus, we must examine, premise by premise, the argument *as we find it* in the *Principles* and the *Dialogues.*

PREMISE 1

(x) $[S_1x \longleftrightarrow (Wx \lor Fx \lor Ax \lor \ldots)]$: In this premise Berkeley does nothing more than show us his use of the term "sensible things." He *shows* us his use; he does not *explain* his use by offering a descriptive account of what a thing must be to be what he calls a "sensible thing." It does not matter whether the use exhibited is a common use, although it is necessary to the effectiveness of the exhibition of examples that the terms used to name the examples be terms in common use. We shall take them to be so, for there is no reason initially to believe that Berkeley is here using such terms as "wood," "fire," and "apple"—and such terms as "houses," "mountains," "rivers," "iron," "flesh," and the like—in any eccentric way. What, in effect, he is saying is that he chooses to call these familiar things "sensible" things. Thus, his "claim" is *pragmatical;* it introduces a use of a term, and there is no reason to quarrel with the term as he uses it.

Once we have decided, with Berkeley, to call such things "sensible things," it is *true* that *if something is a sensible thing, it is wood, or fire, or an apple, or something like that, and vice versa:* our decision as to the use of the term "sensible thing" makes the preceding generalization true.

PREMISE 2

(x) $[(Wx \lor Fx \lor Ax \lor \ldots) \to Kx]$: *Whatever we might consider, if it is wood, or fire, or an apple, or something like that, then it is something that can be known.* Having referred to the "endless variety of ideas or objects of knowledge" (in Section 2 of the *Principles*), Berkeley contends that "there is likewise something which knows or perceives them . . . ." Again, in Section 6, in speaking of the "choir of heaven and furniture of the earth, in a word all those bodies which compose the mighty frame of the world," Berkeley contends that "their *being* is to be perceived or known . . . ." Finally, he describes "Wood, stones, fire, water, flesh, iron, and the like things" as "things that I know." The implication is that, for such things, to be known *is* to be perceived: perception by the senses is the mode of knowing such objects. But, as we have indicated earlier, Berkeley would have been arguing in a circle to insist at the outset that all such objects are *known,* actually *perceived.* What he wanted to show was that such objects are by their very nature such that if they are *perceivable* it follows that they are *perceived.* He wanted to rule out, at the outset, as sensible objects, any esoteric objects, any objects posited by metaphysicians, objects remote from the world of familiar things we encounter in day-to-day experience. Thus, he insisted that sensible things, things like wood, stones, fire, and the like, are "things I know"—that is, the sorts of things I know: *knowable* things, things that *can* be known through sense perception.

Since there is a familiar use of the term "know" such that we would say, in regard to what Berkeley calls "sensible things," that they are "things that we know"; that is, that they are things that *can* be known, the sorts of things that *are* known through perceiving them by the senses, there is no reason why we should object to Berkeley's claim that the things he mentions are "knowable" things. The expression "things that I know" is used in a way which is common and familiar. Again, Berkeley's "claim" is a suggestion that we describe these various things he has mentioned as "things we know," or, more technically, as "knowable" things, in some perfectly familiar sense of the expression "things we know." We may also classify premise 2 as *pragmatical,* then; and in accepting Berkeley's terminological suggestion that we describe the familiar objects of everyday experience as "things that we know"—which we have taken to mean "the sorts of things we know"—we secure the truth of the proposition that wood or fire or apples or things like that are things that can be known. The truth is secured, *not* by *definition,* but by a *decision* as to how the familiar objects of everyday sense experience *are to be described;* that is, by a *pragmatical* decision as to the *use of the expression* "things that we know" or "things that can be known."

PREMISE 3

(x) $[(Wx \vee Fx \vee Ax \vee \ldots) \rightarrow (Kx \longleftrightarrow P_1x)]$: Here Berkeley claims that the things he has been talking about are such that *if known, they are perceived (and vice versa)*; that is, these are things such that *to be knowable and to be perceivable is one and the same.* We certainly grant that such things are things we can know through sense perception; hence, we have no reason to object to premise 3. It is not at all odd to call such things "perceivable" things; we accede to this third *pragmatical* suggestion and thus are willing to treat premise 3 as a true proposition.

PREMISE 4

(x) $[(Wx \vee Fx \vee Ax \vee \ldots) \rightarrow P_1x]$: We have included premise 4 simply because it emphasizes Berkeley's point that the familiar objects of everyday sense experience are the sorts of things we can, in line with ordinary usage, describe as "things that we perceive"; that is, as "perceivable" things. In his writings Berkeley sometimes makes this point separately; sometimes, as in our summary, he relates this premise to the earlier pragmatical claim to the effect that things of the sorts mentioned are "things that I know"; that is, "knowable" things. In acceding to 2 and 3 we are committed *on logical grounds* to accepting 4.

PREMISE 5

(x) $[P_1x \rightarrow \sim Mx]$: In claiming that every *perceivable* thing is something *immediately perceivable,* Berkeley is claiming that sensible things (exemplified by such things as wood, fire, apples, and the like, and subsequently described as "knowable" and "perceivable" things) are capable of being perceived through the use of the senses without any act of inference. In the *Dialogues* Philonous shows how the expression "immediately perceived" is used: "In reading a book, what I immediately perceive are the letters, but mediately, or by means of these, are suggested to my mind the notions of God, virtue, truth, etc." Hylas, a short time later, agrees that "in truth the senses perceive nothing which they do not perceive immediately, for they make no inferences."

If to say that sensible, knowable, perceivable things are "immediately perceivable" means nothing more than that no inferences are needed, once one has sensed such things, to justify the claim that one has sensed, known, or perceived such things, then we have no objection to premise 5. The data are not such as to allow us to clear up the question as to whether a submarine commander, having seen a ship through the periscope, could be said to have seen it "immediately," but the distinction made by contrasting the perception of the letters on a page to the "perception" of the ideas ("notions") symbolized by those letters is clear enough to make it reasonable to suppose that the distinction might be extended so as to include the class of cases to be found in the accounts of the adventures of Sherlock Holmes, who, *immediately perceiving* nothing more than a few ashes, a piece of mud, and a depression in a rug, could deduce—or, we could say, "perceive *mediately*"—what sort of man had been there, how tall he was, what his occupation was, what brand of cigars he smoked, who his companion was, why she was there, and so forth.

If this distinction is the one meant by contrasting cases of "immediately perceiving" something to cases of "mediately perceiving" something, we have no objection to premise 5. In fact, we are tempted to suggest that premise 5 be an *equivalence: Anything perceivable by the senses is immediately perceivable by the senses, and vice versa,* and there is nothing in the above-quoted passages to suggest that Berkeley would not agree to this interpretation; however, a one-way implication is enough for his purposes.

In reading philosophy critically—as in playing a game critically,

when the game involves the use of strategy one can sometimes antici-
pate—one often finds it helpful to ask, "Why did he do that?" So it is
in the critical appraisal of Berkeley's argument. Berkeley has claimed
that sensible things are "knowable"; that is, Berkeley referred to his
examples of sensible things as examples of "things I know." *Why did
he do that?* One is inclined to suppose that he did it in order to contrast *his* position in regard to sensible things, the position, namely,
that sensible things are *known* through sense experience, to the philosophical position represented by Hylas, the position that the existence
of sensible things is always in question, for sensible things are taken
to be the *unknown and unknowable* causes of our sensations. And yet
acceding to Berkeley's use does *not* necessitate the rejection of the
view that sensible things (houses, mountains, stones, rivers, and
things like that) are the *causes* of our sensations and not the sensations themselves; it is still possible to maintain, as the philosopher
George Santayana did in his *Skepticism and Animal Faith,* that
knowledge is *faith* "mediated by symbols" and that "The images in
sense are parts of discourse, not parts of nature [that is, not parts of
the external world]: they are the babble of our innocent organs under
the stimulus of things." Thus, we may accede to Berkeley's use of
some such expression as "things we know"; and we may then agree
with him in saying that sensible things are "things that are known,"
—that is, "the sorts of things we know," "knowable" things—without
being forced to accept Berkeley's "immaterialism," the view that
sensible things of the kinds mentioned are nothing but collections of
sensations. Acceding to his use of the term "know," but anticipating
a later move to exploit that pragmatical concession, we are prepared
to withdraw our acceptance of premises 2 and 3 (which involve the
use of the term "knowable") if Berkeley (or his representative)
insists that to "know" is to "*have,*" as when one *has* a headache or a
pain.

So it is with premise 5: if to say that perceivable things are
"immediately" perceivable means only that such things can be sensed
and that, once sensed, need not be deduced from data, we have no
objection to premise 5. But we ask: Why did he do that? And we
answer: In all probability, to distinguish between his view—by which
it is claimed that sensible things, like sensations (such as pains), are

perceived "immediately"—and the realist position, represented by Hylas, which maintains that only sensations are perceived "immediately" and that sensible things are assumed to be the causes of our sensations. Thus, guessing at Berkeley's strategy, we agree to say that sensible things are perceived "immediately," for here we mean "without the further use of reason"; but we are wary, for we do not want to be coaxed into saying that sensible things are perceived "immediately" if that critical term is used to describe the relation between a sense observer and his *sensations*. So far we have been talking about the relation between a sense observer and the sensible *things* (such as houses, stones, fires) he observes; we are not committed to extending our usage of the expression "perceive immediately" so as to include reference to the relation between a sense observer and his sense responses, his sensations. Such an extension of usage would come easy, for we are not at all tempted to say that sensations (pain, feelings of warmth, cold, and the like) are noticed "mediately." There is a sense of the term "immediate" such that nothing is more immediate than a splitting headache; at such a time, the objects of our physical world seem to be remote. But it would be fatal, having accepted premise 5 on the basis of a pragmatical exhibition in which the letters on a page are described as being "immediately perceivable," to forget the use of the term "immediately" that was a condition of our acceptance and to be seduced into agreeing that, indeed, only sensations are *really immediate*. We would then be committed, because of our inconsistency in the use of the term "perceive immediately," to the conclusion (toward which we know Berkeley is working) that sensible things are *sensations*. Whether or not sensible things are sensations, we do not want to be *driven* to agreeing that they are, as a result of having failed to notice an inconsistency in the use of a critical term.

Let us, then, use "$\sim M_1$" to mean "immediately perceivable, as the letters on a page are perceivable, by the use of the senses: the faculties of vision, hearing, smelling, touching, and tasting." And we shall use "$\sim M_2$" to mean "immediately perceivable, as the sensations of pain, warmth, sweetness, dizziness are perceivable, by a subject, through the subject's having, undergoing, such sensations."

Thus, in considering whether we agree with Berkeley when he

claims that sensible things (which we have agreed to describe as knowable and perceivable by the senses) are "immediately perceivable," it is apparent that such things as houses, mountains, stones, and apples are "immediately perceivable, as the letters on a page are perceivable, by the use of the senses: the faculties of vision, hearing, smelling, touching, and tasting." An apple, for example, may be seen through the use of the eyes; it may be smelled through sniffing it with one's nose; it may be touched with one's finger (or elbow, or toe); and certainly it may be tasted, by taking a bite out of it, by chewing it, by rolling the fragments on one's tongue. Doing these things, one is justified in saying that one knows the apple by having sensed, or perceived, it. It would be odd to say that one "deduced" it was an apple; the apple is perceived, not mediately through an act of reason, but "immediately through the use of the sense faculties." Thus, we *resymbolize* premise 5:

$$(x) \ [P_1x \rightarrow \sim M_1x] \tag{5}$$

The premise is *acceptable* in *this* form.

If, however, we substitute the symbol "$\sim M_2$" for the symbol "$\sim M_1$", premise 5 (a different premise as the result of the substitution) is *unacceptable*; for such things as houses, stones, and apples cannot truly be said to be "immediately perceivable, as the sensations of pain, warmth, sweetness, dizziness are perceivable through having, undergoing, such sensations." An apple, for example, cannot be "had," in the sense of "undergone"; one cannot "have" an apple in the same sense in which one "has" a headache; one cannot "undergo" an apple in the same sense that one can "undergo" suffering (in fact, it is nonsense to talk about "undergoing" an apple).

PREMISE 6

$(x) \ [\sim Mx \rightarrow Qx]$: *Anything immediately perceivable is a sense quality.* We now have the problem of deciding whether the antecedent of premise 6 should be symbolized by "$\sim M_1$" or by "$\sim M_2$". To tie this premise to premise 5, as we have constructed it, we must use "$\sim M_1$" in the antecedent. But now again a problem arises which has come to pervade our criticism of Berkeley's argument: Are we by the term "sense quality" to mean that which we shall symbolize as "Q_1"; namely, *the relational property of a thing definable in terms of the sense response which would be provoked were an observer to attend to the thing* (so that, for example, the sense quality $[Q_1]$ "greenness" of a thing would be considered to be the capacity of the thing to provoke a sensation of a kind associated with the use of the term "green" to describe that which occasioned the sensation)—or are we by the term "sense quality" to mean that which we shall symbolize as "Q_2"; namely, *a kind of sensation?*

How does Berkeley use the term "sensible quality"? Let us attend to the *pragmatical data,* that is, instances of Berkeley's use of terms relating to our problem:

1. "Light and colors, heat and cold, extension and figures—in a word, the things we see and feel—what are they but so many sensations, notions, ideas, or impressions on the sense?" (*Principles,* Section 5)

2. "You will further inform me whether we immediately perceive by sight anything besides light and colors and figures; or by hearing, anything but sounds; by the palate, anything besides tastes; by the smell, besides odors; or by the touch, more than tangible qualities." (Philonous, in *Dialogues, First Dialogue*)

3. "It seems, therefore, that if you take away all sensible qualities, there remains nothing sensible?" (Also Philonous; follows above statement 2)

4. "Colors, sounds, tastes, in a word, all those termed 'secondary qualities,' have certainly no existence without the mind." (Hylas, conceding a point after discussion, *First Dialogue*)

5. ". . . you must know sensible qualities are by philosophers divided into *primary* and *secondary.* The former are extension, figure, solidity, gravity, motion, and rest. And these they hold exist really in bodies." (Hylas, following above statement 4)

6. "I am free to own . . . that all sensible qualities are alike to be denied existence without the mind." (Hylas, conceding

that primary qualities, as well as secondary, are within the mind; *First Dialogue*)

Datum statement 2 (in this set) illustrates the ambiguous use of such terms (for what Berkeley calls "sensible qualities") as "light," "colors," "figures," "sounds," "tastes," "odors," and "tangible qualities." Are these various qualities, or properties, or characteristics, to be defined as we have defined "Q_1"? Are they to be understood through the use of counterfactual conditionals ("if . . . then . . ." statements)—so that, for example, to say that something has color is to say that it is such that *if* it were observed by a visual observer under certain conditions, *then* the observer would undergo a sense experience such that he would be justified in reporting that the thing had color? *Or are we to understand sensible qualities to be, as Philonous claims they are, sensations?*

The *persuasive* statements involving the use of the term "sensible qualities" (or, in a context, statements such that they can be understood to be statements *about* sensible qualities) are statements in which the ambiguity noted above persists. Hylas agrees that we "immediately perceive" by sight nothing but "light, and colors, and figures" because he takes these terms to refer to *causal properties* which are to be understood as capacities to affect sense observers. Thus, when Philonous says (and we take this statement as datum statement 7 in this set):

7. "Sensible things therefore are nothing else but so many sensible qualities or combinations of sensible qualities?" (*First Dialogue*)

—when Philonous says this, Hylas agrees; but when, immediately afterwards, Philonous asks, "Does the reality of sensible things consist in being perceived . . .?" Hylas answers, "To *exist* is one thing, and to be *perceived* is another."

Hylas very much resists accepting as true those statements by which Philonous claims that sensible things are combinations of "sensible qualities" when by "sensible qualities" we understand the reference to be to *sensations*. But when Philonous describes what he calls "the most vehement and intense degree of heat" as a "very great pain," where it is evident that the discussion is about *sensible quali-*

ties, Hylas agrees. Here, however, what is called "heat" is a *sensation* which is painful; and had Hylas been aware of the *pragmatical switch* from discourse about *what he would call* "sensible qualities" to discourse about *what Philonous calls* "sensible qualities," he would *not* have agreed that "vehement . . . heat" is "a very great pain."

Hylas insists that the sensible things under discussion are *external* objects, and he describes the external object as follows:

8. "It is a material substance with the sensible qualities inhering in it." (*First Dialogue*)

In this statement Hylas uses the term "sensible qualities" to mean causal properties. He realizes that he cannot attribute the sensible quality called "great heat" to any material thing *if* by "heat" is meant something that is also describable as "a very great pain"; hence, he retracts his former identification of heat and pain: "Hold, Philonous, I fear I was out in yielding intense heat to be a pain. It should seem rather that pain is something distinct from heat, and the consequence or effect of it."

But, having said this, Hylas immediately makes the mistake of identifying heat with a sensation; the mistake is occasioned by Philonous's drawing Hylas into speaking of "perceiving" *sensations* of heat, as if to perceive *heat*$_1$ (as a causal property [Q_1] of the fire) and *heat*$_2$ (as a sensation [Q_2]) were one and the same. (See discussion in *First Dialogue.*)

Hylas *finally* becomes aware of the need for distinction, and he says firmly (in a passage not previously quoted): "You must distinguish, Philonous, between sound as it is perceived by us, and as it is in itself; or (which is the same thing) between the sound we immediately perceive and that which exists without us. The former, indeed, is a particular kind of sensation, but the latter is merely a vibrative or undulatory motion in the air." (*First Dialogue*)

Philonous then persuades Hylas that only "sensible" sound—that is, sensations—can meaningfully be said to be " 'loud,' 'sweet,' 'acute,' or 'grave.' " Furthermore, Philonous soon has Hylas speaking of *hearing* only "sensible sound" (sensations), and Hylas concedes that it is intolerably paradoxical to insist that *real sounds are never heard.* (Here a distinction is *not* made which, one might argue, *could* have been made between "hearing" as *sensing a sensation* of the sort provoked by sound, that is, as consciously responding in a certain way, and "hearing" as *listening to a sound,* that is, as attending, through the use of the ears, to that which provokes the sensation.)

It is evident from the examination of Berkeley's writings that Berkeley meant to claim that what we ordinarily describe as "colors," "sounds," "odors," "tastes," and so forth, are not the causal properties of external things but the felt qualities (characteristics) of sensations. We have acknowledged Berkeley's use of this claim as a premise by including it in the summary of the argument (as premise 7). Thus, to understand premise 6 *as Berkeley would have it understood,* we must symbolize it as follows:

$$(x) \ [\sim M_2 x \to Q_2 x] \tag{6}$$

In this form, premise 6 is acceptable both to Berkeley and to us; for surely, as we have defined the symbols, *if* anything is immediately perceivable, as the sensations of pain, warmth, sweetness, dizziness are perceivable, through having, undergoing, such sensations, *then* it is a sensation. *If something is perceivable as a sensation, then it is a sensation.*

But premise 5 was acceptable to us only in the form:

$$(x)[\ P_1 x \to \ \sim M_1 x] \tag{5}$$

If to be able to assent to both 5 and 6, we interpret the predicate of premise 5 to mean "immediately perceivable, as the letters on a page are perceivable, by the use of the faculties of sense," so that we use the symbol "$\sim M_1$", while we interpret the antecedent of premise 6 to mean "perceivable *as* a sensation," so that we use the symbol "$\sim M_2$"—if we do this, we break the logical chain represented by the diagram. *Interpreted in this way,* the argument is *invalid.*

Let us, then, in the effort to understand Berkeley and to criticize him fairly, resolve the ambiguity of terms *throughout the argument* and do so in a manner which represents the position so persistently defended by Berkeley's alter ego, Philonous.

The Berkeleian interpretation of the basic argument: Working backwards from premise 6, which has already received an interpretation that the context of Berkeley's presentation demands, we so interpret premise 5 as to permit a logical connection between 5 and 6:

$$(x) \ [P_1x \rightarrow \sim M_2x] \tag{5}$$

But the subject contains an ambiguous predicate term "P_1", interpreted to mean either "capable of being perceived, by means of sensations, as the cause of those sensations," which we shall symbolize with "$P_{1.1}$"; or to mean "capable of being perceived as a sensation, or complex of sensations," which we shall symbolize by using "$P_{1.2}$". Which of the two symbols would be the one to use to represent the interpretation Berkeley would make of premise 5? Surely the latter, for premise 5 makes a claim concerning perceivable things, to the effect that such things are *immediately perceivable as sensations*; therefore, the premise is about *things that are perceivable as sensations*. Thus, we *rewrite* premise 5:

$$(x) \ [P_{1.2}x \rightarrow \sim M_2x] \tag{5}$$

To allow premise 4 to tie in with premise 5, we use the subject term of premise 5 as the predicate term of premise 4:

$$(x) \ [(Wx \vee Fx \vee Ax \vee \ldots) \rightarrow P_{1.2}x] \tag{4}$$

But surely it is not credible that wood, fire, apples, and things like that are *perceivable as sensations* unless somehow these things which Berkeley calls "sensible things" (premise 1) can also be *known as sensations;* for premise 3 states that such things are such that if knowable, they are perceivable. We must, then, if premises 2 and 3 are logically to yield premise 4, modify 3 by specifying the sense of the predicates "K" and "P_1":

$$(x) \ [(Wx \vee Fx \vee Ax \vee \ldots) \rightarrow (K_2x \rightarrow P_{1.2}x)] \tag{3}$$

—where "K_2" means "knowable as sensations."

Premise 2 is modified accordingly:

$$(x) \ [(Wx \vee Fx \vee Ax \vee \ldots) \rightarrow K_2x] \tag{2}$$

But premise 2 is now the proposition that wood (pieces of wood, wooden things), fire (fires), apples, and things like that are *knowable as sensations*. Consequently, if premise 1 is to connect logically with premise 2, the terms "wood," "fires," "apples," and other terms which denote things like that—such terms as "houses," "mountains," "rivers," "stones": terms which Berkeley also used in giving examples of the sorts of things he meant to denote by his use of the term "sensible things"—must be understood to denote "things" which are sensations (or collections of sensations). Now, we know that Berkeley sought, through his argument, to win support for the claim that *sensible things are collections of sensations* by describing the kinds of things he called "sensible things" as "knowable" things, the "knowable things" as "perceivable," the "perceivable" as "immediately perceivable," the "immediately perceivable" as "sense qualities," and the "sense qualities" as "sensations." At that point, by arguing that what he called "sensations" are "ideas" and that "ideas" are "within the mind" and that whatever is "within the mind" is "perceived," Berkeley concluded that, for what he calls "sensible things," to be is to be "perceived." Knowing all this, and having found it necessary, in the attempt to symbolize accurately Berkeley's argument by specifying, through subscripts, the senses of the terms used, we now find it necessary to specify the sense in which the terms "wood," "fire," "apples," and terms like that are used. Berkeley's whole line of argument from premise 2 through 7—in which he claimed that *sense qualities are sensations*—is made possible through discourse about *sensations*. Thus, we found it necessary to devise the symbol "Q_2" to mean *a kind of sensation;* that is, to say that something has the property Q_2 would be to say that it was a *sensation* of a certain kind. For Berkeley, as far as we can tell from the arguments considered, a *sense quality* and a *sensation* are one and the same. We could have used an equivalence symbol in premise 7. However, in contending that in sensing things one is aware of nothing other than "sense qualities," Berkeley meant only to deny that one is ever aware, through sense experience or in any other way, of a "bearer" of properties, a "substance" in which—as Hylas claimed—sense qualities "inhere." Thus, in saying that one is sensibly aware of nothing but sense qualities, Berkeley can be understood to have been claiming that one is aware of *instances* or *cases* of sense qualities: *this* feeling of warmth, *this* sweet taste, and so forth. But entities of these kinds are what he calls "sensations." Thus, there is no difference between "things" which are instances of sense qualities and "things" which are sensations. In this context, a sense quality (or a combination of sense qualities) is the same thing as a sensation (or collection of sensations).

Having devised "Q_2" to mean "instances of sense qualities; that is, *sensations* of certain kinds," we devised "$\sim M_2$" to mean "immediately perceivable *as sensations*," and "$P_{1.2}$" to mean "perceivable as *sensations*," and "K_2" to mean "knowable as *sensations*." Thus, it is evident that Berkeley's argument is *about sensations*; and if it is to be interpreted in such a manner as to make it a consistent argument, the terms "wood," "fire," "apples," and similar terms (in that they denote what Berkeley calls "sensible things") must be understood to make reference to *sensations* or *collections of sensations*—and to interpret them accordingly would be to give these terms, as used in premise 1, a meaning in accordance with the whole line of argument, a meaning made explicit as early as premise 2 (for how could things be *knowable as sensations* were they not sensations?) and stated directly in premise 7 (for in contending that sense qualities are sensations Berkeley meant to provide logical justification for the inference that *sensible things are sensations*).

And now the question is: Does Berkeley so use the terms "wood," "fire," "apple," "house," "mountain," "river," and the like, that we must understand these terms to denote *collections of sensations*? It is of course true, as we have said, that Berkeley comes to the conclusion that such things are collections of sensations: in the *Principles,* for example, having referred to "ideas . . . imprinted on the senses," or what he calls "sensations," Berkeley writes, "And as several of these are observed to accompany each other, they come to be marked by one name, and so to be reputed as one thing. Thus, for example, a certain color, taste, smell, figure, and consistence having been observed to go together, are accounted one distinct thing signified by the name 'apple' . . . ." But Berkeley's *concluding* that what he calls an "apple" is a collection of sensations does not provide evidence to support the claim that he *initially* so uses the term as to denote such a collection and, accordingly, to provide the ground for the semantical claim that, *as Berkeley uses the word,* the word "apple" *means* a certain collection of sensations.

The fact is that Berkeley (and Philonous) uses statements referring to mountains, rivers, apples, fire, and the like in such a way as *presumably* to illustrate the sorts of things he means to include within the range of meaning of the term "sensible things"; but his use of terms is *ambiguous*, in that it allows Philonous to proceed with the construction of an argument which depends on the hidden premise that such things are collections of sensations, while Hylas finds himself acceding to premise after premise because he systematically interprets the terms—including such terms as "wood," "fire," "apples" —as having to do with things understandable by reference to causal properties.

Thus, there is no such thing as *the* meaning of such terms as "wood," "fire," and "apples" as Berkeley (together with Philonous) uses such terms. We shall have to consider the character of the argument interpreted throughout as Berkeley would have it understood, and we shall then be able to compare the consequences of such an interpretation to the consequences of an interpretation that would be agreeable to a critically alert realist.

To complete the interpretation of the argument according to the Berkeleian use of terms—that is, according to the use and meaning to which Berkeley would, in all probability, have given assent (as in so many places in his argument he suggests he would)—we must understand such terms as "wood," "fire," and "apples" to mean *collections of sensations,* even though in the early phases of the argument these things are not described in this way. We shall use the symbols "W_2", "F_2", and "A_2". Premise 1, then, is expressed as follows:

$$(x) \ [S_1 x \longleftrightarrow (W_2 x \lor F_2 x \lor A_2 x \lor \ldots)] \tag{1}$$

You are reminded that "S_1" means "sensible thing," while later in the argument "S_2" means "sensation."

The entire argument, *given the Berkeleian interpretation,* now runs (in summary form) as follows:

1. *Sensible things are things like wood, fires, and apples, considered to be collections of sensations* (as, for example, the mountains, rivers, and stones within the world of our own experience, as in our dreams, our imaginings).

2. *Wood, fire, apples, and things like that are things that are knowable as sensations.*
3. *Wood, fire, apples, and things like that are such that if knowable as sensations, they are perceivable as sensations.*
4. *(Therefore) wood, fire, apples, and things like that are perceivable as sensations.*
5. *Things perceivable as sensations are things immediately perceivable as sensations.*
6. *Things immediately perceivable as sensations are sense qualities, that is, sensations of certain kinds.*
7. *Things which are sense qualities (sensations of certain kinds) are sensations.*
8. *Sensations are ideas.*
9. *Ideas are within the mind.*
10. *Things within the mind are perceived.*

Therefore, *sensible things are things that are perceived. (Or, for sensible things, to be is to be perceived.)*

So interpreted, the argument has the structure of that which we initially called Berkeley's basic argument; and the diagram which we have constructed shows the logical structure of this argument, a structure which is that of a *valid* argument.

Do we object to any of the premises? If Berkeley wishes to talk about the "things" within the inner, private world of his own feelings, sense images, and the like; and if he chooses to call such things "sensible things" and to describe them as "collections of sensations" and then to point out that, interestingly enough, for such things to be perceiv*able* is to be perceiv*ed*—we have no serious objection. We ourselves may be reluctant to call the world of our inner experience—which may, after all, be the fantastic world the madman knows—the "world" and to describe the sense images within our minds as "sensible things," because to do so is to obscure the difference between our sense images and the physical things which resist us, stimulate us, and affect us through the senses. But although we are reluctant to use the terms "world" and "sensible things" (and such terms as "wood," "fire," and "apples") as Berkeley uses them, we find no *error* in his distinctive use of terms, except, perhaps, the practical or rhetorical error of talking unconventionally in such a way as to invite misinterpretation.

The main difficulty with Berkeley's argument—the principal deficiency—is this: what at first struck us as a startling and ridiculous claim, namely, the claim that *mountains, rivers, apples, and things like that are actually perceived,* now turns out to be neither startling nor ridiculous. In fact, the claim is obviously true—*but how trivial it is!* Had Berkeley asserted that pain, emotions, sensations, and things like that are *perceived,* we would not have been inclined to disagree; on the contrary, it is so apparent to us all that such "things" must be "perceived"—that is, "felt" or "had in consciousness"—in order to *be,* to *exist,* that our only surprise would have been at Berkeley's supposing there was some point in stressing the obvious. Why, then, if Berkeley was aware of what he was doing, did he make the claim that *sensible things*—by which he meant *collections of sensations*—are perceived? *Of course,* there could not be a *sensation* that was not *sensed* and, in that sense, *perceived.* Why, then, did Berkeley make this point?

From the outset of his argument Berkeley was concerned to stress what he took to be an important but often neglected truth about the "things we know"—namely, that in their *felt* radiance, vividness, color, movement, these "things" *within* the world of our experience, things we know intimately as our very sensations, are the things that concern us; and that *we need no others.* Philosophers who exercise their skeptical powers by suggesting that perhaps there are no causes of our sensations; or that even if there are such causes, we cannot know that there are; or that even if we can fairly confidently count on the existence of external things, we cannot be sure that they are *like* our sensations—such philosophers are wasting our time and talking nonsense. Such talk is nonsense, Berkeley believed, because nothing can be *like* a sensation but a sensation; just as a pain is like nothing but a pain, so any sensation is like nothing but another sensation. Thus, Philonous argues (in a passage not previously quoted), "Can a real thing, in itself *invisible,* be like a *color;* or a real thing which is not *audible* be like a *sound?* In a word, can anything be like a sensation or idea, but another sensation or idea?" The effort of philosophical realists, then, to maintain that physical, material things are really the external causes of our ideas, causes in no way dependent upon mind, is nonsense (according to Berkeley); for if such presumed objects are in no way *like* what we know *in experience,* how can we significantly even talk about them? Again, Philonous: "I am content, Hylas, to appeal to the common sense of the world for the truth of my notion. Ask the gardener why he thinks yonder cherry tree exists in the garden, and he shall tell you, because he sees and feels it; in a word, because he perceives it by his senses. Ask him why he thinks an orange tree not to be there, and he shall tell you, because he does not perceive it. What he perceives by sense, that he terms a real being and says it 'is' or 'exists'; but that which is not perceivable, the same, he says, has no being."

Berkeley, the immaterialist, then, supposes his point to be proven, and indeed it has been proven, for the use of the terms "wood," "fires," "apples," and other such terms in the argument is such that from the outset an immaterialist—or what we have called a "Berkeleian"—interpretation is possible. The argument is not circular in the sense that the conclusion is introduced as one of the premises; but it is circular in the sense that terms not ordinarily used to refer to "things" within the mind are here used in just that way by Berkeley—but covertly, so as to lead others to suppose he is talking about what anyone else would be talking about in mentioning *houses, mountains, rivers, wood, fires, apples, and things like that.* We have seen that to be true to the line of defense established by Berkeley (and Philonous), we must suppose that Berkeley, *at the very outset* of the argument—while presumably giving, as examples of what he calls "sensible things," things which anyone would recognize as things denoted by everyday terms in common use—was in fact using such terms as "houses," "mountains," "rivers," and "apples" in an unusual way, but in a way agreeable to his purpose, which was that of justifying the claim that sensible things, by their very nature, are perceived. We must concede that Berkeley's conclusion is true, for he so uses the term "sensible things" that one finds such things to be collections of sensations; and, admittedly, for sensations to be, they must be "perceived." But our concession is not remarkable, for we understand that Berkeley's conclusion has been insured by his somewhat extraordinary use of terms; and we realize that, in being provoked by what we took to be the extraordinary and ridiculous claim that physical things ("sensible things") are actually perceived, we were misled by the ambiguity of the terms used in Berkeley's claim.

COMMENTS ON THE ANALYSIS OF BERKELEY'S ARGUMENT

In considering Berkeley's argument we have been considering an argument which gains its persuasive power from the ambiguity of the statements used to present the premises and conclusion of the argument. Taken as an argument about the "world" within the mind, the "world" of sensations, the argument is valid but trivial; taken as an argument about the world of objects which can and sometimes do stimulate us as sense observers, the argument is provocative but unsound.

We would not have been able to come to this critical conclusion had we not made the effort to appraise the logical character of the argument by first of all determining the *meanings* of the terms relative to their *use* in the argument. Beginning with the assumption that in referring to "wood, stones, fire, water, flesh, iron, and the like things," Berkeley was talking about a class of familiar and publicly perceivable objects about which there could be no question which might affect the outcome of the argument, we proceeded with an interpretation we might describe as that of the "commonsense realist," thereby representing the view to which Berkeley refers (in the *Principles*) in the following passage: "It is indeed an opinion strangely prevailing amongst men that houses, mountains, rivers, and, in a word, all sensible objects have an existence, natural or real, distinct from their being perceived by the understanding."

But we found that although such an interpretation allows the commonsense realist to get as far as premise 6 in Berkeley's argument, no logical connection between premises 6 and 7 is possible; for in premise 6 the realist (who is materialistic in that he regards "sensible" or material things to be things which, when observed, *cause* sensations) takes the term "sense qualities" to refer to the causal properties of things, while to accept 7 he must mean by "sense qualities" sensations of certain kinds. Thus, to retain the logical structure which guarantees the validity of the argument, the realist must reject certain premises (for example, he must reject premise 7 if the statement of the premise is taken to mean that *causal* properties are sensations; or, if he makes the predicate of premise 6 a reference to sense qualities considered to be sensations, he must reject 6, for he will not agree that what is immediately perceivable through the use of the sense faculties—say, the letters on a page—is understandable as a collection of sensations). Thus, for anyone who attempts to understand Berkeley's argument in this way, the argument is either invalid and hence unsound despite the truth of its premises, or valid but unsound because of the falsity of some of the premises. What Berkeley claims is startling and provocative but not defensible, *if* the argument is interpreted in this "realistic" way.

We were then interested in discovering the consequences of interpreting the argument along the "immaterialist" lines made eloquent by Philonous. Working backward from the seventh premise, then, we found that we were forced to a reinterpretation even of premise 1, the premise in which our attention is called to certain prime examples or presumably *paradigm cases* of what Berkeley chose to call "sensible things." We realized that, after all, *there was some question* about the sorts of things to which Berkeley referred in mentioning wood, stones, fires, and the like, and we then decided that if Berkeley's use was consistent throughout, he was talking about the "world" within the mind, the "world" of sensations. Hence, his argument can be so interpreted as to retain the structure which makes it valid; but since no one would deny that "things" consisting of sensations are (like aches and pains and other feelings) such that *to be is to be perceived* (if by "perceived" is meant "sensed" or "felt" *as feelings*), the argument comes to a trivial conclusion.

If to be fair to Berkeley—to give him the benefit of any doubt as to his use of terms and thereby to salvage the validity of his argument—we interpret the argument so as to make it provocative but not circular, we find that the argument is unsound. If, then, continuing to make the effort to understand Berkeley and to give his argument every strength which the presentation of it allows, we interpret the argument so as to make it sound (valid, with true premises), we find that the argument is trivial.

Since no further examination of the argument justifies our insisting on the one interpretation in preference to the other, our critical conclusion is that Berkeley's argument is either unsound or trivial.

QUESTIONS FOR DISCUSSION

1. Does a more extensive reading of Berkeley's *Treatise Concerning the Principles of Human Knowledge* or his *Three Dialogues Between Hylas and Philonous* provide evidence to support the claim that in certain respects the above analysis is faulty? If so, what difference does amending those faults make to the critical appraisal of Berkeley's argument?

2. The author of the above analysis attempts to distinguish between statements the purpose of which is to *illustrate* the *use* of a term (*pragmatical* statements) and statements the purpose of which is to give an *explanation* of the *meaning* of a term (*semantical* statements). Consider whether it is true that a person can *show how* he is using a word *without descriptively defining* the word as it is used. Are there statements in Berkeley's argument (see the passages quoted at the beginning of the chapter, or refer to the *Principles* or the *Dialogues*) which clearly seem to be *pragmatical* in function? Are there others which clearly seem to be *semantical*?

3. Draw a logical diagram of Berkeley's argument as the argument would be interpreted by a realist (materialist), making the effort to interpret each of the premises in such a way as to make them all acceptable to the realist. Is the resultant diagram the diagram of a valid or of an invalid argument?

4. The author of the above analysis suggests that to use such terms as "houses," "mountains," "rivers," and "apples" to denote sensations within the mind is an *unusual* way of using the terms. Do you agree? Is Berkeley's use of terms in what the analyst calls the first premise an *ordinary* or an *extraordinary* use of terms?

5. Wouldn't it be possible to read, understand, and appreciate Berkeley's argument *without* considering how he uses the terms, what the terms mean, and what the logical consequences of what he says are? Isn't it enough to assume that he means what he says?

6. How can Berkeley be worthy of a place in the history of philosophy and nevertheless be guilty of having constructed an argument that is either unsound or trivial? Isn't it more likely that the critic is mistaken than that Berkeley was? If the critic is right in what he says, does it follow that Berkeley's importance in philosophy has been exaggerated?

7. If Berkeley was quite clear in his own mind as to the things he meant in talking about mountains, rivers, apples, and so forth, could the critic be justified in contending that the terms "mountains," "rivers," "apples," and so forth are ambiguous as Berkeley uses them?

8. Are atoms physical things? Are they material things? Are they sensible? Are they perceivable? Are they knowable? Are they immediately perceivable?

9. In looking at a blue book, do we perceive its color, its shape, its weight, and its other properties *without* perceiving the book?

10. Everything considered, *do* the objects we can see, hear, taste, smell, or touch exist when unperceived?

VII

ANSELM

THERE IS NO DOUBT THAT THERE EXISTS A BEING, THAN WHICH NOTHING GREATER CAN BE CONCEIVED

ANSELM'S ARGUMENT

. . . I do not seek to understand that I may believe, but I believe in order to understand. For this also I believe,—that unless I believed, I should not understand.

And so, Lord, do thou, who dost give understanding to faith, give me, so far as thou knowest it to be profitable, to understand that thou art as we believe; and that thou art that which we believe. And, indeed, we believe that thou art a being than which nothing greater can be conceived. Or is there no such nature, since the fool hath said in his heart, there is no God? (Psalms xiv. 1). But, at any rate, this very fool, when he hears of this being of which I speak—a being than which nothing greater can be conceived—understands what he hears, and what he understands is in his understanding; although he does not understand it to exist.

For, it is one thing for an object to be in the understanding, and another to understand that the object exists. When a painter first conceives of what he will afterwards perform, he has it in his understanding, but he does not yet understand it to be, because he has not yet performed it. But after he has made the painting, he both has it in his understanding, and he understands that it exists, because he has made it.

Hence, even the fool is convinced that something exists in the understanding, at least, than which nothing greater can be conceived. For, when he hears of this, he understands it. And whatever is understood, exists in the understanding. And assuredly that, than which nothing greater can be conceived, cannot exist in the understanding alone. For, suppose it exists in the understanding alone: then it can be conceived to exist in reality; which is greater.

Therefore, if that, than which nothing greater can be conceived, exists in the understanding alone, the very being, than which nothing greater can be conceived, is one, than which a greater can be conceived. But obviously this is impossible. Hence, there is no doubt that there exists a being, than which nothing greater can be conceived, and it exists both in the understanding and in reality.

And it assuredly exists so truly, that it cannot be conceived not to exist. For, it is possible to conceive of a being which cannot be conceived not to exist; and this is greater than one which can be conceived not to exist. Hence, if that, than which nothing greater can be conceived, can be conceived not to exist, it is not that, than which nothing greater can be conceived. But this is an irreconcilable contradiction. There is, then, so truly a being than which nothing greater can be conceived to exist, that it cannot even be conceived not to exist; and this being thou art, O Lord, our God.

*   *   *   *

But how has the fool said in his heart what he could not conceive; or how is it that he could not conceive what he said in his heart? since it is the same to say in the heart, and to conceive.

But, if really, nay, since really, he both conceived, because he said in his heart; and did not say in his heart, because he could not conceive; there is more than one way in which a thing is said in the heart or conceived. For, in one sense, an object is conceived, when the word signifying it is conceived; and in another, when the very entity, which the object is, is understood.

In the former sense, then, God can be conceived not to exist; but in the latter, not at all. For no one who understands what fire and water are can conceive fire to be water, in accordance with the nature of the facts themselves, although this is possible according to the words. So, then, no one who understands what God is can conceive that God does not exist; although he says these words in his heart, either without any, or with some foreign, signification. For, God is that than which a greater cannot be conceived. And he who thoroughly understands this, assuredly understands that this being so truly exists, that not even in concept can it be non-existent. Therefore, he who understands that God so exists, cannot conceive that he does not exist.

[From *Proslogium* (c. 1078) by St. Anselm (1033–1109; Archbishop of Canterbury); translated from the Latin by Sidney Norton Deane.*]

AN ANALYSIS OF ANSELM'S ARGUMENT

1. THE BASIC CLAIM

St. Anselm's basic claim is that "there is no doubt that there exists a being, than which nothing greater can be conceived." The point of Anselm's assertion is not that no one doubts God's existence but that, whether or not men believe or doubt, there *must* exist *in reality* (that is, not in thought alone) a being "than which nothing greater can be conceived." Anselm identifies this being as God: ". . . and this being thou art, O Lord, our God."

Anselm's attempt is to prove God's existence by arguing that an understanding of God's nature leads to the realization that God must exist and that, properly understood, God cannot be conceived

Edition used: Open Court Publishing Co., 1944.

not to exist. The argument has been called Anselm's "ontological" argument because it is based on a study of God's nature or kind of being.

2. THE BASIC ARGUMENT

To construct St. Anselm's basic argument we must abstract from his written argument those statements which serve as the expressions of his *reasons* for regarding his conclusion as certainly true; such statements provide the data for the logical expression of the premises of the basic argument. Acquiring the data is not enough, however; we know from the critical examination of previous arguments that an understanding of the *logical* structure of an argument requires an understanding of the *meanings* of the statements which express the premises; and we realize also that discovering the meanings of the statements requires careful attention to the author's use of terms.

Let us take the following statements as expressions of St. Anselm's premises:

1. "Lord . . . thou art a being than which nothing greater can be conceived."

2. ". . . the fool . . . when he hears of this being of which I speak —a being than which nothing greater can be conceived— understands what he hears . . . ."

3. ". . . and what [the fool] understands is in his understanding . . . ."

4. "And assuredly that, than which nothing greater can be conceived, cannot exist in the understanding alone. For, suppose it exists in the understanding alone: then it can be conceived to exist in reality; which is greater."

The conclusion then follows:

"But obviously this is impossible [the reference is to the state of affairs described in premise 4]. Hence, there is no doubt that there exists a being, than which nothing greater can be conceived, and it exists in the understanding and in reality."

The symbolization of these premises is made difficult by Anselm's tendency to speak of the subject of his argument, namely, the being than which nothing greater can be conceived, as *existing in the understanding* of the fool who "when he hears of this being . . . understands what he hears . . . ." If we allow ourselves, through our symbolism, to suggest that there *is* such a being, even though only in the understanding, we concede, in a manner different from the one which Anselm attempted to employ, that such a being *exists,* which is the point of the argument. We are *not* making a deliberate effort to resist conceding Anselm's point, but we are making the effort to appraise the argument critically and to accept the conclusion as one that has been proved only when we are satisfied that the argument is valid and the premises true (or acceptable). Consequently, we ask, in regard to the claim that "what [the fool] understands is in his understanding," *how is Anselm using the expression "in his understanding"*? And the conclusion we reach is this: when Anselm speaks of the "being than which nothing greater can be conceived" as one that "is in the understanding" and that "exists in the understanding," he is using those latter expressions as we use such expressions as "I kept you in mind," where there is no suggestion that the *person being thought about* somehow *exists in the mind* of the thinker. The point of such an expression is not that the *being* thought about is *in* the mind or the understanding, but simply that the *thought* of such a being, an *idea about* such a being, is in the mind of the thinker; but to say this is to say nothing more than that *the thinker is thinking* in a certain way.

We might be inclined initially to suppose that if one thinks *about a being,* there must be that being about which one thinks. But a moment's reflection will show that such a supposition is fallacious. We ask: what is it to "think about a being"? The answer is: to think, as we say, "about something," it is not at all necessary that there be that which is thought about; all that is necessary is that we build an idea by conceiving of a *kind* of thing. We may, then—if we are so inclined—find ourselves supposing (expecting that we would discover if we were to investigate) that there is a *thing* of that kind. For example: we may, if we wish, or if some author forces it upon us, think about a *green elephant;* an author might write, for example, "How surprised Alice was to find that, in the place usually reserved for her dolls, there was a green elephant!" We are now thinking about a green elephant. Does it follow that there *is* a green elephant about which we are thinking? Surely not: all that can justifiably be said is that we have *understood* (responded appropriately to the use of) the terms "green" and "elephant" and are now (perhaps) imagining (but, in this case, hardly supposing that there is) a green elephant. Having conceived a *kind* of being, we may now imagine a *thing* of that kind. Does the elephant *exist in our imaginations?* Yes, if by "exist in our imaginations" is meant no more than that we are thinking of a kind of thing and imagining that there is a thing of that kind (through the use of what we call a "mental picture," which no one could possibly confuse with an elephant). But perhaps, instead of saying that a *green elephant* "exists in our imaginations," it is less misleading to say that an *idea* or "mental image" of a kind of animal "exists in our imaginations." Or it might be even better to say that we have "green-elephant thoughts" or that we are thinking in such a way that, were we to report on our thinking, we would make reference to green elephants.

By now, however, it does not matter *how* we say it, for by now we have understood, and we are no longer inclined to think that thinking *about* something is possible only if there is something of the kind about which we are thinking. Nor is it necessary to the analysis of Anselm's argument that we make the effort to clarify further such expressions as "think about," "have thoughts," "mental pictures," and the like; we can now proceed to the symbolization of Anselm's premises:

$$(x) \ [Lx \longleftrightarrow Cx] \tag{1}$$

Here we understand Anselm's first premise to be an implicit definition (a semantical stipulation); Anselm declares, in effect, that in writing about the "Lord," he is considering "a being than whom no greater can be conceived." *If* anything is to be called the "Lord" or "God," *then* it is a being than whom no greater can be conceived; and *if* there is any such being, that being is to be called "Lord." Anselm has written, in effect, "Let us use the term 'Lord' to designate any being that fits the following description . . . ."

It is true that Anselm addresses the Lord: "And so, Lord, do thou, who dost give understanding to faith, give me . . . to understand that thou art as we believe . . . ," but we need not suppose that there is a Lord whom Anselm addresses. Anselm does not argue that there is a God because Anselm addresses him or believes in him or thinks about him; the point of Anselm's argument is that whether or not one addresses the Lord, believes in him, or thinks about him, God exists; he exists necessarily because of the *kind* of being he is.

In symbolizing the second premise, that the fool "when he hears of this being . . . —a being than which nothing greater can be conceived—understands what he hears," we shall simplify the expression of the proposition by using the *individual symbol "f"* to designate "the fool" about whom Anselm speaks. Anselm means *any* fool who doubts God's existence; but he is also writing specifically about *the* fool mentioned in the Bible who said in his heart, "There is no God." We shall use the symbol " *'C'* " for the predicate "is the expression 'a being than which nothing greater can be conceived' (or some expression synonymous in meaning with this expression; for example, the expression 'God')." (In reading the symbol " *'C'* ", however, we shall usually simply refer to "the expression.") The symbol "U_1" is used to mean "understands," in that sense of the term "understands" involved in "He understands the expression." Thus:

$$(Ex) \ [``C"x \cdot U_1 f, x] \tag{2}$$

—which is read: *There is something* (a value of the variable "*x*") *such that it is the expression "a being than which nothing greater can be conceived" (or some expression synonymous with this expression), and the fool understands the expression.*

In symbolizing premise 3—*Anything understood by the fool is in the understanding of the fool*—we do not want to suggest that *the expression* which he hears and understands is what is in the understanding of the fool, nor do we want to say that the *being* (God) meant by the expression is in the fool's understanding. What we shall say is that the fool's conception or *idea* of the meaning of the expression is in his understanding—but we shall mean no more in saying that the "idea" is "in his understanding" than that the fool has understood the expression by conceiving the kind of thing which would fit the description. We do not suggest that there is a mysterious, intangible entity, a "conception" or "idea," which somehow hovers in the mind of the fool; it is more illuminating to suppose that understanding an expression involves a complex dispositional response by which one would be prepared to use the expression in identifying a thing of a certain kind.

In short, we suggest that if there is anything "in the understanding," it is what we call an "idea." Hence, we write:

$$(x) \ [U_1 f,x \longleftrightarrow (Ey) \ (Iy, \ x \cdot U_2 y,f)] \tag{3}$$

—to be read: *If there is anything understood (as an expression) by the fool, then there is the idea of the meaning of that expression, and that idea is in the understanding of the fool, and vice versa.*

This interpretation is justified by Anselm's analogy between the painter and the conceiver of the idea of God. Anselm writes, "When a painter first conceives of what he will afterwards perform, he has it in his understanding, but he does not yet understand it to be, because he has not yet performed it." To conceive of a painting which does not exist, then, is (we could say) "to have an idea"; it is the *idea,* not the painting, which is in the understanding of the artist. By analogy, to conceive of God (who may not exist) is to have an idea; it is the idea, not God, which is in the understanding of the conceiver. Anselm goes on to say, in regard to the artist, that "after he has made his painting, he both has it in his understanding, and he understands that it exists, because he has made it." That which is in the understanding of the artist is the *idea* of the painting; that which the artist understands (knows) to exist "because he has made it" is the *painting.* The suggestion is that, according to this use of the expression, to *"understand that something exists,"* say, a painting or a being than which nothing greater can be conceived, it must be that the thing in question *does exist.* The artist can understand that the painting exists because he *knows* that there is such a painting, for he has made it; knowing that the painting exists, the artist *understands it to exist.* By analogy, then, to *understand* that God, the being than which none greater can be conceived, exists, it must be that God *does exist.* But we cannot know that God exists as the product of our creative effort; therefore, our knowledge of God's existence must be based on our understanding of his nature: *if he is the greatest conceivable being, then he is, for it is greater to be than not to be.*

We now note that since to say that the *idea* of God is in the fool's understanding is pragmatically equivalent to saying that *God* is in the fool's understanding—just as to say that the idea of the painting is in the painter's understanding is pragmatically equivalent to saying that the painting is in the painter's understanding—we may, if we wish, read premise 3 as a premise having to do with the "object" (or "objective") of thought. Thus, *if there is anything understood (as an expression) by the fool, then there is an object of the idea of the meaning of that expression, and that object is in the understanding of the fool; and vice versa.*

To make these pragmatical transitions clear, let us consider the following example. When the expression "square circle" is heard by me, I understand (U_1) what I hear. I *could say* that I have the concept or "idea" "in my understanding" (U_2). What, then, would I say is "the object of my thinking"? Surely, the object would be whatever is meant by the expression "square circle"; namely, the *square circle* kind of figure. My thinking (understanding) has an *object* in that it has an *objective;* I am so disposed, in thinking of what it would be for something to be a square circle, that *were* I to encounter something that had all the characteristics of a square and also all the characteristics of a circle, I would be prepared to call that figure "a square circle." Thus, without actually having to encounter an example of a square circle (and, because of the inconsistency involved in the definition, I *never could* encounter a square circle), I can have whatever is meant by "square circle" as, in the sense described, "the object of my understanding." It does not follow from the fact that the square circle is the object (objective) of my thinking that a figure of that kind *exists. I shall say* (pragmatical decision) that the kind, square circle, is "in my understanding," but I mean no more by that expression than that I understand the expression "square circle."

Analogously, in thinking of God, the fool has as the object of his conception the one and only being that fits the description "a being than which nothing greater can be conceived." But to say this is to say no more than that the fool understands the use and meaning of the expressions used; hence, *we could say* that the fool has the idea "in mind" or "in his understanding," or that (as we may alternatively say) he has God "in his understanding."

According to Anselm's argument, ". . . that, than which nothing greater can be conceived, cannot exist in the understanding alone. For suppose it exists in the understanding alone: then it can be conceived to exist in reality; which is greater." The claim is that since the object of the idea is the greatest being conceivable, that being cannot be "in the understanding" (U_2) and yet not be "understood to exist" (U_3), for (Anselm assumes) it is better to be than not to be when the being in question is a being than which nothing greater can be conceived.

We first show what is involved in the fool's *understanding* (in this case, *knowing*) that a *being* corresponding to his idea of God (fitting the description "*'C'*") *exists:*

$$(Ex) \ (Ey) \ [\text{"}C\text{"}x \cdot Iy,x \cdot U_3y,f] \to (Ez) \ Cz \qquad (4.1)$$

That is, *if the fool understands that something corresponding to his idea of the meaning of the expression "a being . . ." exists, then there is a being that fits the description expressed.* (We note that to say that something corresponding to the *idea* of God is "understood to exist" [U_3] is pragmatically equivalent to saying that the *object* of the idea of God is "understood to exist" or that *God* is "understood to exist.")

The analysis is based on the pragmatical consideration that—as Anselm uses the expression "understands . . . to exist"—it follows from someone's *understanding* that something *exists* that it *does* exist: a condition of understanding that something of a certain sort exists (in this special sense of "understanding . . . to exist") is that a thing of the sort conceived actually exist. The use of the expression "understands . . . to exist" is different from that exhibited in saying, "She understands that he is still alive," when the context is such that we might alternatively say, "It is her understanding that he is still alive" (when he might very well be dead).

We justify our pragmatical claim by referring to the following passage in the argument: "When a painter first conceives of what he will afterwards perform, he has it in his understanding [U_2], but he does not yet understand it to exist [U_3], because he has not yet performed it. But after he has made the painting, he both has it in his understanding, and he understands it to exist, because he has made it."

Analogously, the fool cannot understand God to exist until the fool has sufficient reason to believe that God does exist. That reason is provided, so Anselm claims, by the consideration that "if that, than which nothing greater can be conceived, can be conceived not to exist, it is not that, than which nothing greater can be conceived. But this is an irreconcilable contradiction."

We use the following expression to symbolize the basic point made in the preceding statement:

$$(x)\ (y)\ [(``C"x \cdot Iy,x \cdot U_2y,f \cdot \sim U_3y,f) \to \sim U_2y,f] \qquad (4.2)$$

That is, *if the idea of the meaning of the expression "a being . . ." is in the fool's understanding but nothing corresponding to that idea is understood by the fool to exist, then it is false that the idea (of a being answering to the description expressed) is in the fool's understanding.* In other words, a condition of understanding (U_2) God is that one understand him to exist (U_3).

The conclusion of St. Anselm's argument may now very simply be expressed:

$$\therefore\ (Ex)Cx$$

—from which, together with premise 1, it would follow that:

$$\therefore\ (Ex)Lx$$

—or, *There is a Lord; God exists.*

After presenting his argument, St. Anselm considers the question as to how it was possible for the fool to conceive in his heart that God does not exist. The fool, says Anselm, conceived the idea of the nonexistence of God, for "he said [it] in his heart"; yet the fool could not have said in his heart or conceived the nonexistence of God, "for God cannot be conceived not to exist." The resolution of the paradox is made possible, as always, by realizing that more than one use of the critical terms is involved; as Anselm writes, "there is more than one way in which a thing said is said in the heart or conceived.

ANALYSIS: ARGUMENT · 181

For in one sense, an object is conceived, when the word signifying it is conceived; and in another, when the very entity, which the object is, is conceived." Thus, the fool was able to *say* ("in his heart"), "There is no God," for he used those words; but, according to Anselm, the fool could not have *understood* (and in that sense "conceived") God *not* to exist, for anyone who understands *what* he is talking about realizes that God, since he is the greatest conceivable being, must be thought of as existing and must, on that account, be understood to exist: "So, then, no one who understands what God is can conceive that God does not exist, although he says those words . . . . For, God is that than which a greater cannot be conceived. And he who thoroughly understands this, assuredly understands that this being so truly exists, that not even in concept can it be non-existent. Therefore, he who understands that God so exists, cannot conceive that he does not exist."

Thus, we have understood Anselm to be arguing that in understanding the nature of God one finds an adequate reason for claiming that he does exist; namely, that it is not possible without contradiction to conceive of him as not existing. Thus, one who conceives of God *understands* God *to exist.*

Before we go on to a criticism of Anselm's argument, it might be helpful to consider Anselm's *reductio ad absurdum,* the argument by which he sought to show that the denial of his claim about the Lord's existence involves a contradiction.

Suppose someone attempts to counter Anselm's argument by protesting, "But perhaps the being than which nothing greater can be conceived exists only in the understanding!" Anselm's answer, as we know, is that "suppose it exists in the understanding alone: then it can be conceived to exist in reality; which is greater." The point is that by the term "Lord" we have agreed to mean "a being than which nothing greater can be conceived." But it is greater to exist in reality than merely as an idea in someone's understanding; hence, the Lord, as the greatest being conceivable, must exist in reality. The denial of Anselm's claim, then, is apparently contradictory in that it may be stated as follows: "The being which, as the greatest conceivable being, *must exist in reality* exists *only in the understanding,*" and thus, "The being which, by its very nature, exists not only as idea exists only as idea."

Or suppose that someone denies Anselm's conclusion by saying, "Perhaps God does not exist." Anselm's answer is, in effect, that God is by his very nature an existent being; the denial, then, amounts to the claim that the Lord, a being that must exist, does not exist. To be effective against Anselm's *reductio ad absurdum* defense of his argument, a denial must take a logical form which does not involve an inconsistency of the sort exhibited in these examples. It is not enough to say, as most critics of Anselm have said, that *existence is not a predicate*—that is, that Anselm cannot justifiably demand that God be understood, by definition, to be an *existent* being; one must be able, *without inconsistency,* to deny Anselm's conclusion, and one must find what there is about his argument that is not satisfactory. After all, it appears to be possible to symbolize the argument in such a way that nowhere in the statement of the argument is existence a predicate (in that we have not had to use a symbol, as a predicate symbol, to mean "exists," for we have followed the logical convention of using the existential quantifier). If, after critical examination of the argument, one wishes to be effective in insisting that Anselm's principal fault was that he made existence a predicate, one must be able to explain in what sense it is true that he did this and why it is that making existence a predicate is an error.

3. CRITICISM OF THE BASIC ARGUMENT

St. Anselm's basic argument, as we have summarized and symbolized it, is as follows:

1. $(x) [Lx \longleftrightarrow Cx]$
2. $(Ex) ["C"x \cdot U_1 f,x]$
3. $(x) [U_1 f,x \longleftrightarrow (Ey) (Iy, x \cdot U_2 y,f)]$
4.1. $(Ex) (Ey) ["C"x \cdot Iy,x \cdot U_3 y,f] \rightarrow (Ez) Cz$
4.2. $(x) (y) [("C"x \cdot Iy,x \cdot U_2 y,f \cdot \sim U_3 y,f) \rightarrow \sim U_2 y,f]$

$/\therefore (Ex) Cx$
$/\therefore (Ex) Lx$

Let us construct a diagram of the logical structure of the argument by interpreting the premises in such a way that we no longer have need for quantifiers. We shall devise individual symbols for the expression of the existential statements, and then use any of the individual symbols in expressions that are true of anything (universal statements). Since an existential statement is true of *some* one (or more) individual(s), but perhaps not of all, the individual constant must be understood to represent not any arbitrarily chosen individual, but only any one of those individuals for whom the existential description holds. Thus, if we wanted to represent, without the quantifier, the meaning of "$(Ex)Hx$", when the symbols show the structure of "Something is a human being" or "There are human beings," we could simply write "Ha", with the "a" functioning *as if* it were the name of any one of those individuals whom the description fits—any one of the human beings.

We shall begin with the first existential premise of the argument, premise 2:

$$\text{“}C\text{”}a \cdot U_1f{,}a \tag{2}$$

(Let "a" function as the name of that individual which is the expression "a being . . ." or any synonymous expression: then premise 2 states that a is the expression and that the fool understands a.)

We may use the same individual constant, "a", for the antecedent of premise 3; but we must use a new constant—let us use "b"—for the existential proposition that functions as the consequent of premise 3:

$$U_1f{,}a \longleftrightarrow (Ib{,}a \cdot U_2b{,}f) \tag{3}$$

Premise 4.1, like premise 3, is a universal proposition, even though existential quantifiers begin the statement of 4.1. This is so because 4.1 is an implication statement that could have been written as follows:

$$(x)\ (y)\ [(\text{“}C\text{”}x \cdot Iy{,}x \cdot U_3y{,}f) \rightarrow (Ez)\ Cz]$$

We can substitute constants as follows:

$$(\text{“}C\text{”}a \cdot Ib{,}a \cdot U_3b{,}f) \rightarrow Cc \tag{4.1}$$

(Note that we use the constant "c" for the expression of the existential consequent of premise 4.1.)

Premise 4.2 involves no new constant:

$$(\text{``}C\text{''}a \cdot Ib,a \cdot U_2b,f \cdot \sim U_3b,f) \rightarrow \sim U_2b,f \qquad (4.2)$$

But there is a simpler logical expression of 4.2:

$$(\text{``}C\text{''}a \cdot Ib,a \cdot U_2b,f) \rightarrow U_3b,f \qquad (4.2)$$

(We shall use this more direct statement in the diagram.)

We may now substitute the constant "c" in the expression of premise 1:

$$Lc \longleftrightarrow Cc \qquad (1)$$

And we show the conclusions:

$$\therefore Cc$$
$$\therefore Lc$$

The diagram may now be constructed. A check mark ($\sqrt{\ }$) indicates the assertion of an existential claim:

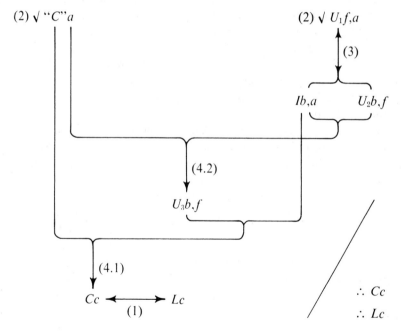

Let us examine the logical structure of Anselm's argument.

Premise 2, an existential premise, asserts that " 'C'a" and "$U_1 f,a$" are true. By 3, as the diagram shows, if "$U_1 f,a$" is true, then both "Ib,a" and "$U_2 b,f$" are true. We now have the three propositions needed to be able to assert the antecedent of premise 4.2; namely, " 'C'a · Ib,a · $U_2 b,f$". The diagram shows that if these three propositions are true, then "$U_3 b,f$" is true. From "$U_3 b,f$", together with " 'C'a" and "Ib,a", according to premise 4.1, proposition "Cc" follows. Since "Cc"—the proposition that there is a being than which nothing greater can be conceived—is a conclusion of the argument, the argument is valid; we have traveled a logical path from the existential premise through the universal premises to the conclusion. The conclusion "Lc", that God exists, follows by definition from "Cc", as the diagram indicates.

We review the line of argument informally: The fool understands what he hears of God, the being than which nothing greater can be conceived (2); hence, he has the idea of God in his understanding (3); hence, he understands God to exist (4.2); hence, God, the being than which nothing greater can be conceived, exists. (The only feature of the argument which is obscured by the logical summary is the consideration which provokes the move from 3 to 4.2; namely, that a being than which nothing greater can be conceived must be understood to exist, for it is greater for such a being to be than not to be.)

The argument is fascinating, like a magical demonstration. How, from an innocuous statement to the effect that the fool has Anselm's conception of "Lord" in his understanding (since he understands what Anselm has said), does it follow that there is a God of the sort Anselm described? The fool must understand God to exist, but the only way to understand something to exist is by knowing it to exist. If the premises are granted, the conclusion must be accepted.

If the logical structure of the argument is that of a valid argument, and if something is wrong somewhere, there must be something wrong with the premises. The form of the argument depends on the meanings of the terms used in the premises; the meanings depend on the uses of terms—thus, we must once again consider Anselm's use of language, for only then can we be confident in our belief that in our reconstruction of Anselm's argument the philosopher has been fairly represented; and only if we know what he has proposed in each of his premises can we responsibly consider whether we are justified in rejecting some part of his argument.

PREMISE 1

"Lord . . . thou art a being than which nothing greater can be conceived." Anselm begins by offering a definitive description of the being he calls "Lord." He does not ask that the reader accept this description as a revealing description of something known to exist; he begins with a statement of what it is he believes, and he readily concedes that some persons, the fool notably, have denied there is a God. Anselm goes on to insist (as, ironically, his critics have) that "it is one thing for an object to be in the understanding, and another to understand that the object exists." All that he asks, at the outset, is that the effort be made to understand that by "Lord" he means "a being than which nothing greater can be conceived." Anselm does not talk *about* the word "Lord"; he does not *mention* the word at all; he talks about what he believes the Lord to be, and to do so he *uses* the word "Lord." (A convenient way to mention a word one has been using or contemplates using is to enclose the word in quotation marks; one could also italicize the word. One then *uses* the quoted word or the italicized word to *mention* the word quoted or italicized.) But, although Anselm does not mention the word "Lord," the *use* of the sentence "And, indeed, we believe that thou art a being than which nothing greater can be conceived" is such that we conclude that by the use of the sentence Anselm intended to accomplish (among other things, perhaps) what he could have accomplished by writing: "Let us so use the term 'Lord' as to mean what the following expression means, 'a being than which nothing greater can be conceived.' " Thus, premise 1 is understood to be, in its functioning if not in its expression, a *semantical stipulation*—not, as with Berkeley's first premise, a pragmatical stipulation consisting of a *demonstration* of the *use* of a critical term; but, rather, a stipulation, an initially specified decision, consisting of a *descriptive explanation* of the *meaning* of a critical term, in this case, the term "Lord."

Do we have any objection to this semantical stipulation, to this proposal concerning the meaning the term "Lord" is to have in the argument?

We have no objections, and for two reasons. At the outset of an argument a man may define his terms as he chooses, provided that he does not claim to be clarifying the meaning of a term already in use. Second, Anselm's definition of the term "Lord," although admirably suited to his purposes in that it gives him the freedom to decide what constitutes greatness, is one which is in accord with the meaning, or meanings, of the term as it is ordinarily used; hence, the argument has a bearing on a matter with which we are to some extent familiar and about which many of us are concerned.

If, during the course of the argument, we were to discover that Anselm had departed from his decision to use the term "Lord" so that it would have the meaning specified, we might object to his not holding to his semantical promise; but we are not inclined to object to the promise itself, and we accept this stipulated definition.

PREMISE 2

". . . the fool . . . when he hears of this being of which I speak— a being than which nothing greater can be conceived—understands what he hears . . . ." There is no reason why we should deny that, in any ordinary sense of "understands what he hears," the fool, in hearing Anselm's definitive description of what he means by "Lord," understands what he hears. We are not now conceding, any more than we did in accepting the definition in the first place, that the fool (or that we, or Anselm) fully comprehends the meaning of the description. After all, we are not prepared to say precisely what it is that constitutes what Anselm would call "greatness" or even what we ourselves would call "greatness"; and we leave open the possibility that the conception of God is relative to various conceptions of greatness.

PREMISE 3

". . . and what [the fool] understands is in his understanding. . . ." *Let us say* that what the fool understands is "in his understanding."

We accept Anselm's pragmatical stipulation, which is, in any case, in accord with the conventional idiom. We may say that the fool has, in his understanding, the *idea* of the meaning of the expression "Lord" or of the expression used by Anselm to define "Lord." The fool understands what Anselm has said, and we here accept another way of saying so.

PREMISE 4

"And assuredly that, than which nothing greater can be conceived, cannot exist in the understanding alone. For, suppose it exists in the understanding alone: then it can be conceived to exist in reality; which is greater."

We have understood the expression "conceived to exist in reality" to be equivalent in meaning to the expression "understand to exist," as the latter expression is used in the example of the painter. According to Anselm's use of the expression "understand to exist," if someone understands something to exist, whatever is understood to exist (something answering to the conception) *does* exist. Premise 4 states that if the fool *understands* the object of his conception (something corresponding to his idea of God) *to exist*, something answering to his conception does exist. If, as we have contended, Anselm so used the expression "understand to exist" that it would follow from someone's understanding that God exists that God did exist, premise 4.1 simply makes the meaning of that expression clear. The question is left open (until our consideration of 4.2) as to whether it follows from the fool's having the object of his conception in his understanding that he understands God to exist. Premise 4.1 is acceptable as making clear the meaning of "understand to exist," as that expression is used by Anselm. The claim here is semantical.

Premise 4.2 states, in effect, that if the fool has the idea of God in his understanding, the fool understands God to exist. Are we willing to concede this point? The issue is critical; for if we grant 4.2, the conclusion must be accepted as true and as having been demonstrated.

In considering whether we are willing to grant that *to think about God* the fool must *understand God to exist,* we find ourselves inclined to be sympathetic to Anselm's effort to require that in thinking about God one think of a being that is more than a product of the imagination. Anselm quite reasonably asks that God, as the *greatest* conceivable being, be considered to be an actual, not an imaginary, being. Let us, by analogy, attempt to make clear the nature of what is reasonable in Anselm's requirement. There is another use of the expression "understand to exist" such that it is reasonable for Anselm to require that the fool, or anyone else attempting to conceive the idea of God, understand God to exist.

Most dictionaries define a "unicorn" as a "fabulous" or "legendary" animal. For example, *Webster's Seventh New Collegiate Dictionary* defines the term "unicorn" as follows: "a fabulous animal generally depicted with the body and head of a horse, the hind legs of a stag, the tail of a lion, and a single horn in the middle of the forehead." The *Oxford Universal Dictionary* defines a "unicorn" as "a legendary animal usually regarded as having a horse's body and a single long horn projecting from its forehead." Suppose an observer were to discover—under conditions excellent for observation and while he himself was in excellent condition to observe—an animal with the body and head of a horse and with a single horn in the middle of its forehead. *Could* the animal be a unicorn? Not according to the definitions cited, for no *actual* animal, no animal capable of being perceived under the conditions specified, is a *fabulous* or *legendary* animal. An actual animal may be of a sort about which fables and legends have been written; but that circumstance would be accidental, and the definitions suggest that to exist in a fable or legend is a condition of something's being a unicorn. If one wished, by definition, to allow for the possibility of discovering a unicorn in one's garden, one would have to define the term "unicorn" to mean "an animal having the body of a horse with a horn in the middle of its forehead." It would not then be sufficient to the existence of a unicorn that it figure in a fable or legend, or that it be in the imagination or understanding alone: for a unicorn to be, it would have to be observable.

Analogously, to preserve the possibility of discovering a mermaid sunning herself on the rocks offshore, one must define the term "mermaid" to mean "a marine creature having the head and trunk of a woman and the tail of a fish." To define the word to mean a "fabulous" or "legendary" or "imaginary" creature is to *rule out the possibility* of ever actually encountering a mermaid. (Thus we recognize once again that *logical possibilities are functions of the meanings of terms.*)

Anselm wished to create the *possibility* of a God that is more than a figure of the imagination. The definition of the "Lord" as a being than which nothing greater can be conceived was intended to require that, in conceiving of such a being, the person who understands Anselm conceive of the being as *not merely in the understanding;* by "Lord" is meant, not a "legendary" or "fabulous" or "imaginary" or "conceptual" being, but a being which is "actual" and "exists in reality." We are inclined to agree that in conceiving God as the *greatest* conceivable being, one quite reasonably supposes that he is something more than a mere idea.

We *could* say, then, that to conceive of God one must "understand him to exist"; but here we mean, not that we must have *knowledge of the existence* of such a being, but that we understand Anselm to be talking about a being of a kind such that, were there such a being, he would not be merely an idea or an image or a conception; such a being must exist outside the understanding.

We would be willing to assent to premise 4.2, then, if in speaking of "conceiving God to exist" or "understanding God to exist" Anselm meant "having the idea of a being that, as perfect, is not simply idea, image, or conception." But if this is what is meant in requiring that if God is in the understanding, he be understood to exist, then premise 4.1 cannot be accepted, for the *existence* of such a being does not follow from the idea that *were there such a being, it would not be imaginary or merely in the understanding.*

Thus, premise 4.2 uses the phrase "understand to exist" either as premise 4.1 explains it, such that if something is "understood to exist," it follows that there is something of the kind conceived—in which case premise 4.2 is unacceptable—*or* premise 4.2 uses the phrase "understand to exist" in such a way that to understand something to exist is simply to think of a kind of being such that if there were a being of that kind, it would be something more than a mere image or conception—in which case 4.1 is unacceptable.

The interpretation of "understand to exist" shown in the symbolic expression of 4.1 is preferable to the interpretation given as an alternative; for if Anselm did not mean to suggest that to *conceive* or *understand* something *to exist* is to have sufficient grounds for believing it to exist, his reference to the painter (as first of all having the idea of the painting in his understanding, and as later on *understanding* the painting *to exist* "because he has made it") would be both irrelevant and misleading.

No matter how we understand Anselm to have used the expression "understand to exist," then, our critical conclusion is that the argument is unsound. We are inclined to regard the argument as *valid but unsound* because of the unacceptability of premise 4.2: We do *not* concede that to have the idea of a being than which nothing greater can be conceived one must "understand [that being] to exist" or "conceive [that being] to exist in reality," as Anselm uses those expressions.

Consequently, either we insist that we can have the conception of God in our understanding and that to do so does not necessitate understanding him to exist (although we agree that were there such a being, he would exist as something more than mere idea); or we confess that we cannot conceive of God at all, if to conceive of him entails knowing of his existence. The former response seems more to the point, for Anselm himself claims that even the fool has God in his understanding.

In his argument Anselm calls attention to his interest in directing thinking about God to the possibility of a being (than which nothing greater can be conceived) that is to be definitively described as not merely imaginary (an image), or conceivable (a concept), or thinkable as idea (an idea). We are not scornful of his faith that there is a being of the sort he describes; and we recognize the concern which led Anselm to declare that if there is a God, he is more than a product of the imagination or intellect. In stressing the value of considering God to be something more than idea, Anselm has done a service to those whose faith is similar to his. But the fact remains that although to think of the sort of being Anselm describes one must think of that being as something other than image or idea, one need not conceive of that being in such a manner that, through conceiving the being, one finds grounds for claiming that being to exist: *one need not understand God to exist* (as Anselm uses the expression "understand to exist").

COMMENTS ON THE ANALYSIS OF ANSELM'S ARGUMENT

Earlier in the analysis we suggested that to be effective against Anselm's *reductio ad absurdum* argument, a denial must take a logical form which does not involve an inconsistency. To say that "God does not exist," if by "God" is meant, in part, "that which must be understood to exist" and, consequently, "that which exists," is to allow a defender of Anselm, using Anselm's *reductio,* to claim that the denial takes the form: "That being which by its nature exists does not exist."

Thus, instead of saying "God does not exist," which may be expressed symbolically as "(Ex) $[Lx \cdot \sim Lx]$", we say—if we choose to deny Anselm's conclusion—"There is no such being as God," or, even better, "It is not true that there is a being which fits the description given for the term 'God.'" This claim may be symbolized as "(x) $\sim Lx$", which means, "Whatever one considers, it is not God," or "Nothing is God." Or we may write, "$\sim (Ex)Lx$", which means, "It is false that something is God." In other words, whatever one considers, it does not fit the definition given of the term "God" (or "Lord"); whatever one considers, it is *not* a being than which nothing greater can be conceived and which, consequently, is understood to exist and, therefore, exists. There is nothing which fits that description; it is false that there is anything that fits it. (These denials may be prefaced by "perhaps" without affecting their form. "Perhaps there is no God" is a noncontradictory statement, if interpreted as suggested here, by reference to a *description* or *kind* of being.)

Critics have argued that existence is not a predicate, meaning thereby to point out that once a definition has been decided upon, to say that a thing of the kind described *exists* is not to attribute to the thing a further property but simply to say that there is a thing of the kind described. Thus, once the term "God" has been defined, to say that God exists is not to attribute to him the further property of "being an existent"; to say that God exists is, rather, to claim that there is a being of the kind definitively described.

This critical point is well taken, but it obscures the fact that sometimes, in defining terms, philosophers want to rule out the possibility that the kind of thing defined (through defining the term) is imaginary, or fabulous, or legendary; and it is the privilege of such philosophers to mean what they please by the terms the meanings of which they devise. What is important is not whether a philosopher makes, in the way mentioned, "reality" or "existence" a feature of the kind of thing he definitively describes; what is important is whether, once the definition is completed, there is anything of the kind described, anything which fits the description offered as the definition of the term. Thus, if by a "mustbee" we mean "a being which by its nature exists (must be)," the question arises as to whether there is any such being, anything *such that by its nature it exists.* So it is with Anselm's argument. We allow Anselm to mean what he pleases by "Lord"; the question remains, after the definition has been stated, as to whether there is any being of the kind he describes: Is there anything which fits the description "being than which nothing greater can be conceived"? Most of us would claim that, in any case, we do not *know* any such being; and we are not being self-contradictory when we say, "Perhaps there is no such being." Neither would it be self-contradictory were we to say, "God does not exist" or "Perhaps God does not exist," even though a defender of Anselm might make it appear to the uncritical person that such a claim does, indeed, involve an inconsistency. One great advantage of using symbolism is that the possibilities of misinterpretation are reduced. If in denying Anselm's conclusion we use the proper symbolism, we are more likely to stay out of the kind of trouble that the *reductio ad absurdum* can make for the unwary.

QUESTIONS FOR DISCUSSION

1. Does a more extensive or careful reading of Anselm's *Proslogium* provide some reasons for regarding the above analysis as being, in certain respects, faulty or deficient? How does a different reading of Anselm affect the results of the logical analysis of Anselm's argument?

2. In the *Critique of Pure Reason* Immanuel Kant (1724-1804) wrote that *"Being* is evidently not a real predicate, or a concept of something that can be added to the concept of the thing." Do you agree? What is a predicate? If to attribute "being" to something does not "add to the concept of the thing," what does it do?

3. One of Anselm's contemporaries, the monk Gaunilon, argued in an essay entitled "In Behalf of the Fool" that by an argument similar to Anselm's one could "prove" that there is a lost island "more excellent than all lands." Anselm's reply was that the non-existence of an island is conceivable but that "the non-existence of that than which a greater cannot be conceived is inconceivable." Criticize Gaunilon's analogy and Anselm's reply.

4. Is it *possible* to prove that God exists; that is, that there is a God? Is the term "God" constant in its meaning? If the term "God" is used in various ways, does that affect the meaning of the term? Is it possible that the term "God" be used in such a way that, relative to that use, it would be possible to prove that there is a God?

VIII

DESCARTES

"I THINK, HENCE I AM" IS INDUBITABLE AND CERTAIN

DESCARTES' ARGUMENT

*I am in doubt as to the propriety of making my first meditations . . .
matter of discourse; for these are so metaphysical, and so uncommon,
as not, perhaps, to be acceptable to every one. And yet, that it may be
determined whether the foundations that I have laid are sufficiently
secure, I find myself in a measure constrained to advert to them. I
had long before remarked that, in relation to practice, it is sometimes
necessary to adopt, as if above doubt, opinions which we discern to be
highly uncertain, as has been already said; but as I then desired to
give my attention solely to the search after truth, I thought that a procedure exactly the opposite was called for, and that I ought to reject
as absolutely false all opinions in regard to which I could suppose the
least ground for doubt, in order to ascertain whether after that there
remained aught in my belief that was wholly indubitable. Accordingly, seeing that our senses sometimes deceive us, I was willing to
suppose that there existed nothing really such as they presented to us;
and because some men err in reasoning, and fall into paralogisms,
even on the simplest matters of Geometry, I, convinced that I was as*

open to error as any other, rejected as false all the reasonings I had hitherto taken for demonstrations; and finally, when I considered that the very same thoughts (presentations) which we experience when awake may also be experienced when we are asleep, while there is at the time not one of them true, I supposed that all the objects (presentations) that had ever entered into my mind when awake, had in them no more truth than the illusions of my dreams. But immediately upon this I observed that, whilst I thus wished to think that all was false, it was absolutely necessary that I, who thus thought, should be [something]; and as I observed that this truth, I think, hence I am, *was so certain and of such evidence, that no ground of doubt, however extravagant, could be alleged by the Sceptics capable of shaking it, I concluded that I might, without scruple, accept it as the first principle of the Philosophy of which I was in search.*

In the next place, I attentively examined what I was, and as I observed that I could suppose that I had no body, and that there was no world nor any place in which I might be; but that I could not therefore suppose that I was not; and that, on the contrary, from the very circumstance that I thought to doubt of the truth of other things, it most clearly and certainly followed that I was; while, on the other hand, if I had only ceased to think, although all the other objects which I had ever imagined had been in reality existent, I would have had no reason to believe that I existed; I thence concluded that I was a substance whose whole essence or nature consists only in thinking, and which, that it may exist, has need of no place, nor is dependent on any material thing; so that "I," that is to say, the mind by which I am what I am, is wholly distinct from the body, and is even more easily known than the latter, and is such, that although the latter were not, it would still continue to be all that it is.

After this I inquired in general into what is essential to the truth and certainty of a proposition; for since I had discovered one which I knew to be true, I thought that I must likewise be able to discover the ground of this certitude. And as I observed that in the words I think, hence I am, *there is nothing at all which gives me assurance of their truth beyond this, that I see very clearly that in order to think it is necessary to exist, I concluded that I might take, as a general rule, the principle, that all the things which we very clearly and distinctly conceive are true, only observing, however, that there is some diffi-culty in rightly determining the objects which we distinctly conceive.*

[From *Discourse on Method* (1637), Part IV, by René Des-cartes (1596–1650); translated from the French and collated with the Latin by John Veitch.*]

Several years have now elapsed since I first became aware that I had accepted, even from my youth, many false opinions for true, and that consequently what I afterwards based on such principles was highly doubtful; and from that time I was convinced of the necessity of undertaking once in my life to rid myself of all the opinions I had adopted, and of commencing anew the work of building from the foundation, if I desired to establish a firm and abiding superstructure in the sciences. . . .

*   *   *   *

. . . I will at length apply myself earnestly and freely to the general overthrow of all my former opinions. But, to this end, it will not be necessary for me to show that the whole of these are false—a point, perhaps, which I shall never reach; but as even now my reason con-vinces me that I ought not the less carefully to withhold belief from what is not entirely certain and indubitable, than from what is mani-festly false, it will be sufficient to justify the rejection of the whole if I shall find in each some ground for doubt. Nor for this purpose will it be necessary even to deal with each belief individually, which would be truly an endless labour; but, as the removal from below of the foundation necessarily involves the downfall of the whole edifice, I will at once approach the criticism of the principles on which all my former beliefs rested.

All that I have, up to this moment, accepted as possessed of the highest truth and certainty, I received either from or through the senses. I observed, however, that these sometimes misled us; and it is the part of prudence not to place absolute confidence in that by which we have even once been deceived.

But it may be said, perhaps, that, although the senses occasion-

**Edition used: Open Court Publishing Co. [no publishing date given].*

ally mislead us respecting minute objects, and such as are so far re-
moved from us as to be beyond the reach of close observation, there
are yet many other of their informations (presentations) of the truth
of which it is manifestly impossible to doubt; as for example, that I
am in this place, seated by the fire, clothed in a winter dressing-gown,
that I hold in my hands this piece of paper, with other intimations of
the same nature. But how could I deny that I possess these hands and
this body, and withal escape being classed with persons in a state of
insanity, whose brains are so disordered and clouded by dark bilious
vapours as to cause them pertinaciously to assert that they are mon-
archs when they are in the greatest poverty; or clothed [in gold] and
purple when destitute of any covering; or that their head is made of
clay, their body of glass, or that they are gourds? I should certainly
be not less insane than they, were I to regulate my procedure accord-
ing to examples so extravagant.

Though this be true, I must nevertheless here consider that I am
a man, and that, consequently, I am in the habit of sleeping, and rep-
resenting to myself in dreams those same things, or even sometimes
others less probable, which the insane think are presented to them in
their waking moments. How often have I dreamt that I was in these
familiar circumstances,—that I was dressed, and occupied this place
by the fire, when I was lying undressed in bed? At the present mo-
ment, however, I certainly look upon this paper with eyes wide awake;
the head which I now move is not asleep; I extend this hand con-
sciously and with express purpose, and I perceive it; the occurrences
in sleep are not so distinct as all this. But I cannot forget that, at other
times, I have been deceived in sleep by similar illusions; and, atten-
tively considering those cases, I perceive so clearly that there exist no
certain marks by which the state of waking can ever be distinguished
from sleep, that I feel greatly astonished; and in amazement I almost
persuade myself that I am now dreaming.

Let us suppose, then, that we are dreaming, and that all these
particulars—namely, the opening of the eyes, the motion of the head,
the forth-putting of the hands—are merely illusions; and even that we
really possess neither an entire body nor hands such as we see. Never-
theless, it must be admitted at least that the objects which appear to us
in sleep, are, as it were, painted representations which could not have
been formed unless in the likeness of realities; and, therefore, that

*those general objects, at all events,—namely, eyes, a head, hands, and
an entire body—are not simply imaginary, but really existent. For, in
truth, painters themselves, even when they study to represent sirens
and satyrs by forms the most fantastic and extraordinary, cannot bestow upon them natures absolutely new, but can only make a certain
medley of the members of different animals; or if they chance to
imagine something so novel that nothing at all similar has ever been
seen before, and such as is, therefore, purely fictitious and absolutely
false, it is at least certain that the colours of which this is composed
are real.*

*And on the same principle, although these general objects, viz.
[a body], eyes, a head, hands, and the like, be imaginary, we are
nevertheless absolutely ncessitated to admit the reality at least of
some other objects still more simple and universal than these, of
which, just as of certain real colours, all those images of things,
whether true and real, or false and fantastic, that are found in our
consciousness* (cogitatio), *are formed.*

*To this class of objects seem to belong corporeal nature in gen-
eral and its extension; the figure of extended things, their quantity or
magnitude, and their number, as also the place in, and the time during, which they exist, and other things of the same sort. We will not,
therefore, perhaps reason illegitimately if we conclude from this that
Physics, Astronomy, Medicine, and all the other sciences that have
for their end the consideration of composite objects, are indeed of a
doubtful character; but that Arithmetic, Geometry, and the other sciences of the same class, which regard merely the simplest and most
general objects, and scarcely inquire whether or not these are really
existent, contain [something] that is certain and indubitable: for
whether I am awake or dreaming, it remains true that two and three
make five, and that a square has but four sides; nor does it seem possible that truths so apparent can ever fall under a suspicion of falsity.*

*Nevertheless, the belief that there is a God who is all-powerful,
and who created me, such as I am, has, for a long time, obtained
steady possession of my mind. How, then, do I know that he has not
arranged that there should be neither earth, nor sky, nor any extended thing, nor figure, nor magnitude, nor place, providing at the
same time, however, for [the rise in me of the perceptions of all these
objects, and] the persuasion that these do not exist otherwise than as*

I perceive them? And further, as I sometimes think that others are in error respecting matters of which they believe themselves to possess a perfect knowledge, how do I know that I am not also deceived each time I add together two and three, or number the sides of a square, or form some judgment still more simple, if more simple indeed can be imagined? But perhaps Deity has not been willing that I should be thus deceived, for He is said to be supremely good. If, however, it were repugnant to the goodness of Deity to have created me subject to constant deception, it would seem likewise to be contrary to his goodness to allow me to be occasionally deceived; and yet it is clear that this is permitted. Some, indeed, might perhaps be found who would be disposed rather to deny the existence of a Being so powerful than to believe that there is nothing certain. But let us for the present refrain from opposing this opinion, and grant that all which is here said of a Deity is fabulous: nevertheless in whatever way it be supposed that I reached the state in which I exist, whether by fate, or chance, or by an endless series of antecedents and consequents, or by any other means, it is clear (since to be deceived and to err is a certain defect) that the probability of my being so imperfect as to be the constant victim of deception, will be increased exactly in proportion as the power possessed by the cause, to which they assign my origin, is lessened. To these reasonings I have assuredly nothing to reply, but am constrained at last to avow that there is nothing of all that I formerly believed to be true of which it is impossible to doubt, and that not through thoughtlessness or levity, but from cogent and maturely considered reasons; so that henceforward, if I desire to discover anything certain, I ought not the less carefully to refrain from assenting to those same opinions than to what might be shown to be manifestly false.

But it is not sufficient to have made these observations; care must be taken likewise to keep them in remembrance. For those old and customary opinions perpetually recur—long and familiar usage giving them the right of occupying my mind, even almost against my will, and subduing my belief; nor will I lose the habit of deferring to them and confiding in them so long as I shall consider them to be what in truth they are, viz., opinions to some extent doubtful, as I have already shown, but still highly probable, and such as it is much more reasonable to believe than deny. It is for this reason I am persuaded that I shall not be doing wrong, if, taking an opposite judgment of deliberate design, I become my own deceiver, by supposing, for a time, that all those opinions are entirely false and imaginary, until at length, having thus balanced my old by my new prejudices, my judgment shall no longer be turned aside by perverted usage from the path that may conduct to the perception of truth. For I am assured that, meanwhile, there will arise neither peril nor error from this course, and that I cannot for the present yield too much to distrust, since the end I now seek is not action but knowledge.

I will suppose, then, not that Deity, who is sovereignly good and the fountain of truth, but that some malignant demon, who is at once exceedingly potent and deceitful, has employed all his artifice to deceive me; I will suppose that the sky, the air, the earth, colours, figures, sounds, and all external things, are nothing better than the illusions of dreams, by means of which this being has laid snares for my credulity; I will consider myself as without hands, eyes, flesh, blood, or any of the senses, and as falsely believing that I am possessed of these; I will continue resolutely fixed in this belief, and if indeed by this means it be not in my power to arrive at the knowledge of truth, I shall at least do what is in my power, viz., [suspend my judgment], and guard with settled purpose against giving my assent to what is false, and being imposed upon by this deceiver, whatever be his power and artifice.

But this undertaking is arduous, and a certain indolence insensibly leads me back to my ordinary course of life; and just as the captive, who, perchance, was enjoying in his dreams an imaginary liberty, when he begins to suspect that it is but a vision, dreads awakening, and conspires with the agreeable illusions that the deception may be prolonged; so I, of my own accord, fall back into the train of my former beliefs, and fear to arouse myself from my slumber, lest the time of laborious wakefulness that would succeed this quiet rest, in place of bringing any light of day, should prove inadequate to dispel the darkness that will arise from the difficulties that have now been raised.

[From *Meditations on the First Philosophy* (1641), Meditation I; translated from the Latin and collated with the French by John Veitch.*]

Edition used: Open Court Publishing Co., 1941.

The Meditation of yesterday has filled my mind with so many doubts, that it is no longer in my power to forget them. Nor do I see, meanwhile, any principle on which they can be resolved; and, just as if I had fallen all of a sudden into very deep water, I am so greatly disconcerted as to be unable either to plant my feet firmly on the bottom or sustain myself by swimming on the surface. I will, nevertheless, make an effort, and try anew the same path on which I had entered yesterday, that is, proceed by casting aside all that admits of the slightest doubt, not less than if I had discovered it to be absolutely false; and I will continue always in this track until I shall find something that is certain, or at least, if I can do nothing more, until I shall know with certainty that there is nothing certain. Archimedes, that he might transport the entire globe from the place it occupied to another, demanded only a point that was firm and immovable; so also, I shall be entitled to entertain the highest expectations, if I am fortunate enough to discover only one thing that is certain and indubitable.

I suppose, accordingly, that all the things which I see are false (fictitious); I believe that none of those objects which my fallacious memory represents ever existed; I suppose that I possess no senses; I believe that body, figure, extension, motion, and place are merely fictions of my mind. What is there, then, that can be esteemed true? Perhaps this only, that there is absolutely nothing certain.

But how do I know that there is not something different altogether from the objects I have now enumerated, of which it is impossible to entertain the slightest doubt? Is there not a God, or some being, by whatever name I may designate him, who causes these thoughts to arise in my mind? But why suppose such a being, for it may be I myself am capable of producing them? Am I, then, at least not something? But I before denied that I possessed senses or a body; I hesitate, however, for what follows from that? Am I so dependent on the body and the senses that without these I cannot exist? But I had the persuasion that there was absolutely nothing in the world, that there was no sky and no earth, neither minds nor bodies; was I not, therefore, at the same time, persuaded that I did not exist? Far from it; I assuredly existed, since I was persuaded. But there is I know not what being, who is possessed at once of the highest power and the deepest cunning, who is constantly employing all his ingenuity in deceiving me. Doubtless, then, I exist, since I am deceived; and, let him deceive me as he may, he can never bring it about that I am nothing, so long as I shall be conscious that I am something. So that it must, in fine, be maintained, all things being maturely and carefully considered, that this proposition (pronunciatum) *I am, I exist*, is necessarily true each time it is expressed by me, or conceived in my mind.

But I do not yet know with sufficient clearness what I am, though assured that I am; and hence, in the next place, I must take care, lest perchance I inconsiderately substitute some other object in room of what is properly myself, and thus wander from truth, even in that knowledge (cognition) which I hold to be of all others the most certain and evident. For this reason, I will now consider anew what I formerly believed myself to be, before I entered on the present train of thought; and of my previous opinion I will retrench all that can in the least be invalidated by the grounds of doubt I have adduced, in order that there may at length remain nothing but what is certain and indubitable. What then did I formerly think I was? Undoubtedly I judged that I was a man. But what is a man? Shall I say a rational animal? Assuredly not; for it would be necessary forthwith to inquire into what is meant by animal, and what by rational, and thus, from a single question, I should insensibly glide into others, and these more difficult than the first; nor do I now possess enough of leisure to warrant me in wasting my time amid subtleties of this sort. I prefer here to attend to the thoughts that sprung up of themselves in my mind, and were inspired by my own nature alone, when I applied myself to the consideration of what I was. In the first place, then, I thought that I possessed a countenance, hands, arms, and all the fabric of members that appears in a corpse, and which I called by the name of body. It further occurred to me that I was nourished, that I walked, perceived, and thought, and all those actions I referred to the soul; but what the soul itself was I either did not stay to consider, or, if I did, I imagined that it was something extremely rare and subtile, like wind, or flame, or ether, spread through my grosser parts. As regarded the body, I did not even doubt of its nature, but thought I distinctly knew

*it, and if I had wished to describe it according to the notions I then
entertained, I should have explained myself in this manner: By body
I understand all that can be terminated by a certain figure; that can
be comprised in a certain place, and so fill a certain space as there-
from to exclude every other body; that can be perceived either by
touch, sight, hearing, taste, or smell; that can be moved in different
ways, not indeed of itself, but by something foreign to it by which it
is touched [and from which it receives the impression]; for the power
of self-motion, as likewise that of perceiving and thinking, I held as
by no means pertaining to the nature of body; on the contrary, I was
somewhat astonished to find such faculties existing in some bodies.*

*But [as to myself, what can I now say that I am], since I sup-
pose there exists an extremely powerful, and, if I may so speak,
malignant being, whose whole endeavours are directed towards deceiving me? Can I affirm that I possess any one of all those attributes
of which I have lately spoken as belonging to the nature of body?
After attentively considering them in my own mind, I find none of
them that can properly be said to belong to myself. To recount them
were idle and tedious. Let us pass, then, to the attributes of the soul.
The first mentioned were the powers of nutrition and walking; but,
if it be true that I have no body, it is true likewise that I am capable
neither of walking nor of being nourished. Perception is another attribute of the soul; but perception too is impossible without the body:
besides, I have frequently, during sleep, believed that I perceived objects which I afterwards observed I did not in reality perceive. Thinking is another attribute of the soul; and here I discover what properly
belongs to myself. This alone is inseparable from me. I am—I exist:
this is certain; but how often? As often as I think; for perhaps it would
even happen, if I should wholly cease to think, that I should at the
same time altogether cease to be. I now admit nothing that is not
necessarily true: I am therefore, precisely speaking, only a thinking
thing, that is, a mind* (mens sive animus), *understanding, or reason,—
terms whose signification was before unknown to me. I am, however,
a real thing, and really existent; but what thing? The answer was, a
thinking thing. The question now arises, am I aught besides? I will
stimulate my imagination with a view to discover whether I am not*

still something more than a thinking being. Now it is plain I am not the assemblage of members called the human body; I am not a thin and penetrating air diffused through all these members, or wind, or flame, or vapour, or breath, or any of all the things I can imagine; for I supposed that all these were not, and, without changing the supposition, I find that I still feel assured of my existence.

But it is true, perhaps, that those very things which I suppose to be non-existent, because they are unknown to me, are not in truth different from myself whom I know. This is a point I cannot determine, and do not now enter into any dispute regarding it. I can only judge of things that are known to me: I am conscious that I exist, and I who know that I exist inquire into what I am. It is, however, perfectly certain that the knowledge of my existence, thus precisely taken, is not dependent on things, the existence of which is as yet unknown to me: and consequently it is not dependent on any of the things I can feign in imagination. Moreover, the phrase itself, I frame an image (effingo), *reminds me of my error; for I should in truth frame one if I were to imagine myself to be anything, since to imagine is nothing more than to contemplate the figure or image of a corporeal thing; but I already know that I exist, and that it is possible at the same time that all those images, and in general all that relates to the nature of body, are merely dreams [or chimeras]. From this I discover that it is not more reasonable to say, I will excite my imagination that I may know more distinctly what I am, than to express myself as follows: I am now awake, and perceive something real; but because my perception is not sufficiently clear, I will of express purpose go to sleep that my dreams may represent to me the object of my perception with more truth and clearness. And, therefore, I know that nothing of all that I can embrace in imagination belongs to the knowledge which I have of myself, and that there is need to recall with the utmost care the mind from this mode of thinking, that it may be able to know its own nature with perfect distinctness.*

But what, then, am I? A thinking thing, it has been said. But what is a thinking thing? It is a thing that doubts, understands, [conceives], affirms, denies, wills, refuses, that imagines also, and perceives. Assuredly it is not little, if all these properties belong to my nature. But why should they not belong to it? Am I not that very being who now doubts of almost everything; who, for all that, understands and conceives certain things; who affirms one alone as true, and denies the others; who desires to know more of them, and does not wish to be deceived; who imagines many things, sometimes even despite his will; and is likewise percipient of many, as if through the medium of the senses. Is there nothing of all this as true as that I am, even although I should be always dreaming, and although he who gave me being employed all his ingenuity to deceive me? Is there also any one of these attributes that can be properly distinguished from my thought, or that can be said to be separate from myself? For it is of itself so evident that it is I who doubt, I who understand, and I who desire, that it is here unnecessary to add anything by way of rendering it more clear. And I am as certainly the same being who imagines; for, although it may be (as I before supposed) that nothing I imagine is true, still the power of imagination does not cease really to exist in me and to form part of my thought. In fine, I am the same being who perceives, that is, who apprehends certain objects as by the organs of sense, since, in truth, I see light, hear a noise, and feel heat. But it will be said that these presentations are false, and that I am dreaming. Let it be so. At all events it is certain that I seem to see light, hear a noise, and feel heat; this cannot be false, and this is what in me is properly called perceiving (sentire), which is nothing else than thinking. From this I begin to know what I am with somewhat greater clearness and distinctness than heretofore.

*   *   *   *

But, finally, what shall I say of the mind itself, that is, of myself? for as yet I do not admit that I am anything but mind. What, then! I who seem to possess so distinct an apprehension of the piece of wax,—do I not know myself, both with greater truth and certitude, and also much more distinctly and clearly? For if I judge that the wax exists because I see it, it assuredly follows, much more evidently, that I myself am or exist, for the same reason: for it is possible that what I see may not in truth be wax, and that I do not even possess eyes with which to see anything; but it cannot be that when I see, or, which comes to the same thing, when I think I see, I myself who think am *nothing. So likewise, if I judge that the wax exists because I touch it, it will still also follow that I am; and if I determine that my imagination, or any other cause, whatever it be, persuades me of the existence of the wax, I will still draw the same conclusion. And what is here remarked of the piece of wax, is applicable to all the other things that are external to me. And further, if the [notion or] perception of wax appeared to me more precise and distinct, after that not only sight and touch, but many other causes besides, rendered it manifest to my apprehension, with how much greater distinctness must I now know myself, since all the reasons that contribute to the knowledge of the nature of wax, or of any body whatever, manifest still better the nature of my mind? And there are besides so many other things in the mind itself that contribute to the illustration of its nature, that those dependent on the body, to which I have here referred, scarcely merit to be taken into account.*

But, in conclusion, I find I have insensibly reverted to the point I desired; for, since it is now manifest to me that bodies themselves are not properly perceived by the senses nor by the faculty of imagination, but by the intellect alone; and since they are not perceived because they are seen and touched, but only because they are understood [or rightly comprehended by thought], I readily discover that there is nothing more easily or clearly apprehended than my own mind. . . .

[From *Meditations on the First Philosophy*, Meditation II.]

AN ANALYSIS OF DESCARTES' ARGUMENT

1. THE BASIC CLAIM

In his *Discourse on Method* Descartes writes that "in relation to practice, it is sometimes necessary to adopt, as if above doubt, opinions which we discern to be highly uncertain . . . ; but as I . . . desired to give my attention solely to the search after truth, I thought that a procedure exactly the opposite was called for, and that I ought to reject as absolutely false all opinions in regard to which I could suppose the least ground for doubt, in order to ascertain whether after that there remained aught in my belief that was wholly indubitable." In the *Meditations,* reporting the circumstances which led to his undertaking the inquiry which is the subject common to both the *Discourse* and the *Meditations,* Descartes writes that he had for many years accepted false opinions as true, and that he was determined to rid himself "of all the opinions I had adopted, and of commencing anew the work of building from the foundation, if I desired to establish a firm and abiding superstructure in the sciences." The overthrow of his opinions was to be accomplished not by an examination of the beliefs considered individually, but by critical attention to the principles upon which the opinions were based. In examining the principles, Descartes adopts the procedural rule of rejecting any belief or principle which is "not entirely certain and indubitable," and he declares that "it will be sufficient to justify the rejection of the whole if I shall find in each some ground for doubt."

We may conclude, then, that Descartes was after "truth" as a firm foundation for his philosophy. He sought, through a systematic examination of the principles of his beliefs, something *indubitable* and consequently *true and certain.*

That Descartes did in fact suppose that the road to certainty was to be found through locating the indubitable is made evident by his suggestion that whatever survived the test of systematic doubt could be taken as "entirely certain and indubitable." When at last he came to a proposition which survived the test of doubt, a proposition he could not reasonably doubt, he accepted it as the first principle of his philosophy, and he then (he reports in the *Discourse*) "inquired in general into what is essential to the truth and certainty of a proposition"; and he reports that "since I had discovered one which I knew to be true, I thought I must likewise be able to discover the ground of this certitude."

We may fairly assume, then, that Descartes' basic claim, in the argument we are considering, is that *the proposition (or statement) "I think, hence I am"* (in the Latin, *Cogito ergo sum*) *is indubitable and, consequently, true and certain.*

2. THE BASIC ARGUMENT

A summary of Descartes' basic argument is provided by the

philosopher himself in Part IV of his *Discourse on Method.* We have only to arrange the statements (adding italics, but not changing the order of expression) so as to emphasize the progression of the argument and to allow a numbering of the parts to be symbolized:

[1] ". . . as I . . . desired to give my attention solely to the search after truth, I thought . . . that I ought to reject as absolutely false all opinions in regard to which I could suppose the least ground for doubt, in order to ascertain whether after that there remained aught in my belief that was wholly *indubitable.*

[2] "Accordingly, seeing that *our senses sometimes deceive us,*

[3] "I was willing to *suppose that there existed nothing really such as they presented to us;*

[4] "and because some men err in reasoning . . . I, convinced that I was as open to error as any other, *rejected as false all the reasonings I had hitherto taken for demonstrations;*

[5] ". . . finally, when I considered that the very same thoughts (presentations) which we experience when awake may also be experienced when we are asleep, while there is at that time not one of them true, I *supposed that all the objects (presentations) that had ever entered into my mind when awake, had in them no more truth than the illusions of my dreams.*

[6] "But . . . *whilst I thus wished* to think that all was false, *it was absolutely necessary that I, who thus thought, should be* [*something*];

[7] ". . . I observed that *this truth, I think, hence I am,*

[8] "*was so certain and of such evidence, that no ground of doubt,* however extravagant, *could be alleged by the Sceptics capable of shaking it,*

[9] "I concluded that I might, without scruple, *accept it as the first principle of the Philosophy of which I was in search.*

[10] ". . . *from the very circumstances that I thought to doubt of the truth of other things, it most clearly and certainly followed that I was;* while, on the other hand, *if I had only*

ceased to think . . . I would have had no reason to believe that I existed;

[11] "I thence *concluded that I was a substance whose whole essence or nature consists only in thinking . . . .*

[12] "And as I observed that *in the words* I think, hence I am, *there is nothing at all which gives me assurance of their truth beyond this, that I see very clearly that in order to think it is necessary to exist,*

[13] "I *concluded* that I might take, *as a general rule,* the principle, *that all the things which we very clearly and distinctly conceive are true . . . ."*

The argument presented in the *Meditations* is substantially the same as that given in the *Discourse on Method*, but the presentation in the *Meditations* is more fascinating because there Descartes supplements the basic argument with a more detailed account of his skeptical train of thought. He supposes that a malevolent and deceiving god might have misled him into considering erroneous beliefs to be certainly true; he then decides not to believe his senses or his memory, and he asks, "What is there, then, that can be esteemed true? Perhaps this only, that there is absolutely nothing certain." But the conclusion is the same: if the deceiver deceives the thinker, the thinker exists. "Doubtless, then I exist, since I am deceived," writes Descartes; "and, let him deceive me as he may, he can never bring it about that I am nothing, so long as I shall be conscious that I am something." And again Descartes settles upon a proposition which, because of its indubitability, he regards as certainly true: "So that it must . . . be maintained . . . that this proposition I am, I exist, is necessarily true each time it is expressed by me, or conceived in my mind."

Let us now symbolize the argument as simply as possible, so as to be able to appreciate its logical character.

$$(D \longleftrightarrow R) \cdot (\sim R \to A) \tag{1}$$

To simplify the logical expression of Descartes' argument we have written the universal proposition *without* quantifiers and variables. Thus, it is *as if* the above expression had been written as follows:

$$(x) \, [(Dx \longleftrightarrow Rx) \cdot (\sim Rx \to Ax)]$$

—which is to be read: *Whatever might be considered* (for all values of *x*), *if it is a proposition for which there is any ground for the slightest doubt, then it is a proposition to be rejected as absolutely false (and vice versa); and if it is a proposition not rejected as absolutely false, then it is a proposition to be accepted as absolutely true; that is, as both true and certain.*

Thus, we incorporate in our symbolic expression of the first premise both Descartes' explicit procedural rule—that he will *reject* any proposition that can *reasonably be doubted* (for Descartes did not intend to doubt irresponsibly, or even to doubt in fact; he sought grounds that might serve as reasons for doubting)—and his implicit rule, that of accepting as certain and true any proposition capable of surviving the rigors of his method of systematic doubt.

$$P \to M \qquad\qquad\qquad (2)$$

We shall read premise 2: *All propositions based upon the senses (the perceptual faculties) are from a class of propositions some members of which are deceiving (misleading); or, all propositions based upon the senses are based upon a source of opinions which is unreliable in that it is sometimes misleading.*

$$M \longleftrightarrow D \qquad\qquad\qquad (3)$$

Our symbolic expression 2 is intended to express the claim that "our senses sometimes deceive us." Premise 3 states the procedural rule that *whatever is misleading is to be doubted;* that is, whatever is derived from a source that has ever misled him through yielding false propositions which he subsequently believed to be true is a proposition which can reasonably be doubted (and vice versa).

From 2 and 3, then, as we have symbolized them, the proposition "$P \to D$" follows (by a logical rule sometimes called "the hypothetical syllogism"). The expression "$P \to D$" should be read: *Any proposition based upon the senses is a proposition which can reasonably be doubted.*

Thus, the logical expression we have included as 3 will be useful in providing a logical connection for other generalizations about sources of propositions. We regard a *proposition* as a matter capable of being proposed as true or as actually the case.

$$L \to M \tag{4}$$

—Propositions based upon the reason (logical arguments) *are propositions derived from a source that is misleading.*

$$I \to M \tag{5.1}$$
$$\therefore I \to R \tag{5.2}$$

—All propositions ever considered (all ideas) *are propositions derived from sources that are misleading.* Therefore, since what is misleading is doubtful, and what is doubtful is to be rejected as false, *whatever has been considered* (each and every idea) *is to be rejected as false.*

In premise 6 Descartes tells us, "I wished to think that all was false . . . ." We now devise the individual constant "*i*", which will serve as the personal pronoun used by Descartes. The symbol "*C*" is a predicate symbol used to mean "am thinking," and "*5.2*" refers to proposition 5.2; namely, "*I → R*". Thus, 6.1 is to be read: *I am thinking that all ideas are to be rejected as false.*

$$Ci,5.2 \tag{6.1}$$

In proposition 6 Descartes writes, "But immediately upon this I observed that, whilst I thus wished to think that all was false, it was absolutely necessary that I, who thus thought, should be [something] . . . ." One might be tempted to suppose that Descartes is here declaring nothing more than that he somehow intuited *himself* as thinker, that he is here claiming that while thinking he noticed something; namely, *himself.* But we suggest that Descartes recognized the propriety of saying, in reporting his experience, either "I am thinking" or "I am"; he discovered that whenever it is appropriate to say, "I am thinking," it would also be appropriate to say, "I am." We do *not* suggest that Descartes recognized his discovery as one involving linguistical considerations; in fact, he appears to have supposed that his argument in no way depended upon the generalization that *whatever is thinking exists.* In replying to a critic Descartes denied that he assumed, as a "prejudgment," the proposition "All that which thinks is or exists"; Descartes claimed that the thinker "experiences in himself that it cannot be that he thinks if he does not exist." But Descartes could not have known intuitively (nondiscursively) and as a particular fact of experience that "it cannot be that I think if I do not exist"; he supposed that "it was absolutely necessary that I, who thus thought, be [something]"; but that supposition, whatever his protestations, was a logical one, deriving whatever strength it had from the linguistic propriety of saying "I am" once one has found evidence to justify saying, "I am thinking." Descartes made a linguistical discovery, but he made it nonlinguistically.

Thus, the claim in premise 6 is twofold: (1) that Descartes is thinking that everything is false (expressed as 6.1), and (2) that if Descartes is thinking, Descartes exists. We now express the second claim as 6.2, and we leave to proposition 7 the conclusion of this particular line of thought. Thus, 6.1 and 6.2 express the premises on the basis of which proposition 7, the famous "Cogito," is asserted. (We here recognize that a philosopher's reading of his own argument may be different from a critic's reading; and we suggest that it is possible that the critic is correct.)

$$Ci \to Si \qquad\qquad (6.2)$$

Proposition 6.2 is to be read: *If I think, I am.* Or we could say, "*Cogito* implies *sum.*" That we are justified in taking this proposition as basic to Descartes' affirmation, "Cogito ergo sum," is borne out by the fact that when (as shown in proposition 12) Descartes attempted to discover the truth in the proposition "I think, hence I am" (proposition 7), he found no reason to be assured of the truth of the proposition other than that "I see very clearly that *in order to think it is necessary to exist*" (italics added). Existence is a condition of thinking; if one is to think, one must be.

But the proposition "If I think, I am" (6.2) is not adequate support for the "Cogito ergo sum," which does not mean "*If* I think, I am," but rather, "I think, and hence I am." Descartes had also to "see very clearly" that he was thinking. Proposition 6.1 asserts that Descartes was thinking (in that he was thinking that everything was false); 6.2 is the claim that *if* he thinks, he is; 7 is the conclusion, "Cogito ergo sum" or "I think, hence I am":

$$\therefore \quad Ci \therefore Si \tag{7}$$

In proposition 7, which figures in later propositions in Descartes' argument, we find *two* conclusions based on previous premises. Descartes asserts that he thinks (Ci) because he finds that he is thinking that everything is false; he asserts that he exists (Si) because he finds that in thinking, he exists. The "hence" marks the transition from "I think" to "I am" by way of the conditional proposition 6.2: "If I think, I am" (a logical claim based on a linguistical consideration suggested by the report of Descartes' experience of thinking).

Proposition 8 tells us that Descartes found proposition 7 to be "so certain and of such evidence, that no ground of doubt, however extravagant, could be alleged by the Sceptics capable of shaking it," but he offers no further reasons for regarding proposition 7 to be certain and indubitable.

We suggest that, in this connection, a sentence from the *Meditations* is especially helpful. Descartes declares that even if there is a deceiver "of the highest power and the deepest cunning," Descartes can be assured of one indubitable truth: "Doubtless . . . I exist, since I am deceived; and let him deceive me as he may, he can never bring it about that I am nothing, so long as I shall be conscious that I am something." He concludes that "it must, in fine, be maintained, all things being maturely and carefully considered, that this proposition (*pronunciatum*) I am, I exist, is necessarily true each time it is expressed by me, or conceived in my mind."

The problem now is to explain what (if anything) there is about the proposition "I exist" (or the proposition "I think") which makes it indubitable and true every time it is conceived or thought. (It is not at all evident that the proposition "I think" is true *if it is stated,* for a man may speak without thinking; but the proposition "I exist" or "I am" is true if a man states it, for if he states it, he is. However, for Descartes, stating a proposition would not be sufficient to existence: to *be* one must *think*—as proposition 10 makes clear.)

Let us use the following as a symbolic expression of what we take to be a hidden premise in Descartes' argument:

$$(x) \; [(Ci,x \rightarrow Tx) \longleftrightarrow \sim Di,x]$$

That is, *if in thinking something, "x", x is made true, then I cannot reasonably doubt x; that is, if x becomes true in virtue of my thinking it, x is indubitable; and vice versa.*

Now, proposition 7 (in fact, either proposition separately asserted in 7: *"Ci"* or *"Si"*) fits the description given in the antecedent, for (to consider *"Ci"* first) *if I think that I think, it is made true that I think* (or, if I think 7, then 7 is made true); hence, 7 is indubitable.

If, now, we consider *"Si"*, we find that it also is indubitable, for *if I think that I am, it is made true that I am* (or, if I think the proposition meant by *"Si"*, the proposition is made true). This claim is based on the previous claim (6.2) that *if* I think, I am. Thus, if I think I am, I am, for if I think, I am. And, as noted in the discussion of *"Ci"*, if I think that I think, I think, for if I think, I think. Since both *"Ci"* and *"Si"* are indubitable, premise 7, which is the joint assertion of the two, is indubitable (for if I think that I think and I am, I think and I am, for if I think, I think, and if I think, I am).

Proposition 8, then, asserts that premise 7 is being thought by Descartes and is indubitable. We have suggested that the reason for asserting the indubitability of proposition 7 is that 7 is such that its truth is secured whenever Descartes considers (thinks) it. To say that a proposition is "indubitable," then, *as Descartes uses the term,* is to say that the proposition is such that *if* thought, it cannot reasonably be doubted. Proposition 7 could not reasonably be doubted (although it could *unreasonably* be doubted), for if one were to doubt it, since doubting is a kind of thinking, one would make it true; and if doubting makes it true, then the proposition could not be misleading (that is, Descartes could not be deceived in believing what believing makes true) and, consequently, could not reasonably be doubted. (The diagrams to follow will show the reasoning involved here.)

We may now state proposition 8:

$$Ci,7 \cdot \sim Di,7 \tag{8}$$

Descartes tells us that he observed the "Cogito" and found it to be indubitable; that is, "so certain . . . that no ground of doubt, however extravagant, could be alleged by the Sceptics capable of shaking it . . . ." And what is a skeptic?—a professional doubter. Read

8: *I think "I think, therefore I am," and "I think, therefore I am" is indubitable (relative to me).*

Descartes now declares that the "Cogito" is not to be rejected as false and that it is certain and true, absolutely (not contingently) true:

$$\therefore \sim R7 \cdot A7 \tag{9}$$

Descartes turns to a consideration of what he is, and he decides that—since if he thinks, he exists, but if he does not think, nothing remains which he would choose to call himself—he will define himself as a thinking being, as "a substance whose whole essence or nature consists only in thinking . . . ." We first of all symbolize the basic proposition expressed as follows: "from the very circumstance that I thought to doubt of the truth of other things, it most clearly and certainly followed that I was; while, on the other hand, if I had only ceased to think . . . I would have had no reason to believe that I existed . . . ."

$$(Ci \to Si) \cdot (\sim Ci \to \sim Si) \tag{10}$$

—which means, *If I think, I am; and if I don't think, I am not.* Or, if I think, I exist (already given as premise 6.2); while if it is not true that I am thinking, it is not true that I exist (that something exists which is I). We have taken the point in the latter half of Descartes' remark to be, not that were he not thinking he could then have no reasons for believing in his existence in that he could not, then, as not thinking, consider anything, but that, considering what he would say in describing what would remain once thinking had ceased, he finds that nothing would remain which he would count as worthy of being called "I."

From proposition 10, 11 follows logically:

$$\therefore Ci \leftrightarrow Si \tag{11}$$

Now, although in what we have called premise 12 Descartes declares that what assures him of the truth of 7 is the clarity and distinctness of proposition 6.2, on which, together with 6.1, proposition 7 is based, we are true to the direction of Descartes' thinking here (a direction made evident by proposition 13) if we take 12 to mean that Descartes found that premise 7, which he regarded as indubitable, certain, and true, was a proposition capable of being conceived "very clearly and distinctly" to be true. The clarity and distinctness of Descartes' conception of 7 appears, then, to be dependent upon the clarity and distinctness of his conception (or thinking) of propositions 6.1 and 6.2.

$$Vi,7 \tag{12}$$

—Or: *I see very clearly and distinctly the truth of "I think, therefore I am."*

$$(x) \ [Vi,x \rightarrow Ax] \tag{13}$$

The "general rule" stated as proposition 13 is derived from 12 and the implicit premise "$(Vi,7 \cdot A7) \rightarrow (x) \ [Vi,x \rightarrow Ax]$." In other words, having found the "Cogito" proposition (7) to be certain and true (that is, *supposing* himself to have discovered the certain truth of 7), Descartes discovered (so he reports) that he saw the proposition very clearly and distinctly to be true (that is, he *presumed* that he discovered a special feature of his conceiving 7 to be true), and he then generalized to the effect that if the "Cogito" is seen clearly and distinctly to be true *and* is certain and true, then *any proposition seen clearly and distinctly to be true is certain and true.* Proposition 13 is the conclusion of this line of reasoning.

3. CRITICISM OF THE BASIC ARGUMENT

Descartes' argument, as we have summarized and symbolized it, is as follows:

1. $(D \leftrightarrow R) \cdot (\sim R \rightarrow A)$
2. $P \rightarrow M$
3. $M \leftrightarrow D$
4. $L \rightarrow M$
5.1. $I \rightarrow M$
∴ 5.2. $I \rightarrow R$
6.1. $Ci,5.2$
6.2. $Ci \rightarrow Si$

∴ 7. Ci ∴ Si
 8. $Ci,7 \cdot \sim Di,7$
∴ 9. $\sim R7 \cdot A7$
 10. $(Ci \rightarrow Si) \cdot (\sim Ci \rightarrow \sim Si)$
∴ 11. $Ci \longleftrightarrow Si$
 12. $Vi,7$
 13. $(x) [Vi,x \rightarrow Ax]$

Before constructing the diagram of the argument, let us abstract from the argument any intermediate conclusions, for such conclusions can presumably be derived from other premises, and we should not put them into the diagram. After constructing the diagram, however, we should determine whether the completed diagram *shows* the intermediate conclusions (and, hence, demonstrates that the intermediate conclusions were legitimately derived from the other premises). Thus, we shall not, in drawing the diagram, include the intermediate conclusion 5.2 nor the intermediate conclusions 7, 9, and 11. We notice that premise 6.2 and the left side of the conjunction in 10 are the same; thus, to complete the drawing of premise 10, when an arrow from "Ci" to "Si" has already been provided in the representation of 6.2, we need only draw an arrow head at the end of the shaft that points at "Ci", for the proposition "$\sim Ci \rightarrow \sim Si$" is logically equivalent to "$Si \rightarrow Ci$". The rule for the reading of statements which involve the use of the arrow is suggested by the following: "$A \rightarrow B$" means that *if A, then B* or (what is logically equivalent) *if not-B, then not-A*. Thus, *if the direction is reversed, the terms are negated:* $(A \rightarrow B) \longleftrightarrow (\sim B \rightarrow \sim A)$.

In reading the diagram of Descartes' argument it is necessary to remember that universal propositions are shown without individual symbols; such propositions are understood to be true for all values of the variable "x". When a universal involves part of another expression—as, for example, in propositions 6.2 and 10, which involve reference to "Ci", which has appeared as part of 6.1 $(Ci,5.2)$ —an arc marks that part of the other expression (6.1) which is involved in the universal (6.2 and 10). Also, proposition 13 is about *anything* which "I see very clearly and distinctly to be true"; it uses, as its antecedent, part of proposition 12 $(Vi,7)$; hence, an arc marks that part of proposition 12 which is involved in the universal proposition 13.

When an expression involves the negation of a term already used positively in the diagram, a bar indicates the negation. Thus, the second part of premise 1, which is "$\sim R \rightarrow A$", is shown in the diagram by using the bar to negate the consequent of the first part of premise 1 and then drawing an arrow to "A". To show in the diagram proposition 8, "$Ci,7 \cdot \sim Di,7$", we use "7" as an individual symbol to accompany "Ci"; we *check it ($\sqrt{}$) to remind ourselves* that the premise claims "$Ci,7$" to be the case (something that would be necessary if "$Ci,7$" functioned as the antecedent of a conditional proposition and were also asserted categorically), and we note that this part of the logical structure is derived from proposition 8. To show "$\sim Di,7$", also from 8, we insert a denial sign ($\times$) to the side of the complex symbol "$7,iD$".

We have noted, to the right of the long diagonal line in the lower right-hand corner of the diagram, the intermediate conclusions included in the statement of the argument.

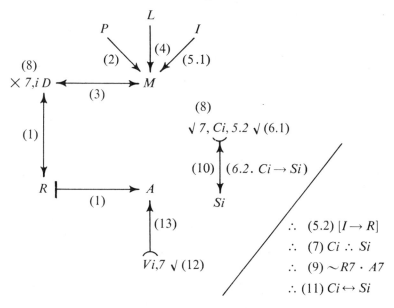

This first diagram, however, does not show what led Descartes to suppose that the "Cogito" is an indubitable proposition. We shall attempt to remedy that omission by providing two other diagrams. However, it is possible to determine, by a consideration of the present diagram, whether Descartes validly established his conclusions. A consideration of the transition from the statement of the "Cogito" to the assertion of its indubitability and consequent certainty can then be undertaken separately.

Let us now determine, by reference to the diagram, whether Descartes validly reached his conclusions. Premise 5.1 states, $I \to M$; the diagram shows that if M, then D; if D, then R. Thus, $I \to R$, the first intermediate conclusion to be considered, is validly based on the premises given.

Premise 6.1 states that "$Ci,5.2$" is the case; if "$Ci,5.2$", then "Ci", and (by 6.2 and 10) if "Ci", then "Si". Hence proposition 7, the "Cogito"—"Ci ∴ Si", has validly been established.

The latter half of premise 8 states, "$\sim Di,7$"; since the diagram shows that "$R \to D$", we realize that "$\sim D \to \sim R$". It also shows that if "R" is false, "A" is true; hence, "$\sim R7$" and "$A7$" are validly deduced from the premises. Thus, conclusion 9 is validly drawn.

Proposition 11, as we have already indicated, follows from 10; the double-headed arrow expresses both 10 and 11, for the two propositions are logically equivalent.

We notice that propositions 12 and 13 are claims established independently of the premises. Proposition 12 states that Descartes saw very clearly and distinctly that the "Cogito" was true; proposition 13 states the general rule that Descartes adopted (perhaps inadvisedly) for determining truths to be certain. If, indeed, seeing with clarity and distinctness the truth of a proposition were a dependable procedure for determining absolutely true propositions, no one could legitimately object to Descartes' general rule; but, as he himself points out, immediately after declaring that he has decided to use the rule of clarity and distinctness, "there is some difficulty in the proper discernment of distinct propositions."

We shall now proceed to an appraisal of the premises, for the argument is admittedly successful in validly establishing the conclusions stated.

PREMISE 1

In premise 1 Descartes announces his intention to reject as false any proposition which gives rise to the slightest doubt in his mind, and he suggests that any proposition which does not arouse doubt in his mind is not to be rejected. He then adds that any proposition not rejected after being considered by him is to be accepted as absolutely true and certain.

We shall later consider whether we are willing to agree that every indubitable proposition (as defined by Descartes' operational criterion) is certain and true; but for the time being we shall understand Descartes' first premise to be a procedural rule, the specification of his method of systematic doubt, the spelling out of the screening process by which he hoped to isolate at least one indubitable, true, and certain proposition. Since premise 1 states what is to be done with propositions considered by Descartes, there is no need to consider the acceptability of premise 1. We do not object to his procedural decision.

PREMISE 2

Descartes claims that our senses sometimes deceive us, the suggestion being that propositions based upon sense experience may not be true. We are in agreement with Descartes' claim that the senses are misleading; hence, we accept premise 2.

PREMISE 3

Descartes' rejection of the senses suggests the procedural rule: whatever has been or could be misleading as a source of beliefs is to be doubted (reasonably). This is a radical principle, but it is understandable given the desire to found philosophy on an absolutely secure truth. We are primarily witnesses of Descartes' practice; we do not choose to judge his procedure; we accept the rule which premise 3 states.

PREMISE 4

Descartes rejects, as coming from a source that has sometimes yielded false opinions, those propositions supported by logical reasoning. Descartes claims that he is "as open to error as anyone"; we know ourselves to be fallible, and we realize how often logical claims may appear to be justified when, in fact, only a weakness in us makes them credible at all. Hence, we concur with Descartes' claim that propositions based on logical reasoning are based on a source which has sometimes misled us.

PREMISE 5

Sometimes we are not certain that we are awake; sometimes we are not certain that we are asleep. *Perhaps* no belief is absolutely reliable. Descartes, giving his skepticism full rein, offers what we have called premise 5 not as an expression of a proposition he is prepared to defend as true, but as an expression of a radical view he is prepared to act upon. The point of premise 5 is that *at that stage in his inquiry* Descartes could not bring himself to accept as certain and true *any* proposition *so far considered*. In deciding, later on, that certain propositions were indubitable, true, and certain, Descartes did not reject premise 5, for 5 is here understood to be concerned with everything *so far considered* by Descartes. Descartes does not assert, however, that all his ideas to this point are false; what he asserts is that he "supposed" that everything that he had ever believed was false. Premise 5, then, is the statement of a supposition; it provides material for reflection; it is idle to consider further any question as to its truth or falsity.

PREMISE 6

Premise 6.1 is the proposition that "I [Descartes] . . . thus thought [that] all was false." Let us agree (as any reasonable man would, were he free of Descartes' stringent criteria for the acceptability of propositions) that Descartes was thinking what he says he was thinking; namely, what we have called premise 5.2. *We* may agree with premise 6.1; however, there is a serious question as to whether, having established certain rules to govern his inquiry, *Descartes* ought to have accepted what we call 6.1. Consequently, the question arises as to whether, even if we are agreeable, we ought to accept premise 6.1.

Under ordinary circumstances, no one would deny that Descartes was thinking and that, if he says so, he was thinking (making the effort to believe) that everything he had ever considered was false. But the circumstances, as Descartes makes clear, are *not* ordinary: a proposition is to be accepted as true only if it is certainly true.

Could Descartes have been mistaken in supposing that he was thinking that everything he had ever considered was false? Not if "I . . . thus thought [that] all was false" is a statement that does no more than express (and, one must say, in an unconventional way) some *uninterpreted data*. But the statement was surely meant to be more than an inarticulate cry which, being only a cry, could not have been in error. Descartes' claim that he is thinking that all is false is an empirical claim; it represents an interpretation or report of experience; it states (what under ordinary circumstances would not be questioned) that Descartes understands his experience to be that of the activity we call "thinking." Let *us* grant that Descartes was thinking that everything he had ever thought was false. Nevertheless, *as far as he knew,* restrained as he was by his extraordinary criteria of acceptability, he was not *thinking;* perhaps, as far as he knew, he was mistaking feelings of erratic brain action for signs of thinking. If, in desperation, he were to decide: "But this, whatever it is, is what I *mean* by 'thinking,' " he would be settling for a cry when what he sought was a certain and true proposition.

Let us be clear about the direction of the present critical remarks. We have not yet considered whether "I think" is indubitable. Furthermore, we are not considering whether, as a matter of fact, Descartes was thinking; nor are we considering whether, if he was thinking at the time he was reportedly thinking everything false, he was thinking that everything was false—for we are certainly inclined to believe that Descartes was thinking, and that among the things he thought was that everything was false. What we are considering is whether, having set out to discover some absolutely true belief, Descartes ought to have accepted, as a premise in his argument, the proposition that he was thinking everything was false. He *says,* "I wished to think that all was false," and perhaps he did; we think he did. But perhaps he was not *wishing;* perhaps he was not wishing *to think;* perhaps he was not *thinking;* perhaps he was not thinking *that all was false.* It is unlikely that Descartes was mistaken in thinking that he thought that everything was false—but it does not follow that he could *not possibly* have been mistaken or even that he was not, in fact, mistaken.

Of course, if Descartes was mistaken, at least he was thinking. But the question remains as to whether it was at the time beyond all reasonable doubt (relative to Descartes' very stringent criteria of reasonableness) that he was thinking that all was false.

Even if, as we grant, it is indubitable and true that, as Descartes put it, "I am thinking," and even if it were true, as we do not grant, that indubitable propositions are certain and true, Descartes would nevertheless not have been justified in claiming "I . . . thought [that] all was false," for he could not have known with certainty that the proposition in question was indubitable. To know that it was true, he would have had to rely on his experience as a manifestation of the activity the presence of which he presumed to have discovered; but in premise 3 he rejected all sense experience. To know that the proposition that he was thinking was indubitable, he would have had to rely on his powers of logical analysis, but in premise 4 he rejected logical reasoning as a source of the indubitable. In fact, neither experience nor logical reasoning is the source of the indubitable (relative to Descartes' use of the term), for the indubitable depends on the character of the proposition itself (as we shall discover). It is one thing for a proposition to be indubitable; it is something else to know that it is indubitable. The proposition that "the proposition 'I think' is indubitable" is not itself indubitable: it is only certain and true; but Descartes, following his procedure, could not have known the certainty of this proposition.

To make this clear, we must analyze the claim that "I think" is indubitable. We shall attempt to do so in criticizing premise 8, in which it is claimed that the "Cogito" is indubitable.

Premise 6.2 is the claim that "If I think, I am." This simple assertion to the effect that if an individual is active, there is such an individual—an assertion not to be confused with the "Cogito"—is a logical claim which we accept (although, again, we wonder whether Descartes, who officially doubted logical reasoning and would have had to rely on sense experience to support this linguistical claim, ought to have accepted it).

The outcome of our appraisal of 6.1 and 6.2 is that—despite our misgivings about the philosophical propriety of Descartes' accepting as premises what, according to his criteria, ought to have been rejected as false—we accept 6.1 as an empirical claim and 6.2 as a logical claim, both of which we presume to be true.

PREMISE 7

The "Cogito" ($Ci \therefore Si$)—"I think, hence I am [Cogito ergo sum]"—is acceptable if 6.1 and 6.2 are acceptable. For if it is true that Descartes was *thinking* that everything he had ever thought was false, then it is true that he was thinking. And (as 6.2 states) if to think is to be, then he was. Premise 7 is derived from 6; it adds nothing new.

PREMISE 8

Now Descartes asserts that he thinks premise 7, the "Cogito." Probably he did; his claim is empirical; he could not have been certain (under the circumstances he provided for judging such matters). We are willing to concede that he thought 7.

Descartes also claims that proposition 7 is indubitable. To decide whether he was right in *saying* so, we review the meaning of "indubitable" *as Descartes used the word. A proposition is indubitable if it is such that, if thought, the thinking of it makes it true.* We represent the definition as follows:

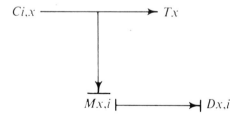

We read the diagram: *If, when I think something, it is made true, then it cannot be misleading; and if it cannot be misleading, then it cannot reasonably be doubted by me (that is, it is indubitable, relative to me).*

The trouble with the senses, with reason, and with experience in general, whether acquired while dreaming or awake, is that any proposition based on such sources can be misleading, as, on occasion, some propositions based on those sources have been misleading—so Descartes claimed. But the propositions "I think" and "I am" are "indubitable" because if one thinks them—even if one doubts them—one secures their truth. If their truth is secured by the thinking of them, how, in thinking them, could one be mistaken? If one could not be mistaken in thinking them, one cannot reasonably doubt them; such propositions are indubitable. In general, then:

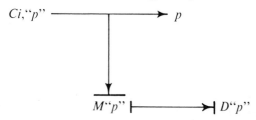

Or, if my thinking "p"—that is, that p is true—has as a consequence the truth of p, then it is not the case that what I am thinking is misleading; consequently, it is not the case that what I am thinking is reasonably to be doubted: what I am thinking is indubitable.

So it is with the proposition "Ci", for if *I think* that I am thinking, then what I am thinking—namely, "I think"—is true in virtue of my thinking it:

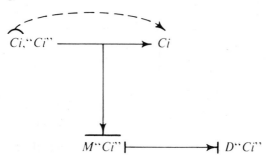

(The broken arrow shows what there is about thinking "Ci" that yields the truth of the proposition thought.)

Let us now consider the proposition "Si". Inserting the premise

"$Ci \rightarrow Si$" (proposition 6.2)—and again we use the broken arrow—we find the following logical situation:

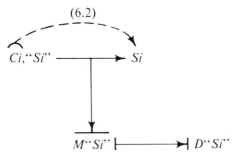

(6.2)

$Ci, "Si" \longrightarrow Si$

$M"Si" \longmapsto\!\!\!\to D"Si"$

The diagram shows that if I think that I am, I am, for (by 6.2) if I think, I am. Thus, the truth of "Si" is secured by the thinking of it. Consequently, "Si" is not misleading; hence, it is indubitable.

For Descartes to have been justified in *accepting* the "Cogito," however, it was not enough that the "Cogito" be indubitable and true; it also had to be certain—and, even more, Descartes had to be certain that it was certain, as well as that it was indubitable and true. To be certain that it was indubitable, he would have had to rely on his logical powers, which he doubted; to be certain it was true, he would have had to rely on his experience, which he doubted; to be certain that it was certain, he would have had to have been mistaken.

Descartes would have to have been mistaken to have been certain that the "Cogito" was certain; for, in fact, the "Cogito," although indubitable and probably true, was not certain. (The dilemma is inescapable, for even if the "Cogito" were certain, to be certain that it was certain Descartes would have had to rely on his logical powers, which he doubted.)

The matter is considered further in the consideration of proposition 9.

PREMISE 9

In asserting, as we have symbolized it, "$\sim R7 \cdot A7$", Descartes was, in effect, declaring himself to be justified in not rejecting as false the "Cogito" and in taking it to be certain and true (absolutely, without qualification, and not contingently true).

Let us define our terms. A proposition is *contingently* true if its truth value depends on something other than itself. Propositions which by their structure could not be false are true, not contingently, but logically; not probably, relative to empirical evidence, but certainly, relative to logical form. Thus, the proposition "If anything is a red flower, then it is a flower," or "If anything is a red flower, then it is red," or even, as we use the terms, "If anything is a rose, then it is a flower" is certainly (logically) true. But "I am smelling a rose" is the statement of a contingent proposition.

I may invite consideration of the proposition "I am smelling a rose" by stating the proposition. The time of uttering the statement determines, in part, the reference of the statement; that is, the moment of utterance is the moment meant. When I say now (as I write this) that it is false that I am smelling a rose, I am not claiming that while you read this I am not smelling a rose. Who knows?

So it was with Descartes. In writing "I think," the meaning of what he stated was determined in part by the time and manner of his statement. If Descartes is not now thinking, we should not say that "I think," *as he stated it at the time,* is now false; as he stated it at the time, the proposition was (and is) probably true; and any gracious and reasonable person, not bound by Descartes' procedural rules for doubting, would be inclined to say, "Oh, certainly, it was true!" But such a concession is not an acknowledgment of the *logical* certainty of the proposition Descartes stated; it is as if one declared, "Oh, in all probability it was true!" But even the "all" does not, in such a use, mean what the logician means by "all." If Descartes, in declaring the "Cogito" to be certain meant only that he found his experience to be, for him, overwhelming in its support of the empirical claim he was making, he had, by that time, overcome his distrust of experience and, consequently, abandoned his own rules for systematic doubting.

We must distinguish, as we have, between a *statement* of a proposition and the *proposition* stated. I may make a proposal, but the proposal I make need not have been made; it could have been considered, but not made; it need not even have been considered. So it is with propositions, which are the meanings of statements that need not be made. To say that a proposition is a meaning does not mean that a proposition must be meant, but only that, were a statement made, the proposition would be what was meant. A proposition made in English could be made in French, but it need not be made at all. If a statement is made, however, the proposition meant is at least in part determined—as something that has been stated—by the time and character of the statement. Propositions, then, are the meanings of possible statements of the sort ordinarily described as being either "true" or "false."

Thus, Descartes need not have considered the proposition he stated by saying, or writing, at the time, "I think." Had he not stated the proposition at that time, it would probably have been true anyway, for he was busy thinking. But whether he stated it or not, the proposition is not certain, for its truth depends, not on its form, its logical content, but on what Descartes was then doing. The proposition "I think," stated by Descartes, need not have been stated by Descartes, and, although probably true, the proposition need not be (or, we could say, "have been") true. Descartes should have seen that propositions of this type are not certain and then, by his rules of procedure, he should not have felt justified in claiming the proposition to be certain; if fact, by his rules, he would not have been justified in claiming the proposition to be *not* certain, for, having ruled out both experience and reason, he had nothing left on the basis of which to be justified in saying anything at all.

PREMISE 10

Descartes decided to define himself as that which thinks. Perhaps he said something meaningless or false in claiming that he was *thinking substance,* but here we are not concerned to discuss that question. We are inclined to say that, were we unconscious, our existence would not then be appreciated by us; but we are not inclined to say that our existence ceases whenever we are unconscious. But Descartes chose to think of himself as a thinker and of his body as merely that which carried the burden. A definition may be impractical and the offering of it may be ill-advised; but unless the definition purports to be an account of the meaning a term has acquired in its use (a semantical *claim*), it cannot be false, nor can it be true. Hence, it is of no particular consequence to our appraisal of the argument that we accept premise 10.

PREMISE 11

The proposition "*Ci* ←→ *Si*" is simply the logical equivalent of premise 10.

PREMISE 12

We do not deny that his experience led Descartes to say that he saw "very clearly and distinctly" the truth of the "Cogito." But he may not have been justified *in saying so,* for there remains, as we have suggested, the question as to the criteria by reference to which one can determine whether what one supposes oneself to be seeing very "clearly and distinctly" is, relative to this use of terms, *in fact* being "seen very clearly and distinctly."

PREMISE 13

Consequently, we are not at all inclined to find useful the rule proposed in what we have called proposition 13.

COMMENTS ON THE ANALYSIS OF DESCARTES' ARGUMENT

In criticizing Descartes' argument we find ourselves in a curious position. Premises acceptable to us ought not to have been acceptable to Descartes. Hence, the criticism seems, to some extent, to be *ad hominem,* to be directed to the man for failing to abide by his own procedural rules. However, were our appraisal of the argument conducted by reference to less stringent criteria of acceptability, we should nevertheless be forced to conclude that Descartes' most significant claims are not true. The "Cogito," which Descartes regarded as certain, is not certain, but only indubitable. The proposition "The 'Cogito' is indubitable," which Descartes, in order to be justified, had to regard as indubitable, is not indubitable, but only certain. The defense of these critical claims depends on the clarification of the meanings of the terms "indubitable" and "certain," as Descartes used the terms. The analysis, insofar as it is useful, is useful because it clarifies the meanings of the terms used and relates those meanings to the logical claims made by the author of the argument analyzed.

QUESTIONS FOR DISCUSSION

1. Read Descartes' argument in both the *Discourse on Method* and the *Meditations*. Do you agree with the critic when he suggests that Descartes was seeking a proposition that was both indubitable and certain? Consider Descartes' use of the term "indubitable." Does it seem to you that a proposition could be indubitable but not certain? Do you agree that the "Cogito ergo sum" is a proposition which is indubitable but not certain? Do you agree that the proposition "The 'Cogito' is indubitable" is certain but not indubitable? In what way, if any, is the analysis unfair to Descartes?

2. Do you believe that Descartes actually doubted that he had a body? Could he have been justified in doubting that he had a body? How could he have been justified?

3. Descartes claims that he is "a substance whose whole essence or nature consists only in thinking . . . ." What is a substance? Could Descartes have been certain he was a substance, even if he could have been certain that he was thinking?

4. If a person will not trust himself while thinking, is it possible for him to know anything?

5. Descartes was skeptical about beliefs based on sense experience and reason. What is the value of being skeptical? Is skepticism the way to certainty? If not, is it nonetheless a useful critical tendency?

6. Distinguish between a *proposition* (that which is or may be proposed for consideration) and a *statement*. Need a proposition be stated? Need the proposition "I think" be stated? If I think "I think," am I thinking the same proposition Descartes was thinking when he thought what he stated as "I think"? Is it possible that the proposition "I am alive" be false?

7. If a person under hypnosis, upon being told to say "I am thinking," then said, "I am thinking," would he be stating a proposition? Would he be making a proposition? If so, would that proposition be true? Would it be certain? Would it be indubitable?

8. If on Monday I say, "I am thinking," and then on Tuesday I say it again, have I stated the same proposition twice? Have I used the same statement twice? Have I made the same statement twice?

IX

PLATO

The soul is immortal [the argument of
concrete opposites]

PLATO'S ARGUMENT

[Socrates is speaking.] *Suppose we consider the question whether the
souls of men after death are or are not in the world below. There
comes into my mind an ancient doctrine which affirms that they go
from hence into the other world, and returning hither, are born again
from the dead. Now if it be true that the living come from the dead,
then our souls must exist in the other world, for if not, how could they
have been born again? And this would be conclusive, if there were
any real evidence that the living are only born of the dead; but if this
is not so, then other arguments will have to be adduced.*

Very true, replied Cebes.

*Then let us consider the whole question, not in relation to man
only, but in relation to animals generally, and to plants, and to
everything of which there is generation, and the proof will be easier.
Are not all things which have opposites generated out of their opposites? I mean such things as good and evil, just and unjust—and
there are innumerable other opposites which are generated out of*

opposites. And I want to show that in all opposites there is of necessity a similar alternation; I mean to say, for example, that anything which becomes greater must become greater after being less.

True.

And that which becomes less must have been once greater and then have become less.

Yes.

And the weaker is generated from the stronger, and the swifter from the slower.

Very true.

And the worse is from the better, and the more just is from the more unjust.

Of course.

And is this true of all opposites? and are we convinced that all of them are generated out of opposites?

Yes.

And in this universal opposition of all things, are there not also two intermediate processes which are ever going on, from one to the other opposite, and back again; where there is a greater and a less there is also an intermediate process of increase and diminution, and that which grows is said to wax, and that which decays to wane?

Yes, he said.

And there are many other processes, such as division and composition, cooling and heating, which equally involve a passage into and out of one another. And this necessarily holds of all opposites, even though not always expressed in words—they are really generated out of one another, and there is a passing or process from one to the other of them?

Very true, he replied.

Well, and is there not an opposite of life, as sleep is the opposite of waking?

True, he said.

And what is it?

Death, he answered.

And these, if they are opposites, are generated the one from the other, and have their two intermediate processes also?

Of course.

Now, said Socrates, I will analyze one of the two pairs of op-posites which I have mentioned to you, and also its intermediate processes, and you shall analyze the other to me. One of them I term sleep, the other waking. The state of sleep is opposed to the state of waking, and out of sleeping waking is generated, and out of waking, sleeping; and the process of generation is in the one case falling asleep, and in the other waking up. Do you agree?

I entirely agree.

Then, suppose that you analyze life and death to me in the same manner. Is not death opposed to life?

Yes.

And they are generated one from the other?

Yes.

What is generated from the living?

The dead.

And what from the dead?

I can only say in answer—the living.

Then the living, whether things or persons, Cebes, are gene-rated from the dead?

That is clear, he replied.

Then the inference is that our souls exist in the world below?

That is true.

And one of the two processes or generations is visible—for surely the act of dying is visible?

Surely, he said.

What then is to be the result? Shall we exclude the opposite process? and shall we suppose nature to walk on one leg only? Must we not rather assign to death some corresponding process of genera-tion?

Certainly, he replied.

And what is that process?

Return to life.

And return to life, if there be such a thing, is the birth of the dead into the world of the living?

Quite true.

Then here is a new way by which we arrive at the conclusion that the living come from the dead, just as the dead come from the

*living; and this, if true, affords a most certain proof that the souls of
the dead exist in some place out of which they come again.*

*Yes, Socrates, he said; the conclusion seems to flow necessarily
out of our previous admissions.*

[From *Phaedo* by Plato (427?–347 B.C.); translated by Benjamin Jowett.*]

AN ANALYSIS OF PLATO'S ARGUMENT

1. THE BASIC CLAIM

In the *Phaedo* Plato represents Socrates as a man who, on the
day of his death, argues that the true philosopher "is always pursuing
death and dying . . . ." Socrates maintains that the philosopher is a
lover of truth and that truth is to be acquired only by freeing the
soul from the body. Consequently, the question as to whether the
soul exists after death is one of great importance to the philosopher,
and Socrates spends his last hours advancing various arguments in
support of the claim that man's soul is immortal. The argument of
concrete opposites and the more subtle and sophisticated argument
of essential opposites are of particular interest to those who would
get at the heart of the Socratic method.

The argument of concrete opposites is advanced by Socrates in
response to a remark made by Cebes to the effect that men fear that
on the day of death the soul perishes. Conceding that the pursuit of
wisdom would be facilitated were man not distracted by the senses
and bodily desires, Cebes suggests that "it requires a great deal of
argument and many proofs to show that when the man is dead his
soul yet exists, and has any force or intelligence."

Socrates argues that if the living come from the dead, souls
must exist in the world below. The argument for the immortality of
the soul, then, is designed to support the claim that the soul is born
again. Socrates concerns himself with the problem of demonstrating
that the living are born from the dead in order to be justified in con-

*Edition used: Oxford University Press, 1892.

cluding that the souls of men do not perish at the moment of death.

The basic claim of the argument, then, is that *the soul is immortal* in that *the souls of men after death exist in the world below from which they are born again.*

2. THE BASIC ARGUMENT

There is nothing haphazard about the progression of the argument under consideration. Socrates begins by sketching the general features of his problem: if he can demonstrate that the souls of the living come from the dead, he can show that the soul does not perish at the moment of death, for the soul cannot come from the world below if it is not initially there.

The argument is by analogy: just as a man who awakes must have been sleeping, and a man who falls asleep must have been awake, so a man who is born must have been in the world below, and a man who dies must progress from the world of the living to the world of the dead. The summary of the argument will be adequate, then, only if it maintains the analogy.

We summarize the argument, in Socrates' words (as reported by Plato), as follows:

1. ". . . all things which have opposites [are] generated out of their opposites . . . . I mean such things as good and evil, just and unjust . . . I mean to say, for example, that anything which becomes greater must become greater after being less."
2. "And in this universal opposition of all things . . . there [are] also two intermediate processes which are ever going on, from one to the other opposite, and back again . . . ."
3. "The state of sleep is opposed to the state of waking . . . ."
4. ". . . out of sleeping waking is generated, and out of waking, sleeping . . . ."
5. ". . . the process of generation is in the one case falling asleep, and in the other waking up."
6. ". . . death [is] opposed to life . . . ."
7. "And they are generated one from the other . . . ."

8. "Then the living, whether things or persons . . . are generated from the dead . . . ."
9. "Then the inference is that our souls exist in the world below . . . ." " . . . for if not, how could they have been born again?"
10. "And one of the two processes of generation is visible . . . the act of dying . . . ."
11. " . . . we [must] assign to death some corresponding process of generation . . . . Return to life . . . the birth of the dead into the world of the living . . . ."

The conclusion, then, is:

" . . . the souls of the dead exist in some place out of which they come again."

We shall now symbolize the argument and construct a diagram of its logical structure. In the process of symbolization we shall distinguish between premises and intermediate conclusions, and we shall supply missing premises, if any.

Socrates' first premise is a generalization about what he calls "concrete opposites." We shall consider the meaning of this expression by reference to his examples, but we reserve critical comment until the completion of the symbolization of the argument.

$$(x) \ (y) \ [Ox,y \rightarrow (Gx,y \cdot Gy,x)] \tag{1}$$

Read: *For all values of* "x" *and* "y", *if* x *and* y *are concrete opposites, then* x *is generated from* y, *and* y *is generated from* x.

The second premise is also a generalization; the generalization applies to any pair such that one is generated from the other:

$$(x) \ (y) \ [Gx,y \rightarrow (Ez) \ Pz,y\text{-}x] \tag{2}$$

We have devised the symbol "y-x" to suggest the process-relation between terms. The meaning of the symbolic expression is as follows: *For all values of* "x" *and* "y", *if* x *is generated from* y, *then there is a process—call it* "z"—*from* y *to* x.

Premise 3 introduces the first example, which is to serve as the basis of Socrates' analogy:

$$Os,w \tag{3}$$

We are here faced with the problem of deciding whether to interpret premise 3 as a proposition about "states": the "state of sleep" and the "state of waking"—or about *things* (living things) which have these states. Since a state of being is a state of a thing, there is no danger of misinterpreting Plato in deciding to talk about things rather than states, or vice versa. But we must be careful to remember that the concrete opposite of a thing *in a certain state* (say, sleep) is *itself in the opposite state*. Thus, the concrete opposite of a person asleep is *that very same person awake*. We read premise 3 as a generalization, and we choose to read it as a generalization about concrete things which admit of opposite states. A more complicated logical expression would show the distinctions being made here, but we prefer the simpler expression because of its usefulness in making the basic analogy clear. Thus, we read 3: *Sleeping things are the concrete opposites of themselves as awake.* Remember that the relation of being a concrete opposite is *symmetrical*: a sleeping thing is the concrete opposite of itself as awake; a person who is awake is the concrete opposite of himself as sleeping.

Premise 4 is an intermediate conclusion based upon premises 1 and 3:

$$Gw,s \cdot Gs,w \tag{4}$$

The conjunction is reversed to be in accord with the statement being symbolized; but since the order of a conjunction is logically irrelevant, it is apparent that 4 as symbolized represents, as the context suggests, an inference from 1, a generalization about all concrete opposites, and from 3, an assertion to the effect that a sleeping thing is the concrete opposite of itself as awake. Thus, *waking things are generated from themselves as asleep, and sleeping things are generated from themselves as awake.*

Premise 5 introduces some relevant terminology, the naming of the intermediate processes with which Socrates is here concerned:

$$(x) [Px,w\text{-}s \longleftrightarrow \text{"}F\text{"}x] \cdot (x) [Px,s\text{-}w \longleftrightarrow \text{"}A\text{"}x] \tag{5}$$

Read: *The process in which a thing is involved which makes the transition from the state of being awake to that of being asleep is called "falling asleep"; and the process in which a thing is involved which makes the transition from the state of being asleep to that of being awake is called "waking up"—or "awaking."*

The argument now proceeds to an analysis of a presumably analogous pair of concrete opposites: things as dead and the same things as living. Once again the opening generalization is about states or conditions: death and life; but since the argument is about *things*— as both the context and Socrates' own appraisal at the opening of the argument of essential opposites make clear—we are justified in simplifying the symbolization of the argument by regarding the following as a generalization about *things*:

$$Od,l \qquad (6)$$

Read: *Dead things are the concrete opposites of themselves as living.* Thus, we remind ourselves: *Living things are the concrete opposites of themselves as dead.*

Thus, from 1 and 6, the intermediate conclusion 7:

$$Gd,l \cdot Gl,d \qquad (7)$$

Read: *Things as dead are generated from themselves as living, and things as living are generated from themselves as dead.*

From 7, premise 8 is derived:

$$Gl,d \qquad (8)$$

At the outset of his argument Socrates made the following statement: "Now if it be true that the living come from the dead, then our souls must exist in the other world, for if not, how could they have been born again?" Let us, then, introduce the following supporting premises:

$$Gl,d \rightarrow (d) \ (Ex) \ [Sx,d \cdot Bx] \qquad (9.1)$$

Having simplified the generalizations about living and dead things by using the symbols "*l*" and "*d*", we now generalize about the dead by using the form of a universal quantifier for "*d*". (It is as if we wrote: $(x) \ (Ey) \ [Dx \rightarrow (Sy,x \cdot By)]$—that is, for all values of "*x*", if *x* is dead, then there is a *y* such that *y* is the soul of *x*, and *y* [the soul] will be born again.) We read 9.1: *If living things are generated from themselves as dead, then for each dead thing there is something which is the soul of that dead thing, and the soul will be born again.*

The expression "(Ex) (d) Sx,d" would mean that there is one soul for *all* the dead; that is, that the dead share a single soul. But the expression used as the consequent of 9.1 is used to mean, in part, that *each* dead thing has a soul of its own; and we shall assume, but not show symbolically, that no dead thing shares its soul with another. To say that something is the soul "of" a dead thing will mean only that there is a soul which is the soul that formerly was the life bearer of the thing now dead.

$$(x) \ [Bx \rightarrow Wx] \tag{9.2}$$

—*Anything which will be born again is a thing in the world below.*

The conclusion that "our souls exist in the world below"—that is, that *the souls of the dead exist in the world below,*—may now be stated:

$$\therefore \ (d) \ (Ex) \ [Sx,d \cdot Bx \cdot Wx] \tag{9.3}$$

We recall that the argument of concrete opposites was undertaken in the effort to settle the question as to whether "the souls of men after death are or are not in the world below." Since the conclusion has been reached that the living are generated from the dead and that the souls of the dead exist in the world below and are born again, there is no need to go further. But Socrates adds a kind of postscript to his argument, an appeal to experience, by which, one presumes, he seeks to win further support for a conclusion already established on other grounds. He points out that "one of the two processes or generations is visible—for surely the act of dying is visible . . .":

$$(Ex) \ [Px,l\text{-}d \cdot Vx] \cdot (x) \ [Px,l\text{-}d \leftarrow\rightarrow \text{``}D\text{''}x] \tag{10}$$

—*There is a process of generation from life to death, and it is visible; and that process is called "dying."*

Socrates then claims that there is a corresponding process or passage, that from death to life, and it is called the "return to life":

$$(Ex) \ [Px,d\text{-}l] \cdot (x) \ [Px,d\text{-}l \longleftrightarrow \text{"}R\text{"}x] \qquad (11.1)$$

And the "return to life" is "the birth of the dead into the world of the living":

$$(x) \ [\text{"}R\text{"}x \rightarrow (d) \ (Ey) \ (Sy,d \cdot By \cdot Wy] \qquad (11.2)$$

"Then here is a new way by which we arrive at the conclusion that the living come from the dead," Socrates declares, the "new way" being the present appeal to our experience of the process of dying, together with a consideration of the claim (not here symbolized) that nature does not "walk on one leg only . . . ." At the outset of the argument, as we noted in the remark prefacing the introduction of the symbolized statements for proposition 9, Socrates contended that if the living come from the dead, souls exist in the other world. The problem, then, was to show that the living come from the dead. Once again, Socrates has come to the point of concluding that there is a rebirth of souls from the world of the dead. Now we write the conclusion: $(d) \ (Ey) \ [Sy,d \cdot By \cdot Wy]$.

3. CRITICISM OF THE BASIC ARGUMENT

Socrates' argument of concrete opposites includes a general claim about the generation of concrete opposites and two particular examples of such generation. The logical analysis of the argument is facilitated if one so constructs the diagrammatic representation of the argument as to show how the argument by analogy is carried out. Premises 1 and 2 set forth the general scheme; 3, 4 and 5 present the particular case of waking-sleeping things; and the remainder of the argument is devoted to a consideration of the process of generation from life to death and from death to life. Of that remainder, premises 6 through 9.3 form one argument (a logical analogy) and 10 through 11.2 provide an empirical consideration in support of the conclusion.

The argument of concrete opposites, as we have symbolized it, is represented by the following sets of premises and conclusions:

1. $(x)\ (y)\ [Ox,y \rightarrow (Gx,y \cdot Gy,x)]$
2. $(x)\ (y)\ [Gx,y \rightarrow (Ez)\ Pz,y\text{-}x]$
3. Os,w
∴ 4. $Gw,s \cdot Gs,w$
5. $(x)\ [Px,w\text{-}s \longleftrightarrow \text{``}F\text{''}x] \cdot (x)\ [Px,s\text{-}w \longleftrightarrow \text{``}A\text{''}\ x]$
6. Od,l
∴ 7. $Gd,l \cdot Gl,d$
∴ 8. Gl,d
9.1. $Gl,d \rightarrow (d)\ (Ex)\ [Sx,d \cdot Bx]$
9.2. $(x)\ [Bx \rightarrow Wx]$ / ∴ 9.3. $(d)\ (Ex)\ [Sx,d \cdot Bx \cdot Wx]$
10. $(Ex)\ [Px,l\text{-}d \cdot Vx] \cdot (x)\ [Px,l\text{-}d \longleftrightarrow \text{``}D\text{''}x]$
11.1. $(Ex)\ [Px,d\text{-}l] \cdot (x)\ [Px,d\text{-}l \longleftrightarrow \text{``}R\text{''}x]$
11.2. $(x)\ [\text{``}R\text{''}x \rightarrow (d)\ (Ey)\ (Sy,d \cdot By \cdot Wy)]$
   / ∴ $(d)\ (Ey)\ [Sy,d \cdot By \cdot Wy]$

Premise 2 states that whenever one thing is generated from an other (itself in the opposite state), there is a process of generation from that which generates to that which is generated. Thus, we decide to show premises 1 and 2, logically related, by means of the following diagram:

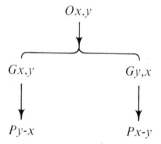

The diagram shows that whenever x and y are concrete opposites there is a generation of x from y and of y from x. When there is a generation of x from y, there is a process of generation from y to x; and when there is a generation of y from x, there is a process of generation from x to y.

Now we introduce the diagram of the first particular case. We simply use "s" and "w" in place of x and y:

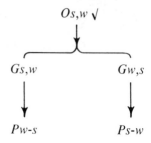

To this point we have a logical analogy, a pattern of relationships which corresponds to that established by the first generalization. The diagram shows that whenever a sleeping thing is the concrete opposite of a waking thing, there is a generation of the sleeping thing from the waking and of the waking from the sleeping. Furthermore, when there is a generation of the sleeping from the waking, there is a process of generation from waking to sleeping; and when there is a generation of the waking from the sleeping, there is a process of generation from the sleeping to the waking. The check mark indicates that Socrates has *asserted* "Os,w"—that sleeping things are the concrete opposites of themselves as awake.

Premise 5 provides names for the generative processes:

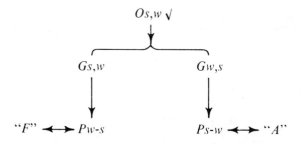

Again building on the general pattern established in premises 1 and 2, Socrates offers an analogical argument concerning living things as concretely opposed to themselves as dead. Just as, in the example concerning sleeping and waking things, Socrates moved from a claim relating terms as concrete opposites to the claim that the opposites generate each other (basing the inference on premises 1 and 2), so, having established living things as the concrete opposites of themselves as dead, Socrates (again by premises 1 and 2) moves to a claim concerning generation, then to a claim concerning the processes of generation, and then to various critical implications leading to the conclusion that there are souls in the world below (the world of the dead) which are born again. We construct a complete logical analogy and diagram the remaining argument:

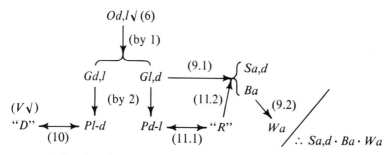

Notice that the diagram indicates that the universal premises 1 and 2 are used to justify the inferences from "Od,l". We use the individual constant "a" to signify the soul of any arbitrarily chosen dead thing. We indicate by checking "V" that Socrates claims that the process from life to death ("dying") is "visible" and has been observed. We simplify the assertion made in 11.2 so as to bring out the train of thought by which Socrates, for the second time, came to the conclusion that for each dead thing there is a soul which will be born again from the world of the dead.

We make no independent effort to include the conclusions 4, 7, 8, and 9.3. If the argument is valid, these conclusions will be traceable from the diagram of the premises.

Let us now determine, by reference to the diagram, whether the argument is valid. We shall then consider the acceptability of the premises.

Given 6, Od,l, it follows, by premise 1, that Gd,l and Gl,d. From the latter, by 9.1, it follows that both Sa,d and Ba are true. If Ba, then Wa. Since Sa,d, Ba, and Wa have been deduced from the premises, the conclusion, which asserts the conjunction of all three propositions, has validly been established.

Also, from Gl,d it follows that $Pd-l$ is true. But $Pd-l$ is equivalent to and hence leads to "R". In turn, "R" leads to the conjunction of Sa,d and Ba. Ba implies Wa. The conclusion, $Sa,d \cdot Ba \cdot Wa$, has validly been established once again.

The reference to the "visibility" of the process from life to death has no useful logical implications here; it was intended, one presumes, to add plausibility to the supposition that there is a corresponding process from death to life; hence, a return to life; hence, a being born again of the soul, with the consequence that the souls of the dead must be in the world below.

We conclude from our study of the logical structure of the argument from concrete opposites that the argument is valid: if the premises are accepted and the analogies conceded, the conclusions must be admitted. We turn, then, to a consideration of the basic premises; we shall not appraise the intermediate conclusions.

PREMISE 1

Is it *true* that "all things which have opposites [are] generated out of their opposites . . ."? We cannot decide whether this claim is true, or whether it makes sense to say that it is true, or even whether what is being stated here is a claim, until we determine the meaning of what is said. But the meaning depends on the use of the language of the expression. We must consider Socrates' (Plato's) use of such critical terms as "opposites" and "generated." To do so, we turn to the text.

Socrates states, "Then let us consider the whole question, not in relation to men only, but in relation to animals generally, and to plants, and to everything of which there is *generation* . . . ." (Italics added.) Here the term "generation" is used with reference to "men" "animals generally," and "plants."

If no further use were made of the term "generation," we would be inclined to regard the term as signifying *the process of producing offspring*. But as examples of "things" which are "opposites *generated* out of their opposites," Socrates mentions "such things as good and evil, just and unjust . . . ." We know from the context (and from an explicit distinction made later in the argument of essential opposites) that by "such things as good and evil" Socrates means, *not* goodness and evil, but good *things* and evil *things*. It also quickly becomes evident that the "opposites" are not two distinct things, but a thing as opposed to itself because of having come to have the opposite of a character it formerly had: "anything which becomes greater must become greater after being less." Thus, a good thing is "generated out of" its opposite; namely, itself as not good, but bad. By now it is apparent that the term "generation" is *not* being used to mean *the process of producing offspring,* for no one would be inclined in the least to say that a good thing which has become bad produced, as its offspring, itself as bad. The expression "succession of opposite states" might very well be used to state what the expression "generation of opposites" means in this Socratic context.

But a question remains as to the meaning of "opposites." The "concrete opposite" of a thing, we have decided, is *itself* as in the "opposite" state of being—but in what sense of the term "opposite"? The pairs "good and evil," "just and unjust" are *opposites* in a sense we may distinguish by using the term "contraries." A person who has been good may become bad; the person as bad is in a state contrary to, diametrically opposed to, that of being good. A state contrary to that of being less is that of being greater; of being weaker, that of being stronger; of being worse, that of being better (all these are Socratic examples). If a state is contrary to another, the other is contrary to it: the relation of contrariety is *symmetrical.*

What about the concrete opposites which figure centrally in the Socratic argument of concrete opposites; namely, the pairs *sleeping* thing and *waking* thing, and *live* thing and *dead* thing? Are these pairs examples of *contraries?* Yes, for to be in a state contrary to, diametrically opposite to, that of being asleep is to be awake; to be in a state contrary to that of being alive is to be dead; and vice versa in each case.

We thus take the claim that "all things which have opposites [are] generated out of their opposites" to mean that anything which is in a state to which there corresponds a *contrary* state has *succeeded* itself as in the contrary state.

Thus, we may now ask: is it *true?* Is it true that all things which have opposites are generated out of their opposites; that is to say, is it true that anything which is in a state to which a contrary state corresponds has succeeded itself as in that contrary state?

We shall consider the question by considering the examples which figure prominently in Socrates' argument; thus, we ask: Are all things which are awake things things that have succeeded themselves as asleep? Let us think about an infant, just born. The infant is born, let us suppose, awake; must it be the case that, prior to being awake, the infant was asleep? The answer seems to be, *not necessarily,* for the infant prior to birth, while yet within the womb, may have been awake.

But it might be argued that the Socratic argument is built around cases of *becoming*. Nothing can *become* awake which has not been sleeping; nothing can *fall* asleep which has not been awake; nothing can *become* dead which has not been alive. Socrates intends his generalization to apply, it might be urged in addition, *not* to cases of the *becoming* (the coming into being) of things, but to cases of *things becoming* opposite to what they were. Thus, even if an infant has always been awake—so that we could not say that the infant, as awake, succeeds itself as asleep—we cannot take the case of the perpetually awake infant as a case of a thing's becoming opposite to what it was. But if we consider an infant who has come to be asleep after having been awake, or awake after having been asleep, it is certainly true that, in such a case, the opposite has been generated out of its opposite. And so, it might be insisted, all opposites which become opposites to what they were succeed themselves as in the opposite state.

Let us give Socrates the benefit of the doubt by supposing that when he said he wanted to consider the question "in relation . . . to everything of which there is generation" he meant to limit his generalization concerning the generation of opposites to those cases only which can be taken to be instances of a thing's becoming, in its state or condition, opposite to what it was.

But now premise 1 is taken to mean: *All concrete opposites are things which have become opposite (contrary) to what they were and shall become opposite to what they are.*

Let us consider the implications of this reading of premise 1 if we attempt to apply premise 1 to the presumed opposites: *living thing* and the (same) *thing dead*. If a body, once living, becomes dead, surely its status as a dead thing is subsequent to, and immediately succeeds, its status as a living thing. But we have no reason to suppose that a living thing is a thing in which life has been generated in the manner described; that is, we have no reason to suppose (and ample reason to deny) that a living body has succeeded itself as dead. Thus we cannot concede that the pair *living thing* and *itself as dead* is a pair of concrete opposites "of which there is generation."

Thus, even if we grant premise 1 because of its stipulated semantical character (its function as a prescribed definition), we need not grant premise 6, namely, that dead things and living things are concrete (and generated) opposites. But if we fail to grant premise 6 we are not committed to accepting the conclusion of the argument.

Our conclusion regarding the acceptability of premise 1, then, is: either premise 1 is *semantically tautological* (simply asserting by definition that all "concrete opposites" are things which were themselves in the contrary state) *or* it is *factual* (in that it asserts that all things which are in a state to which there is a contrary were themselves in that contrary state)—but *if* premise 1 is *stipulatively semantical,* and hence acceptable as a proposal, the question as to whether the pair *living thing* and *itself as dead* is a case of concrete and generated opposites is left open (and we would answer the question negatively); while *if* premise 1 is *factual* in the way indicated, then it is obviously not the case that all opposites are generated out of their opposites (for not all things that are awake were once asleep; not all good things were once bad; not all just things were once unjust; not all living things were once dead). Thus, either premise 1 is *trivial* and does not apply to the critical case, or it is *false*.

PREMISE 2

Is it *true* that "in this universal opposition of all things . . . there [are] also two intermediate processes which are ever going on, from one to the other opposite, and back again . . ."?

If by the "generation of opposites" is meant "the succession of opposite states in things" (so that if a thing, once black, becomes white; or, once asleep, becomes awake; or, once good, becomes bad —we would say that these are cases of the "generation of opposites"), then it seems inaccurate to say that in *every* such case there is a "process from one to the other opposite." Although a thing which is white may, by stages, *progress* (through varying shades of gray) to the state of being black, not every case of the generation of opposites is a case in which there is a *passage* or progression from one state to the other. A person may, perhaps, in some literal sense of the expression, be "half asleep" or "half awake" (depending on which direction he is headed); and he may, in some metaphorical sense of the expression, be "half dead" or "half alive," but in *no* literal sense of the expression can *someone* be "half dead."

The "process" of which Socrates speaks, then, is not a *passage* or a *gradual change*. However, it was to Socrates' advantage to lead his listeners to suppose that all passage from one opposite to the other was a matter of the putting off and taking on of opposite states —so that, later in the argument, it seemed quite in line with the course of the discussion to maintain that there must be a *soul* to serve as the constant bearer of opposite states, a *thing* making the mysterious passage from the world of the dead to the world of the living. But the progression with which we are here involved is a *logical* progression: even if the transition from one state to its opposite is immediate, we *can say* that a thing "passes" from one state to the other—but we must remember that a logical transition is not a journey. We say that the transition is "logical" because if a thing *becomes*, it *must* (as following from the meaning of "becomes") previously *not have been* whatever it is it becomes. The necessity here follows from the meanings of the terms used; it is a *logical* necessity.

We grant, then, that in every case in which a thing becomes the opposite of what it was there has been an "intermediate process" from being in the one state to being in the other; but we regard the process as not necessarily a matter of change by degrees, or biological generation, or natural evolution: the process is merely *logical*. Here, again, the claim is tautological; hence, trivial (relative to Socrates' grand expectation that premises 1 and 2, once granted, would provide a basis for proving the immortality of the soul).

PREMISE 3

Socrates argues that "The state of sleep is opposed to the state of waking . . . ," and we understand him to mean that a sleeping thing is the concrete opposite of itself as awake. We shall proceed by giving premise 1 the interpretation which allows us to regard it as true;

namely, *All things which come to be the opposite (contrary) of what they once were succeed themselves as in the opposite state.* We grant that anything (any *thing*) which becomes awake after having been asleep succeeds itself as asleep; anything which comes to be asleep (which falls asleep) after having been awake succeeds itself as awake. But we are *not* conceding that if a thing which is awake comes to be, in that there is the coming to be of the thing, the thing succeeds itself as in the contrary state.

PREMISE 4

Premise 4 is an intermediate conclusion; its acceptability depends on the acceptability of the preceding premises.

PREMISE 5

Since premise 5 is nothing more than the naming, in a conventional way, of the logical transition (or "processes") from being awake to being asleep (a transition to be called "falling asleep") and of the transition from being asleep to being awake (to be called "waking up"), we have no objection to 5. We shall not say that premise 5 is "true," for the premise is not a claim; it is a terminological suggestion.

PREMISE 6

Socrates claims that "death [is] opposed to life," and we take him to be claiming that, in all cases of a thing's *becoming* its own concrete opposite—that is, *assuming* or *coming* to have the state of being alive or being dead—the thing succeeds itself as in the opposite state. Thus, according to Socrates, any *living* animal or plant which *becomes* dead does so *after having been* alive; and any dead animal or plant which *becomes* alive does so *after having been* dead.

What Socrates *suggests*—although what he *says* may be startling to those who do not get the *logical* point—is *true: if* a thing (animal, vegetable, or whatever) *dies* (becomes dead), it must have been alive; and if a dead thing *returns to life* (becomes once again alive), it must have been dead (or what we call "dead").

But the critical question within the context of this argument for immortality is whether every thing which becomes alive was formerly

dead. It is necessarily true that any thing which becomes the opposite
of what it was succeeds itself as in that opposite state (and on such
an interpretation we can admit the truth of premise 6); no one would
be justified in denying that a thing which returns to life after having
been "dead" succeeds itself as "dead." But what we are wondering
here, since the question is one of immortality (and not of the logical
implications of "become"), is whether every *thing* which becomes
alive was formerly dead. We *could* say that a certain chemical complex, given the final necessary component, has become a *live thing;*
and yet, under the circumstances, we would not be justified in saying
that the thing (the complex) which becomes alive was formerly *dead.*
In such a case the "opposite" is *not* the *contrary* state but the *logical
complement;* namely, *not-alive.*

We are now prepared to consider the following distinguishable
kinds of becoming: (a) the coming-to-be of a thing which did not
previously exist, (b) the change of a thing from one state to its contrary, and (c) the change of a thing from one state (or absence of a
state) to the logical complement of that state. Thus, we distinguish
between (a) the *origin* of a thing, (b) a thing's *becoming the contrary* of what it was, and (c) a thing's *becoming what previously it
was not.* For example, the birth (or beginning to be in the foetal
state) of a *human* being is an instance of generation, or procreation,
which is a matter of *origination;* prior to the beginning-to-be of *this*
human being there was *no* human being to be identified with this one.
That which was formerly *not* alive, or not-alive, was not the *human*
being, but the being (a chemical complex) which became alive; such
a transition from nonlife to life is a case of what we might call the
"generation of complements." A body (person) that dies makes the
transition not only from nondeath to death (generation of complements), but also from life to death (generation of contraries). Similarly, a person who, having died (having been declared dead according to an operational definition), comes to life again makes the
transition from nonlife to life (a process from one state to its logical
complement) and also from death to life (a process from one state
to its logical contrary).

We realize now that not everything which comes to be as a thing which is awake succeeds itself as asleep. It may be that the thing (a human being, for example) *originates,* begins its existence, as a thing which is awake; it need not previously have been sleeping, for it need not previously have been. Even a thing which, not being awake, becomes awake, need not have been sleeping; it may have been neither awake nor sleeping; it may have been a chemical complex that was not alive.

Analogously, we realize that not everything which comes to be as a living thing succeeds itself as dead. It may be that the thing (a human being, for example) *originates,* begins its existence, as a thing which is alive; it need not previously have been dead, for it need not previously have been. Even a thing which, although not alive, becomes alive, need not have been dead; it may have been neither alive nor dead; it may have been a chemical complex that was neither awake nor sleeping, a complex exhibiting none of the vital processes.

Having made these distinctions we grant that "death [is] opposed to life," *provided that* what is meant is that in every case of a *thing's coming to be* dead (dying), that thing must previously have been alive (a state which is the contrary of death), and in every case of a *thing's coming to be* alive, that thing must previously *not have been alive.* It would be odd to say that everything which is not alive is *dead:* my desk is not alive, yet it is not dead. Hence, if we are to grant that death is opposed to life, we must either use the term "death" in an unusual way (as we *sometimes* do, as when we speak of "dead rocks" or "dead sand" or "dead water"), or interpret the generalization in such a manner that the transition from death to life is attributed only to those things which, having been dead, become alive. If we take the latter course, we understand "death is opposed to life" to mean that if any living thing becomes dead, it must have been living; if any dead thing becomes alive, it must have been dead. The question would then remain, in any instance of the origination of life, whether the case on hand was one of (1) the beginning of a thing, or (2) a thing's changing from not being alive (but not necessarily dead) to being alive, or (3) a thing's changing from being dead to being alive. To win his argument Socrates would have to show that the generation of a human life is an instance of the third kind of generation, but he could do so only by begging the question (assuming what he is trying to prove). Thus, premise 6 does nothing to settle the question of immortality or even to contribute to the resolution of the problem, for the premise applies only to cases of a thing's converting to a state contrary to the state it had; the premise does not settle the question as to whether the generation of a human life is a case of a thing's (soul's) converting to a state (life) contrary to the state it had (death). *Of course* (as logical analysis shows), all living things (if any) *that undergo the change from the contrary state of being dead things* are things that are generated from themselves as dead, but the question remains as to whether all living things are in that manner generated. Logical analysis will not settle a question which only empirical inquiry can resolve.

PREMISE 9.1

If the living are generated from themselves as dead, argues Socrates, then there are souls (of the dead) to be born again.

But we are not prepared to agree that *all* living things are generated from themselves as dead. Thus, we are not interested in premise 9.1, for we cannot utilize it in the argument.

In any case, even if we confine our attention to those living things which are the product of a change of a thing from the state of being dead to the contrary state of being alive, we do not need to concede that such a change involves a *soul,* nor that the soul is "born again from the world of the dead." When a person dies and then, through the efforts of physicians, is brought back to life, it may be that not the soul (whatever that is) but the human organism is once again able to act in a manner which is constitutive of life; it may be that what was once vitally functioning ceased, for a time, so to function—and then began again. Why assume that something (the "soul") made a journey to another world and then, hurriedly, returned?

The assumption of the soul as something distinct from the bodily organism which can function and cease to function is entirely gratuitous. No premise prepares the way for the introduction of this entity called "soul"; no definition makes its nature clear; no experience provides evidence in support of a claim as to what it is or whether it is.

PREMISE 9.2

Socrates argues that if the souls of the dead are born again, they must be born *from the world of the dead*. There is no harm in conceding that *if* souls, whatever they are, are born again, then, *if* we call the state of nonlife "death," and being in that state "being in the world of the dead," souls are born again from the world of the dead. But we have *not* conceded that there are souls, nor that it is meaningful to talk about souls (that is, that the term "souls" is meaningful), nor that souls are born again. Hence, we lose nothing and gain nothing by allowing premise 9.2 to stand.

PREMISES 10 and 11.1

Socrates calls the transition from life to death "the act of dying." We have already objected to calling the transition from one state to its contrary a temporal process, and here we object to the use of the expression "act of dying"; for although there is an event at or near the end of a man's life which we call the "act of dying," we are concerned in this argument with the logical transition from the one state to the other, a transition which is itself neither a state, nor a process, nor an act. However, we have no objection to using the word "dying" to talk about the transition from life to death.

Socrates then calls the transition from death to life the "return to life," and he maintains that there is such a transition. In premise 9.1 it was suggested that such a transition is a matter of being born again from the world of the dead. Names do not change facts, but both expressions—"return to life" and "birth from the world of the dead"—suggest a great deal more than the bare logical transition from the state of not being alive to the opposite (complementary) state of being alive. The naming becomes a persuasive device to foster the notion that the generation of the living is a dramatic process involving a mysterious traveler, the soul, which partakes in a neverending cycle of birth and rebirth. We have been able to think of only one kind of instance we would choose to describe as an example of the "return to life," and that was the case of one who, having been declared medically dead, was restored to a state of organic activity constitutive of life. Such a "rebirth" is not literally comparable to the original *birth* of the person, nor does it involve a return from the world of the dead as part of a never-ending journey.

Socrates claims that the process from life to death is visible. It is true that we have seen men, plants, and animals die. Thus, we accept this part of premise 10.

But we are not thereby inclined to suppose (as 11.1 proposes) that there is a corresponding "process of generation" from death to life (except for the kind of case already mentioned: the restoration of a medically dead person). The available empirical evidence suggests that each life is created anew from available chemical material; we say, therefore, that a human being is born, that he finds his origin in the womb, and that his procreation or generation is not an instance of the generation of concrete opposites.

PREMISE 11.2

If there is a return to life, says Socrates, there are souls that are born again from the world of the dead. The discussion pertinent to premise 9.1 applies here as well.

Our examination of the premises of Socrates' argument has led us to conclude that for a number of reasons we cannot regard the conclusion as having been established soundly. If the generalization concerning concrete, generated opposites is meant to apply only to things involved in perpetual change from one state to its contrary, there is no reason to suppose that human beings, as alive, are the concrete, generated opposites of themselves as dead; hence, there is no ground for applying the generalizations given in premises 1 and 2 to human beings. Furthermore, even in the cases (extremely rare) of persons being restored to life (to organic functioning) after being medically dead, we do not recognize the invariant and reciprocal generation of opposites of which Socrates speaks. Finally, the assumption of a "soul" as the bearer of one or the other of opposing states is a wholly gratuitous assumption, and the empirical argument involving reference to the visibility of the process from life to death in no way inclines us to the view that nature "walks on one leg only" in giving rise to new life through the human procreative process.

Socrates undertakes the argument of concrete opposites in the effort to provide "real evidence" that the living come from the dead.

Although there is ample evidence to support the claim that the dead come from the living, and although the appeal is made that nature is uniform and does not "walk on one leg only," there is no way, apparently, of finding direct empirical evidence for the generation of the living from the dead. Socrates thus resorts to an argument by logical analogy.

But surely Socrates was aware of the difference between the empirical and the logical; he could not seriously have supposed that since the word "become"—as used in instances of the sort he advanced—suggests a change of state, a case for immortality can be fashioned logically. Why, then, did he advance the argument of concrete opposites?

Perhaps he meant to suggest that in the class of cases with which he was concerned—cases of "generation"—a clarification of the logical relations uncovered by the analysis of the discourse about generation throws light on nature itself: an interplay of opposites in nature corresponds to the interplay of contraries in our discourse.

But an analysis of language throws light on nature only to the degree that one becomes aware of the way language is used with reference to nature. *If* a living thing were, in Socrates' sense of the term, the "concrete opposite" of itself as dead and, hence, involved in an endless cycle of generation, an analysis of the logical principles involved in discourse about contrary states might call our attention to certain matters about life and death that otherwise we would miss. *But* to make the logical points useful, one has to assume what the argument purports to prove; namely that living things *are* instances of the concrete opposites (contraries) of themselves as dead.

COMMENTS ON THE ANALYSIS OF PLATO'S ARGUMENT

What we regard as Socrates' (Plato's) failure to prove his point by the analogical argument of concrete opposites suggests a useful truth about arguments by analogy: logical analogies cannot reveal anything about nature until nature has revealed enough about itself to justify our discourse about it. Arguments by analogy may be useful as suggesting how diverse things, in some respect similar, may also in other respects be similar; but the final justification for claims about things in nature can come only from observation of the things. The analysis of Plato's argument shows, we believe, that it is futile to seek to find in grammar what only a study of nature can yield.

QUESTIONS FOR DISCUSSION

1. The critic assumes that Plato's argument of concrete opposites is an argument by analogy. Is it possible that Plato meant to base his argument on the universal experience of generation in nature? Is the argument by empirical analogy (involving the reference to the observable process of dying) an argument which makes more credible and meaningful the analogies which Plato constructs?

2. Distinguish between concrete opposites and opposite states.

3. Distinguish between contrary states and logically complementary states.

X

PLATO

THE SOUL IS IMMORTAL [THE ARGUMENT OF ESSENTIAL OPPOSITES]

PLATO'S ARGUMENT

[Phaedo, the narrator of the dialogue to Echecrates of Phlius, reports Socrates as making the following comment.] . . . *I shall have to go back to those familiar words which are in the mouth of every one, and first of all assume that there is an absolute beauty and goodness and greatness, and the like; grant me this, and I hope to be able to show you the nature of the cause, and to prove the immortality of the soul.*

Cebes said: You may proceed at once with the proof, for I grant you this.

Well, he said, then I should like to know whether you agree with me in the next step; for I cannot help thinking, if there be anything beautiful other than absolute beauty should there be such, that it can be beautiful only in so far as it partakes of absolute beauty—and I should say the same of everything. Do you agree in this notion of the cause?

Yes, he said, I agree.

He proceeded: I know nothing and can understand nothing of any other of those wise causes which are alleged; and if a person says to me that the bloom of colour, or form, or any such thing is a source of beauty, I leave all that, which is only confusing to me, and simply and singly, and perhaps foolishly, hold and am assured in my own mind that nothing makes a thing beautiful but the presence and participation of beauty in whatever way or manner obtained; for as to the manner I am uncertain, but I stoutly contend that by beauty all beautiful things become beautiful. This appears to me to be the safest answer which I can give, either to myself or to another, and to this I cling, in the persuasion that this principle will never be overthrown, and that to myself or to any one who asks the question, I may safely reply, That by beauty beautiful things become beautiful. Do you not agree with me?

I do.

And that by greatness only good things become great and greater greater, and by smallness the less become less?

True.

Then if a person were to remark that A is taller by a head than B, and B less by a head than A, you would refuse to admit his statement, and would stoutly contend that what you mean is only that the greater is greater by, and by reason of, greatness, and the less is less only by, and by reason of, smallness; and thus you would avoid the danger of saying that the greater is greater and the less less by the measure of the head, which is the same in both, and would also avoid the monstrous absurdity of supposing that the greater man is greater by reason of the head, which is small. You would be afraid to draw such an inference, would you not?

Indeed, I should, said Cebes, laughing.

In like manner you would be afraid to say that ten exceeded eight by, and by reason of, two; but would say by, and by reason of, number; or would you say that two cubits exceed one cubit not by a half, but by magnitude?—for there is the same liability to error in all these cases.

Very true, he said.

Again, would you not be cautious of affirming that the addition of one to one, or the division of one, is the cause of two? And you would loudly asseverate that you know of no way in which anything comes into existence except by participation in its own proper essence, and consequently, as far as you know, the only cause of two is the participation in duality—this is the way to make two, and the participation in one is the way to make one. You would say: I will let alone puzzles of division and addition— wiser heads than mine may answer them; inexperienced as I am, and ready to start, as the proverb says, at my own shadow, I cannot afford to give up the sure ground of a principle. And if any one assails you there, you would not mind him, or answer him, until you had seen whether the consequences which follow agree with one another or not, and when you are further required to give an explanation of this principle, you would go on to assume a higher principle, and a higher, until you found a resting-place in the best of the higher; but you would not confuse the principle and the consequences in your reasoning, like the Eristics—at least if you wanted to discover real existence. Not that this confusion signifies to them, who never care or think about the matter at all, for they have the wit to be well pleased with themselves however great may be the turmoil of their ideas. But you, if you are a philosopher, will certainly do as I say.

What you say is most true, said Simmias and Cebes, both speaking at once.

Ech. *Yes, Phaedo; and I do not wonder at their assenting. Any one who has the least sense will acknowledge the wonderful clearness of Socrates' reasoning.*

Phaed. *Certainly, Echecrates; and such was the feeling of the whole company at the time.*

Ech. *Yes, and equally of ourselves, who were not of the company, and are now listening to your recital. But what followed?*

Phaed. *After all this had been admitted, and they had agreed that ideas exist, and that other things participate in them and derive their names from them, Socrates, if I remember rightly, said:—*

This is your way of speaking; and yet when you say that

Simmias is greater than Socrates and less than Phaedo, do you not predicate of Simmias both greatness and smallness?

Yes, I do.

But still you allow that Simmias does not really exceed Socrates, as the words may seem to imply, because he is Simmias, but by reason of the size which he has; just as Simmias does not exceed Socrates because he is Simmias, any more than because Socrates is Socrates, but because he has smallness when compared with the greatness of Simmias?

True.

And if Phaedo exceeds him in size, this is not because Phaedo is Phaedo, but because Phaedo has greatness relatively to Simmias, who is comparatively smaller?

That is true.

And therefore Simmias is said to be great, and is also said to be small, because he is in a mean between them, exceeding the smallness of the one by his greatness, and allowing the greatness of the other to exceed his smallness. He added, laughing, I am speaking like a book, but I believe that what I am saying is true.

Simmias assented.

I speak as I do because I want you to agree with me in thinking, not only that absolute greatness will never be great and also small, but that greatness in us or in the concrete will never admit the small or admit of being exceeded: instead of this, one of two things will happen, either the greater will fly or retire before the opposite, which is the less, or at the approach of the less has already ceased to exist; but will not, if allowing or admitting of smallness, be changed by that; even as I, having received and admitted smallness when compared with Simmias, remain just as I was, and am the same small person. And as the idea of greatness cannot condescend ever to be or become small, in like manner the smallness in us cannot be or become great; nor can any other opposite which remains the same ever be or become its own opposite, but either passes away or perishes in the change.

That, replied Cebes, is quite my notion.

Hereupon one of the company, though I do not exactly remember which of them, said: In heaven's name, is not this the direct contrary of what was admitted before—that out of the greater came the less and out of the less the greater, and that opposites were simply generated from opposites; but now this principle seems to be utterly denied.

Socrates inclined his head to the speaker and listened. I like your courage, he said, in reminding us of this. But you do not observe that there is a difference in the two cases. For then we were speaking of opposites in the concrete, and now of the essential opposite which, as is affirmed, neither in us nor in nature can ever be at variance with itself: then, my friend, we were speaking of things in which opposites are inherent and which are called after them, but now about the opposites which are inherent in them and which give their name to them; and these essential opposites will never, as we maintain, admit of generation into or out of one another. At the same time, turning to Cebes, he said: Are you at all disconcerted, Cebes, at our friend's objection?

No, I do not feel so, said Cebes; and yet I cannot deny that I am often disturbed by objections.

Then we are agreed after all, said Socrates, that the opposite will never in any case be opposed to itself?

To that we are quite agreed, he replied.

Yet once more let me ask you to consider the question from another point of view, and see whether you agree with me:—There is a thing which you term heat, and another thing which you term cold?

Certainly.

But are they the same as fire and snow?

Most assuredly not.

Heat is a thing different from fire, and cold is not the same with snow?

Yes.

And yet you will surely admit, that when snow, as was before said, is under the influence of heat, they will not remain snow and heat; but at the advance of the heat, the snow will either retire or perish?

Very true, he replied.

And the fire too at the advance of the cold will either retire

*or perish; and when the fire is under the influence of the cold, they
will not remain as before, fire and cold.*

That is true, he said.

*And in some cases the name of the idea is not only attached
to the idea in an eternal connection, but anything else which, not
being the idea, exists only in the form of the idea, may also lay
claim to it. I will try to make this clearer by an example:—The odd
number is always called by the name of odd?*

Very true.

*But is this the only thing which is called odd? Are there not
other things which have their own name, and yet are called odd,
because, although not the same as oddness, they are never without
oddness?—that is what I mean to ask—whether numbers such as
the number three are not of the class of odd. And there are many
other examples: would you not say, for example, that three may
be called by its proper name, and also be called odd, which is not
the same with three? and this may be said not only of three but also
of five, and of every alternate number—each of them without being
oddness is odd; and in the same way two and four, and the other
series of alternate numbers, has every number even, without being
evenness. Do you agree?*

Of course.

*Then now mark the point at which I am aiming: not only do
essential opposites exclude one another, but also concrete things,
which, although not in themselves opposed, contain opposites;
these, I say, likewise reject the idea which is opposed to that
which is contained in them, and when it approaches them they
either perish or withdraw. For example; Will not the number three
endure annihilation or anything sooner than be converted into an
even number, while remaining three?*

Very true, said Cebes.

*And yet, he said, the number two is certainly not opposed to
the number three?*

It is not.

*Then not only do opposite ideas repel the advance of one
another, but also there are other natures which repel the approach
of opposites.*

Very true, he said.

Suppose, he said, that we endeavor, if possible, to determine what these are.

By all means.

Are they not, Cebes, such as compel the things of which they have possession, not only to take their own form, but also the form of some opposite?

What do you mean?

I mean, as I was just now saying, and as I am sure that you know, that those things which are possessed by the number three must not only be three in number, but must also be odd.

Quite true.

And on this oddness, of which the number three has the impress, the opposite idea will never intrude?

No.

And this impress was given by the odd principle?

Yes.

And to the odd is opposed the even?

True.

Then the idea of the even number will never arrive at three?

No.

Then three has no part in the even?

None.

Then the triad or number three is uneven?

Very true.

To return then to my distinction of natures which are not opposed, and yet do not admit opposites—as, in the instance given, three, although not opposed to the even, does not any the more admit of the even, but always brings the opposite into play on the other side; or as two does not receive the odd, or fire the cold—from these examples (and there are many more of them) perhaps you may be able to arrive at the general conclusion, that not only opposites will not receive opposites, but also that nothing which brings the opposite will admit the opposite of that which it brings, in that to which it is brought. And here let me recapitulate—for there is no harm in repetition. The number five will not admit the nature of the even, any more than ten, which is the double of five, will admit the nature of the odd. The double has another opposite, and is not strictly opposed to the odd, but nevertheless rejects the odd altogether. Nor again will parts in the ratio 3:2, nor any fraction in which there is a half, nor again in which there is a third, admit the notion of the whole, although they are not opposed to the whole: You will agree?

Yes, he said, I entirely agree and go along with you in that.

And now, he said, let us begin again; and do not you answer my question in the words in which I ask it: let me have not the old safe answer of which I spoke at first, but another equally safe, of which the truth will be inferred by you from what has been just said. I mean that if any one asks you 'what that is, of which the inherence makes the body hot,' you will reply not heat (this is what I call the safe and stupid answer), but fire, a far superior answer, which we are now in a condition to give. Or if any one asks you 'why a body is diseased,' you will not say from disease, but from fever; and instead of saying that oddness is the cause of odd numbers, you will say that the monad is the cause of them: and so of things in general, as I dare say that you will understand sufficiently without my adducing any further examples.

Yes, he said, I quite understand you.

Tell me, then, what is that of which the inherence will render the body alive?

The soul, he replied.

And is this always the case?

Yes, he said, of course.

Then whatever the soul possesses, to that she comes bearing life?

Yes, certainly.

And is there any opposite to life?

There is, he said.

And what is that?

Death.

Then the soul, as has been acknowledged, will never receive the opposite of what she brings.

Impossible, replied Cebes.

And now, he said, what did we just now call that principle

which repels the even?
  The odd.
  And that principle which repels the musical or the just?
  The unmusical, he said, and the unjust.
  And what do we call that principle which does not admit of
death?
  The immortal, he said.
  And does the soul admit of death?
  No.
  Then the soul is immortal?
  Yes, he said.
  And may we say that this has been proven?
  Yes, abundantly proven, Socrates, he replied.

  [From *Phaedo* by Plato (427?–347 B.C.); translated by
  Benjamin Jowett.*]

AN ANALYSIS OF PLATO'S ARGUMENT

1. THE BASIC CLAIM

  Before beginning his argument Socrates stated to Cebes, ". . .
I hope to be able to show you the nature of the cause, and to
prove the immortality of the soul." The remark was made in the
context of a discussion concerning "the causes of existence."
Socrates suggested a "new method" for getting at the "cause" of
generation and corruption, a method that would yield results superior to those attained through the investigation of nature. The
method, as described by Socrates, is as follows: ". . . I first assumed
some principle which I judged to be the strongest, and then I
affirmed as true whatever seemed to agree with this, whether
relating to the cause or to anything else; and that which disagreed
I regarded as untrue." The argument which follows, the argument
of essential opposites, is offered as a proof of the immortality of
the soul, a proof made possible, according to Socrates, by the

  Edition used: Oxford University Press, 1892.

new method of seeking first principles and their logical implications. We may take as the conclusion of the argument the simple proposition "The soul is immortal."

2. THE BASIC ARGUMENT

We abstract from the text those passages which present what we consider to be the basic premises of Plato's argument of essential opposites:

1. ". . . first of all assume that there is an absolute beauty and goodness and greatness, and the like . . . ."
2. ". . . [nothing] comes into existence except by participation in its own proper essence . . . ." ". . . . ideas exist, and . . . other things participate in them and derive their names from them . . . ."
3. ". . . [no] opposite which remains the same [can] ever be or become its own opposite, but either passes away or perishes in the change."
4. ". . . not only do essential opposites exclude one another, but also concrete things, which, although not in themselves opposed, contain opposites; these, I say, likewise reject the idea which is opposed to that which is contained in them, and when it approaches them they either perish or withdraw."
5. ". . . nothing which brings the opposite will admit the opposite of that which it brings . . . ."
6. ". . . whatever the soul possesses, to that she comes bearing life . . . ."
7. "[Death is] opposite to life . . . ."
8. "[The immortal is] that principle which does not admit of death . . . ."
Conclusion: "Then the soul is immortal . . . ."

Socrates begins his argument by asking that all present assume "that there is an absolute beauty and goodness and greatness, and the like . . . ." Later in the argument a term is used which has become the conventional name for such an entity as "absolute beauty"; namely, the term "Idea" (we shall avoid confusion by capitalizing the word). An alternative name for the Idea of something is the term "essence," as we find in what we have called premise 2: ". . . [nothing] comes into existence except by participation in its own proper essence . . . ," and "ideas exist, and . . . other things participate in them and derive their names from them . . . ."

The Ideas or essences are definitive features or characteristics which are common to things of the same kind. Thus, absolute beauty is the Idea *beauty* considered in abstraction from beautiful things, all of which are said to share the essence or Idea called "beauty." It is obvious that the Socratic use of the Greek term ιδεα, usually translated "Idea," is quite different from that use of the term illustrated by the sentence "I had a brilliant idea yesterday." Philosophers using English as the language of their art have tended to use the term "universal" in much the same way that Socrates used the term "Idea" (that is to say, its Greek equivalent).

We shall not prejudice the critical consideration of the Platonic argument of essential opposites by claiming at the outset that the Platonic theory of Ideas makes no difference to the meaning or structure of the argument; for even if it is true that the theory makes no difference to the argument, we can be justified in saying so only if we understand the theory and also the meaning and structure of the argument. Let us begin, then, by setting forth Plato's theory of Ideas.

In Book X of the *Republic,* Socrates, preparing the way for the rejection of imitative poetry from the ideal republic, introduces his theory of Ideas; he begins by asking what imitation is:

Can you tell me what imitation is? for I really do not know. A likely thing, then, that I should know.

Why not? for the duller eye may often see a thing sooner than the keener.

Very true, he said; but in your presence, even if I had any faint notion, I could not muster courage to utter it. Will you enquire yourself?

Well then, shall we begin the enquiry in our usual manner: Whenever a number of individuals have a common name, we

*assume them to have also a corresponding idea or form:—do you
understand me?*

I do.

*Let us take any common instance; there are beds and tables
in the world—plenty of them, are there not?*

Yes.

*But there are only two ideas or forms of them—one the idea
of a bed, the other of a table.*

True.

*And the maker of either of them makes a bed or he makes a
table for our use, in accordance with the idea—that is our way of
speaking in this and similar instances—but no artificer makes the
ideas themselves: how could he?*

Impossible.

*   *   *   *

*God, whether from choice or from necessity, made one bed
in nature and one only; two or more such ideal beds neither ever
have been nor ever will be made by God.*

Why is that?

*Because even if He had made but two, a third would still
appear behind them which both of them would have for their
idea, and that would be the ideal bed and not the two others.*

Very true, he said.

*God knew this, and He desired to be the real maker of a real
bed, not a particular maker of a particular bed, and therefore He
created a bed which is essentially and by nature one only.*

So we believe.

Other passages, from the *Timaeus*, further set forth Plato's
conception of Ideas (forms, essences) as alone having real being:

[Timaeus is speaking.] . . . *What is that which always is and
has no becoming; and what is that which is always becoming and
never is? That which is apprehended by intelligence and reason is
always in the same state; but that which is conceived by opinion
with the help of sensation and without reason, is always in a process of becoming and perishing and never really is. Now everything
that becomes or is created must of necessity be created by some*

cause, for without a cause nothing can be created. The work of the creator, whenever he looks to the unchangeable and fashions the form and nature of his work after an unchangeable pattern, must necessarily be made fair and perfect; but when he looks to the created only, and uses a created pattern, it is not fair or perfect. Was the heaven then or the world . . . always in existence and without beginning? or created, and had it a beginning? Created, I reply, being visible and tangible and having a body, and therefore sensible; and all sensible things are apprehended by opinion and sense and are in a process of creation and created. . . . the world has been framed in the likeness of that which is apprehended by reason and mind and is unchangeable, and must therefore of necessity, if this is admitted, be a copy of something. Now it is all-important that the beginning of everything should be according to nature. And in speaking of the copy and the original we may assume that words are akin to the matter which they describe; when they relate to the lasting and permanent and intelligible, they ought to be lasting and unalterable, and, as far as their nature allows, irrefutable and immovable—nothing less. But when they express only the copy or likeness and not the eternal things themselves, they need only be likely and analogous to the real words. As being is to becoming, so is truth to belief. . . .

* * * *

Now the nature of the ideal being was everlasting, but to bestow this attribute in its fulness upon a creature was impossible. Wherefore he [the creator] resolved to have a moving image of eternity, and when he set in order the heaven, he made this image eternal but moving according to number, while eternity itself rests in unity; and this image we call time.

* * * *

. . . And is all that which we call an intelligible essence nothing at all, and only a name? Here is a question which we must not leave unexamined or undetermined, nor must we affirm too confidently that there can be no decision . . . .
Thus I state my view:—If mind and true opinion are two

*distinct classes, then I say that there certainly are these self-
existent ideas unperceived by sense, and apprehended only by the
mind; if, however, as some say, true opinion differs in no respect
from mind, then everything that we perceive through the body is
to be regarded as most real and certain. But we must affirm them
to be distinct, for they have a distinct origin and are of a different
nature; the one is implanted in us by instruction, the other by
persuasion; the one is always accompanied by true reason, the
other is without reason; the one cannot be overcome by persuasion,
but the other can: and lastly, every man may be said to share in
true opinion, but mind is the attribute of the gods and of very few
men. Wherefore also we must acknowledge that there is one kind
of being which is always the same, uncreated and indestructible,
never receiving anything into itself from without, nor itself going
out to any other, but invisible and imperceptible by any sense, and
of which the contemplation is granted to intelligence only. . . .*

We shall not begin our study of Plato's argument by quarrel-
ing about his theory of Ideas. If and when we discover that an
adequate appraisal of the argument of essential opposites entails
acceptance or rejection of the theory of Ideas, we shall pass
judgment at that time. But for the present, in the attempt to
summarize the basic argument, it is enough to realize that Plato
assumes that *there are Ideas* (or essences, or universals, or properties, or characteristics), and that things come into being "by
participation" in the Ideas. Plato, then, assumes that there are
Ideas, which may be the essences of things; and he claims that
nothing can be of a certain kind without having as its property
the Idea which makes it of that kind.

For example: There is the Idea beauty; things become beautiful by acquiring (participating in) the Idea called "beauty";
anything participating in the Idea can be described by a term
derived from the name of the Idea: hence, the thing can be said
to be "beautiful."

Since Plato's argument involves references to relationships between properties (Ideas) and their opposites, he begins with the
claim that there are Ideas; later on he argues, by example, that

there are Ideas which have essential opposites (themselves Ideas).
It is enough for our purposes if we begin by showing, as part of a
logical diagram, that Plato (Socrates) claims that there are essential opposites (Ideas which have Ideas as opposites):

Oa,b

This expression, which is to function as part of the logical diagram
of Plato's argument of essential opposites, is to be understood to
mean that *there is at least one entity (call it "a") such that it is
an Idea essentially opposite to another Idea (call it "b").*

(We shall now proceed to build the logical diagram *without*
first of all stating the premises in the conventional quantified form.
In this way the logical expression of the argument is simplified,
for the diagram *relates* the parts of the argument to one another
and *shows* what parentheses, brackets, and braces can only awk-
wardly indicate.)

We shall now devise a diagram for premise 3, for 3 is a generalization which relates to the essential opposites mentioned in
premise 1. Perhaps it would be wise to show that we (like Plato)
are using the predicate "essential opposite" in such a way that if
one Idea is the essential opposite of another, the other is the essential opposite of the first. Thus, we write:

Ox,y

Oy,x

Plato states, through Socrates, that no essential opposite can
"ever be or become its own opposite" (premise 3), and then in 4
he says that "essential opposites exclude one another" and "reject
the idea which is opposed. . . ." We shall use the predicate symbol
"*R*", suggested by the term "reject," in such a way as to mean by
"Rx,y" that x is incompatible with y, that it cannot be or become
y, and that it rejects y.

We must also show that any essential opposite, by virtue of
rejecting its opposite, either "passes away" (we shall use "*W*",

suggested by the "withdraws" of premise 4) or "perishes" (we shall use "*D*", suggested by "dies," reserving "*P*" for the relationship of "participation" which obtains between a thing and the Idea which constitutes its essence) if its own opposite "approaches" (*A*):

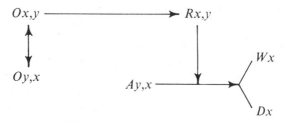

To show premise 1, we need only place the constant symbols "*a*" and "*b*" above the variable symbols "*x*" and "*y*" on the diagram:

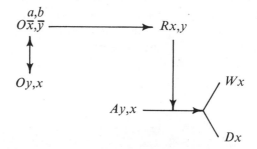

Wherever "*x*" appears on the diagram we may now understand "*a*" as a value of the variable, and wherever "*y*" appears we may understand "*b*" as a value of the variable. (For example, *a* rejects *b*, and thus if *b* approaches *a*, *a* either withdraws or perishes.)

"Not only do essential opposites exclude one another," says premise 4, "but also concrete things . . . likewise reject the idea which is opposed to that which is contained in them, and when it approaches them they either perish or withdraw."

Thus, we show that for all values of x, if x is a concrete thing, then there is an Idea (call it c) in which x participates:

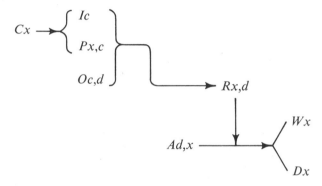

$$Cx \longrightarrow \begin{cases} Ic \\ Px,c \end{cases}$$

The diagram can serve to express premise 2: ". . . [nothing] comes into existence except by participation in its own proper essence . . . ," and prepares us for premise 4:

Premise 4, as diagrammed, shows that *if anything is a concrete thing, there is an Idea, "c", such that the thing participates in c. If, in addition, c is the essential opposite of an Idea we call "d," then the concrete thing rejects d, thereby entailing that if d approaches the thing, the thing either withdraws or perishes.*

(We notice the logical similarity between the diagrams for premises 1 and 3 and the diagrams for premises 2 and 4. The former diagrams show that an essential opposite rejects its opposite; the latter show that a concrete thing rejects the essential opposite of the Idea in which the concrete thing participates.)

Premise 5 is similar to 4, the difference being that 4 is about concrete things which "contain" Ideas—that is, which participate in Ideas—while 5 is about things which "bring" or "bear" Ideas, in some undefined sense of those terms. To show the structure of the claim that "nothing which brings the opposite will admit the opposite of that which it brings," we devise:

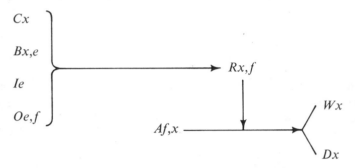

That is, *for all values of "x," if* x *is a concrete thing and there is an Idea (call it "e") which it bears, and* e *is the essential opposite of* f, *then* x *(the concrete thing which bears e) rejects* f, *and thus if* f *approaches* x, x *either withdraws or perishes.*

Premise 6 tells us that "whatever the soul possesses, to that she comes bearing life." What is pertinent here is that the soul (that is, any soul) is the life bearer. Let us treat "the soul" as a value of *"x"* in the diagram of premise 5; for in speaking of the soul, whatever else it may be, we are speaking of *that which* (according to Plato) *bears life,* and thus we are not speaking of an Idea but of a "concrete thing" which has a specific function essential to its status as the soul.

Premise 7 states that death is the essential opposite of life, and thus (if we use *"m"* as the symbol for the Idea "death") we may substitute *"l"* (for the Idea "life") for *"e"* (in the diagram for premise 5) and *"m"* for the essential opposite symbolized by *"f"*. (The diagram may be found at the top of the facing page.) Read, *there is a value "s" for the variable "x" [used in the diagram for premise 5], and there are individual values for the constant symbols "e" and "f"—so that since the soul is the bearer of life (an Idea which has as its essential opposite death), the soul rejects death; and when death approaches, the soul either withdraws or perishes.*

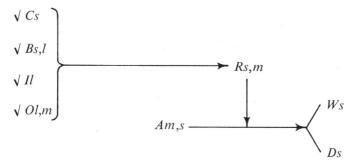

Premise 8, "[The immortal is] that principle which does not admit of death . . . ," leads us to draw an arrow from *"Rs,m"* to the negation of *"Ds"*; for if the soul rejects death (in that it does not admit death), the soul is immortal (which we take to be the negation of the proposition that the soul perishes):

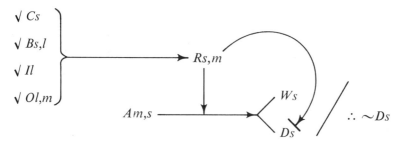

The conclusion, ". . . the soul is immortal . . . ," is the negation of *"Ds,"* as shown.

3. CRITICISM OF THE BASIC ARGUMENT

If we are to begin our critical appraisal of the argument of essential opposites by considering the validity of the argument, we must first of all decide whether Socrates meant his generalizations about *essential opposites,* about *concrete things having opposites,* and about *concrete things bearing opposites* to be logically related in such a way that from the first generalization the latter two generalizations follow. Did Socrates (Plato) anywhere claim that *if* essential opposites reject each other, *then* it follows logically that concrete things reject the Idea opposite to the Idea in which they participate? Apparently not, for he argues, not that *since* the one, then the other, but that *"not only* do essential opposites exclude one another, *but also* concrete things . . ." (italics added), thereby suggesting that the second generalization, although compatible with the first, is *not* advanced as logically entailed by the first.

Nevertheless, although Socrates does not deduce the second generalization (about concrete things which *have* opposites) from the first (about essential opposites), there is a logical attractiveness in claiming that *since* essential opposites reject each other, *things* participating in Ideas which have opposites reject the opposites of the Ideas they have. On what does this "logical" attractiveness depend?

The answer, it appears, is that an implicit linguistic suggestion is made to which we are inclined to give assent. If essential opposites reject each other ("exclude one another"), *why not say* that a thing which *participates* in an Idea (essence) opposed to another Idea *also* (like the Idea which it has) "rejects" the opposing Idea? *Why not say* that a thing which *bears* an Idea to which another Idea is opposed *also* (like the Idea which it bears) "rejects" the opposing Idea? The transition, which is agreeable, is *pragmatical* (in our special sense of that term) in that it depends upon agreement as to the *use of the term* "rejects."

We are inclined to agree with the transitions from generalization to generalization because in each case the rejection or exclusion claim is based upon the logical fact of the incompatibility of essential opposites. Essential opposites *do* exclude each other in that they are contrary characters or states of being. Consequently, if a concrete thing has, as its character, an Idea which has an essential opposite, then, so long as the thing continues to have that character it cannot have the opposite character; the concrete thing may be said to "reject" the opposite character in that the thing has a character which, as an essential opposite, rejects its own opposite. Analogously, a thing which "bears" an Idea which has an essential opposite may be said to "reject" the Idea opposite to the Idea which it bears in that the Idea which it bears is an essential opposite which rejects its own opposite.

Once the pragmatical concession is made—so that there is no longer any question about the propriety of the transitions from generalization to generalization—logical appraisal may be confined to the climactic phase of the argument as presented in premises 5, 6, 7, and 8, and the conclusion. We turn our attention, then, to the last diagram (p. 279).

The check marks indicate that Socrates has asserted that the soul bears life, that life is an Idea, and that life is the essential opposite of death. He has already won the concession that anything which bears an essential opposite rejects the opposite of the Idea it bears. Therefore he is justified in asserting *"Rs,m"*; namely, that the soul rejects death. But if the soul rejects death, then (as the arrow from *"Rs,m"* indicates) one is justified in asserting the negation of *"Ds"*; and the negation of the proposition that the soul perishes may be stated affirmatively by saying that the soul is immortal. The logical argument is unassailable; if we grant the truth of the premises, we cannot consistently deny the conclusion.

One further comment on the logical character of the argument is relevant. We recall that Socrates introduced the argument of *concrete* opposites by saying, "Suppose we consider the question whether the souls of men after death are or are not in the world below." The present argument has something to say on this matter, for if *"Rs,m"* is true, then *"Am,s"* (death approaches the soul) implies either *"Ws"* (the soul withdraws) or *"Ds"* (the soul perishes). But *"Rs,m"* implies the *negation* of *"Ds"*; consequently, *"Am,s"* implies *"Ws"*: if death approaches the soul—that is, if there is any essential change—it cannot be the soul which perishes; *the soul withdraws*—presumably, to another world.

Let us now consider the acceptability of the premises. The logical form of the argument is a function of the meanings of the premises *as interpreted in a certain way;* and we are to remain alert to the possibility that our initial understanding of Plato's use of terms may need correction and that on the basis of that correction a new logical analysis may be advisable.

PREMISE 1

Shall we assume that "there is an absolute beauty and goodness and greatness, and the like"? What is "absolute" beauty? Socrates' claim that "nothing makes a thing beautiful but the presence and participation of beauty in *whatever way or manner obtained*" (italics added) supports our interpretation to the effect that *whatever* metaphysical convictions Plato may have had about the independent existence (or subsistence) of essences, he meant by "absolute" beauty to designate *beauty* itself, the property called "beauty," considered in abstraction from beautiful things, which are said to "partake" of beauty or to "participate in" beauty. Thus, there is no need for us to agree with the Platonic theory that Ideas are independently existing prototypes; we can accept premise 1 as amounting to an invitation to turn our attention to the *properties* of things, in contrast to the previous argument in which our attention was called to *things* having properties.

PREMISE 2

Having agreed to consider relationships among properties of things, we are inclined to agree that "ideas exist, and . . . other things participate in them and derive their names from them." We relate this claim to the grammatical convention which involves using adjectives to talk about the properties of things (so that by the "property of a thing" we mean whatever it is we talk about in using an adjective to describe a thing); the word "Ideas" is here used to talk about whatever it is we denote when we use nouns as the names of properties. No metaphysical concession (as to essences in another world!) is made here, and none need be made. (If an apologist for Plato insisted upon such a concession on the ground that it is the toughness and recalcitrance of independently subsisting eternal essences that accounts for the "essential opposition" to which Plato's argument alludes, we would reject premises 1 and 2 and, thus, the argument. But in our opinion such an apologist would fail to do justice to Plato's argument, which has a logical appeal that is quite independent of any metaphysical development of the basic claims.)

We do wonder, however, about the phrase "its own proper essence." We agree that for a thing to come into being—that is, for it to come to be that there is a thing of a certain sort—it must come to be that an "Idea," that is, a characteristic, is the characteristic of something. The Idea or "essence" is the thing's "own proper essence" only in the sense that we may choose to understand the thing as identifiable by the property it has. For example, if for something to be what *we would call* a "blackboard" it must be black—so that if a board were green it would not be a blackboard—then, relative to our linguistic practice, the Idea called "blackness" would be part of the blackboard's "own proper essence." But if to concede that there are Ideas which constitute the proper essences of things is to concede that essences are given to things, that the nature of all things is determined before their existence by some power that assigns defining properties, and that all change (or generation) is to be accounted for in terms of the shuffling about of essences capable of existing on their own (so that they "approach," "reject," "withdraw," "exclude one another," and so forth, as if they were human beings), then we *cannot* concede that there are Ideas which are the proper essences of things.

But once again we appeal to the basic simplicity of Plato's argument, which rests, we are convinced, on nothing more esoteric than the claim, grounded in our grammar, that if a thing has a certain property, it cannot, while having that property, have the opposite property as well. If something is alive it cannot, while alive, also be dead; if a number is odd it cannot, while correctly identifiable as an "odd" number, also be even.

PREMISE 3

We agree that no essential opposite can ever be or become its own opposite. Our concession is based upon the consideration given above, for the strength of Plato's claim is drawn from the *principle of contradiction: the conjunction of a proposition and its negation is a false proposition*. If something is a property which has an essential opposite, then it cannot be or become its own opposite; for if it were its opposite, it would not be itself, and it cannot both be and not be itself. This statement is not a fundamental law of nature; the principle of contradiction is a *logical tautology:* it is true because the conventions of our language make it true.

But now let us consider the claim that if there is change, the essential opposite which is displaced "either passes away or perishes in the change." There cannot be change *in* an essential opposite; no property which has an opposite can be anything other than itself. But a change is possible *in a thing* which has a property to which another property is essentially opposite. Thus, a room which is cold can become warm; there is a change from the state of being cold to a state essentially opposite, the state of being warm. *Coldness,* the property of being cold, does not change (no opposite can ever be or become its own opposite), but the room (temperature) changes. The problem now is: What happens to the coldness of a room when there is a change and the room becomes warm? Plato says (through Socrates) that the essential opposite which is supplanted "either passes away or perishes in the change." Let us consider these alternatives.

When there is a change, does the essential opposite which formerly characterized the thing which is changed *pass away?* Our problem here is a pragmatical one; we are to decide whether we are willing to describe a displaced property as one which has "passed away." We are tempted to do so, just as we are tempted to say that the former essential opposite (the property that the thing had prior to the change) has been *displaced*—removed from its place. But we are not inclined to claim that a displaced property now literally resides in another place; we are not led to say that it has gone to another world. It would be better to say, simply, that the former property is no longer the property of the thing which has undergone change. There is no need to specify—and, indeed, there would be no sense in specifying—what has happened to the former property; a property is not a thing, and it does not have adventures.

Moreover, a displaced property does not *perish.* For what literal sense is there in saying that the coldness of the room has *died?*

Let us, then, assent to premise 3 with the understanding that the truth of premise 3 is derived from the principle of contradiction; and we shall assume that when there is change, the thing which has changed cannot have the property essentially opposite to the property it has. Those who wish to do so can say that the "displaced" property has "passed away" or "perished"; we prefer to say that the changed thing no longer has the property it used to have.

PREMISE 4

In our discussion of the logical structure of the argument of essential opposites we granted the attractiveness of saying that concrete things reject the Idea "which is opposed to that which is contained in them . . . ." To say that a thing "rejects" the Idea or property opposite to its own property is only to say that nothing which has a property can, at the same time and in the same respect, have the property which is essentially opposite. The reasons which led us to accept premise 3 also operate to support our acceptance of premise 4.

However, it *does* make sense to talk about *things* as "passing away," "perishing" or "withdrawing." *Shall we say* that if a thing changes in some respect, it has "perished" or "withdrawn?" If a room, formerly cold, becomes warm, shall we say that the room has perished or withdrawn? Surely not. But the room *as cold* no longer exists; that is, there is no such room. Shall we say in regard to the *room as cold* that it has perished or withdrawn? It would not be advisable to say so, for it might be supposed that the cold room has gone somewhere or (even worse) died. But, then, we could mean no more in speaking of the perishing or withdrawal of the cold room than that it is no longer true that the room is cold. So interpreted, Plato's claim that concrete things "perish or withdraw" whenever there is essential change can be granted.

PREMISE 5

Are we prepared to grant that "nothing which brings the opposite will admit the opposite of that which it brings . . ."? Benjamin Jowett, in translating from the Greek, adds, *"in that to which it is brought";* while Harold North Fowler, translating the same passage, writes, "nothing which brings an opposite to that which it approaches will ever admit *in itself* the oppositeness of that which is brought" (italics added). Although scholars may (and should) quarrel as to which of the two translations comes closer to the meaning of the original Greek passage, we need not in this case be disturbed by the difference. As Plato's example shows, the number three, which is odd, will not admit the Idea of the even; for that reason, "things which are possessed by the number three must not only be three in number, but must also be odd." Hence, such things, as odd, are also opposed to the even; and it is the number three, as possessing such things, which does not admit the even *in the collection,* for the number three does not admit the even *in itself.*

The critical function of this generalization is apparent once the argument moves to the consideration of the soul as the bearer of life. The soul, as the bearer of life, will not admit death *in itself;* that is, the soul itself rejects death. Consequently, as long as the soul possesses a body, that body will not admit death, for the soul in not admitting of death *in itself* does not admit death *in that to which it brings life.* Plato's emphasis, however, is not on the function of the soul as keeping death *from the body,* but on the essence of the soul as the life bearer and, hence, as that which does not admit death in itself. (Plato acknowledges, later on, that "when death attacks a man, the mortal portion of him may be supposed to die"; but he insists that the soul, as that which will not admit death, "retires at the approach of death and is preserved safe and sound . . . .")

Our present problem is that of deciding whether we are to grant that "nothing which brings the opposite will admit the opposite of that which it brings . . . ." Since we are prepared to grant that anything which gives to another thing a property to which there is an essential opposite both rejects the opposite in itself and in that which it possesses, we accept premise 5. Our conclusion is qualified, however, just as Plato himself qualifies his claim. For example, Plato writes, "Will not the number three endure annihilation or anything sooner than be converted into an even number, *while remaining three?*" (Italics added.) Nothing, *while having a certain property,* will admit the property opposite to the property it has.

PREMISE 6

The claim that "whatever the soul possesses, to that she comes bearing life" depends, for its acceptance, on the admission that there are souls and that it is the "inherence" of the soul which "renders the body alive."

Socrates prepares the way for the soul by prefacing a critical query with the injunction ". . . do not you answer my question in the words in which I ask it: let me have not the old safe answer of which I spoke at first . . . . I mean that if any one asks you 'what that is, of which the inherence makes the body hot,' you will reply not heat (this is what I call the safe and stupid answer), but fire, a far superior answer . . . ." The critical question, the answer to which is to be governed by the injunction, is the question "Tell me, then, what is that of which the inherence will render the body alive?" Cebes cannot honor the Socratic injunction by answering, "Why, life, of course," for to do so would be to give an answer "in the words" in which the question was asked; it would be to give what Socrates here calls "the safe and stupid answer . . . ." (The "old safe answer" of which Socrates speaks is the claim in regard to the "cause" of anything: ". . . I stoutly contend that by beauty all beautiful things become beautiful. This appears to be the safest answer which I can give, either to myself or to another . . . .") Since Cebes cannot say, while being obedient to Socrates, that it is by life that all living things become living—which would be no more than to say that living things somehow originate—he must invent, or have recourse to, the metaphysical conviction that there is an entity which is the "bearer" of life and which by "possessing" the body makes it alive. Just as a flame, being by nature hot, brings heat to the bonfire it ignites (and, thus, so long as the fire burns there, opposes the cold and enables the pile of burning material also to reject the cold), so, presumably, there is an entity, the soul, which is by nature (that is, by definition of the term "soul") living and which brings life to the body it enlivens (and, thus, as long as the soul enlivens the body, the soul opposes death and enables the living body also to reject death).

We cannot accept this analogy as providing a reason for assenting to the metaphysical claim that there are souls which bring life to bodies; for although it *sometimes* happens that something acquires a property through being affected by something else that has the property itself (as, for example, a pile of wood, not itself aflame, is set aflame when something else, already flaming, is introduced), it is often the case that a thing changes through being affected by something *different in kind* from what it becomes. A match, not itself aflame, *may* be set aflame by a flaming match, but it can also be set aflame through the heat of engendered friction. Again, although a child, not itself abnormally warm, may be made warmer through the application of a hot-water bottle, the child can also be made warmer through the action of bacteria, not themselves feverish or abnormally warm.

And, indeed, empirical evidence supports the view that a living thing begins to function not through being "possessed" by or affected by another thing, itself alive, but simply through the action of certain chemical compounds on certain other chemical compounds. The cell exists when certain chemical changes occur. One cell, itself living, may be affected by another cell, also living, in such a manner that an organism develops; but the fertilizing cell does not bring life to the inanimate egg, for the egg is itself already alive; the fertilizing cell stimulates the egg into a growth process, even though the sperm cell is not itself already involved in that growth process. (This account, suggested by the results of the inquiry made by biologists, is supported by evidence as dependable as the evidence that leads us to the conclusion that it is not only by the introduction of a flame that something becomes aflame. The significant difference in the cases here compared—the match that becomes aflame through friction and the chemical compound that becomes alive through chemical action—is that the cell is *never* made alive through being affected by something else already alive, but the match may be set aflame by something else already flaming.

We do sometimes say that decaying flesh is "alive" with maggots, themselves alive, but the less said about that, the better.)

We are inclined to reject premise 6, therefore, on the ground that there is no need to suppose that life begins in a body as a result of the body's being possessed by something which renders the body alive.

Premise 6 suffers from the further difficulty that even if there were souls (by definition, bearers of life), their being bearers of life would not guarantee their being able, through "inherence" or "possession," to endow bodies with life and, therefore, with that which is essentially opposed to death. Suppose that the souls were bearers of life in the sense of literally carrying life to the body. Quite apart from the difficulty (probably insurmountable) of conceiving how the property life could be transported, there is the perplexing problem (probably insoluble) of conceiving how the property life, once delivered to the body, could thereupon become a property of the body in such a manner that the body, formerly inanimate, would subsequently be alive. Life cannot be dumped upon a body or stored inside; how, then, can a life bearer, through entering the body, render the body alive?

Suppose, now, that the soul is conceived to be, not a carrier of life, but a thing itself somehow alive. Just as a man inside a papier-mâché monster cannot make that monster alive, even though the man himself is alive and while alive cannot be dead; so a soul, itself alive, could not, by possession alone, bring life to a body. But if not by possession or inherence, then how? Are we to conceive of the soul (a mystery but for its alleged function) as a busy and creative agent somehow able—through being alive or through carrying life—to affect the chemical organization of a body so as to render it alive? If so, why call that busy agent "soul"? Why not call it "the chemical agent which, under certain specifiable circumstances, is productive of life"? But such an agent could not legitimately be said to be either alive or a bearer of life.

Plato cannot prove to our satisfaction that the soul is immortal if he cannot demonstrate that there are souls. The most he could hope to prove is that if there were souls, they would be immortal.

We shall consider whether he proves even this latter proposition to be true, but we are no longer inclined to suppose that the argument of essential opposites provides any acceptable defense of the claim that the soul is immortal.

PREMISE 7

Is death "opposite" to life? Death is certainly the *contrary* of life: "Oh, he is still alive! Wait, no . . . on the contrary, he is dead." But there is another opposite of life: nonlife. The table is not alive; the opposite is true: it is nonalive. But the argument of essential opposites has already been shown to be unsatisfactory; there is no need to deny that at least in some sense of the term "opposite," death is opposite to life.

PREMISE 8

Cebes agrees with the Socratic claim that "the soul . . . will never receive the opposite of what she brings," and on that account he agrees to describe the soul as "immortal," for he agrees with Socrates in calling "that principle which does not admit of death" the "immortal."

But the ambiguity of the term "life bearer" continues to cause trouble, for if the soul literally "comes bearing life," although the soul could not, insofar as it bore life, be bearing death, which is life's essential opposite, there is no contradiction in supposing that the soul, the *bearer,* and not the *life* which it bears, might die. Thus, we cannot concede, as Cebes does, the point that "the soul . . . will never receive the opposite of what she brings," and hence we are not compelled to describe the soul as being immortal.

Suppose, again, that the soul bears life in the sense that it is itself alive. *While alive* a soul could not be dead, but this tautological circumstance (guaranteed by the logical incompatibility of the predicates "alive" and "dead") does not insure a soul against extinction. (After all, a human being while alive cannot be dead; it does not follow that human beings are immortal.) Thus, although if we define the soul as a *living* entity (that is, if we define the term "soul" to mean, at least in part, a living entity, so that it would be a contradiction in terms to speak of a dead soul) we cannot admit the possibility of a soul that is not alive, we need not, in the first place, admit that there are souls, and, in the second place, we need not suppose that if there are souls, they are immortal. A soul might *be* (and, hence, while being, be alive); and then it might be the case that there *was* no such soul. There is, thus, no justification for describing as "immortal" an entity the existence of which has not been demonstrated, and such that even were it to exist, it need not continue to exist.

Plato's argument of essential opposites is unsatisfactory to us because it depends on the assumption that something which "bears" life is involved in the process of rendering the body alive; the argument is also unsatisfactory in that it commits the same kind of logical error Anselm committed in the ontological argument for the existence of God: a term is defined in such a way that for something to fit the definitive description it must be alive (or be more than an idea in mind); it is then contended that since it would be contradictory to say that the thing so defined was *not* alive (or outside the mind), the thing must exist and be immortal. One avoids the semblance of contradiction by framing the disclaimer to read that *perhaps there is no such thing.*

Is there, then, anything of value in Plato's argument? We do find interesting the effort to enlist the metaphysical theory of Ideas in the campaign to demonstrate the immortality of the soul. The theory of Ideas is intriguing on its own account, and we appreciate the philosophical imagination which led Plato to suppose that he could employ the essential opposition of the Ideas of life and death in his argument to show the soul to be immortal. But the premises of the argument are vulnerable to critical challenge whether or not the theory of Ideas is true; hence, the theory of Ideas, whatever its value as either a historical curiosity or as providing an insight into a realm beyond that of the senses, has nothing to do with the worth and meaning of the argument of essential opposites.

The dimension of the argument which is essential to the argument and which probably represents a central concern of its author is the metaphysical claim that there are souls. As one who believed in the independent reality of Ideas, Plato was faced with the problem of bringing the Ideas to earth. The problem of generation, first handled in the argument of concrete opposites and then on a more sophisticated level (intellectually) in the argument of essential opposites, can be considered to be the problem of showing the role of the Ideas in any instance of generation or change. How does something *acquire* a property, given the assumption that properties, characteristics, have a reality of their own which is in no way dependent upon their being exemplified in things? The world of Ideas and the world of bodies must somehow be brought together if change is to be made explicable—so Plato assumed.

Turning his attention to the world of bodies, Plato found that change is often the consequence of the action upon a body of another body already possessing a certain Idea: a piece of wood, originally not aflame, may be set aflame by another piece of wood already aflame. Sometimes creation is the result of the action of an artisan (who in another sense of the term "possesses" an Idea) upon the material of his craft: by reference to the Idea, the artisan fashions the material. But how is one to account for bodies having become alive in the first place? How is one to account for the origin of life on earth? And since in neither of the above-mentioned ways could a body become alive, how is one to account for individual cases of a thing's becoming alive?

Plato was led to suppose that perhaps something, not itself a body and hence not observable, is uniquely fitted to be the life carrier, the agent that brings the eternal, immaterial, and ultimately real Idea of life to the body; and the word "soul" was already available, by virtue of common use, to serve as the term to denote any such agent. Somehow the Idea of life must be able to "inhere" in a body and thereby to make the body alive; the soul could be assumed to be the agent which (in some manner never explained) makes such inherence possible. Since the soul is itself the life-bearing agent, it cannot, like a body, die; for to die is to have the Idea of life removed by that which bears the Idea. If whatever cannot die is immortal, the soul is immortal.

Plato's supposition is intriguing for it suggests that the relation of the posited soul to the Idea that it is presumed to "bear" is different from any other relation of an Idea to a thing. It is different from the relation of an Idea to the body of which the Idea is the property; it is different from the relation of an Idea to a mind which conceives a kind of thing; and, finally, it is presumably different from any gross, literal relation of a bodily carrier to that which the carrier transports. The soul cannot be presumed to be merely a transporter of the Idea of life, for the function of the soul (by definition) is not merely to bear the Idea but to make possible the Idea's inherence in a body.

Unfortunately, at least for those who enjoy this sort of speculation, Plato did not make clear the relation or function which presumably is meant by the term "bearing." We find it difficult to appraise Plato's metaphysical claim—that there are souls, by definition "life bearers"—for we are not able to be clear as to what constitutes "bearing" the Idea "life."

Nevertheless, it is the combination of this metaphysical (or, perhaps, nonsensical) dimension of the argument and the logical play with essential opposites, together with the appeal of the theory of Ideas (to which Aristotle offered a more down-to-earth alternative, by saying that characteristics exist only *in things*), that accounts for Plato's persuasive power. The argument itself appeals to almost no one, but the imaginative intellect which fashioned the argument and which is strikingly exhibited in the course of developing the argument continues to provoke admiration and respect.

COMMENTS ON THE ANALYSIS OF PLATO'S ARGUMENT

Plato's argument of essential opposites is technically interesting because it represents an effort to create a cosmic drama of generation, a drama in which the soul, as the hero, is portrayed as an eternal traveler, moving forever from the world of the living through the world of the dead and back again to the world of the living, forever bearing life, which by its dynamic character as essence or Idea holds off death and enables the soul to enliven any body it possesses. But this drama of life and death, this poignant account of the invulnerable and immortal soul, like all great myths that promise to uncover the powers of light and darkness, is pervaded by mystery. However one strives to comprehend that curious realm of Ideas from which the soul abstracts the life it bears, however one tries to understand how a functional property like life can be "borne" and be made to "inhere" in a body, one fails.

What to the pious and the reverent is *mystery* is *nonsense* to the logical analyst. After we have studied Plato's argument we reject the metaphysical claim which undergirds it, not because we find that we do not share Plato's faith in something possible—namely, the bearing of life by the soul—but because we find nothing possible in Plato's account. The term "soul" is defined by reference to a function, that of bearing life, but the function is not itself definitively described. In any case, a simpler explanation is possible, one which conceives of life as an organic process initiated in certain chemical compounds by the action of other compounds. The latter type of explanation is simpler because it finds its meanings in the world of experience; it makes no appeal to undefined worlds beyond worlds: the world of the Ideas, the world of the dead, of souls restless with the life they bear.

The analysis makes it clear that Plato's theory of Ideas, itself a metaphysical view with elements of mystery, need not be considered in the examination of the argument of essential opposites. The argument depends partly on the metaphysical postulation of the soul, as we have remarked; but an equally integral part of the argument is the claim that any concrete thing (body) which "contains" life is able, because of the essential opposition of life and death, to "reject" death. But we have shown that this power of rejection to which the dramatic language of the dialogue alludes is nothing more than the metaphorical analogue of a logical incompatibility (between "being alive" and "being dead"). The ontological argument for the immortality of the soul fails because the argument illegitimately exploits the logical opposition involved.

QUESTIONS FOR DISCUSSION

1. Some critics claim that Plato, in writing of the "opposition" of essential opposites, expresses a belief that Ideas are active both in forming things and in opposing themselves to their essential opposites. If the argument of essential opposites is considered on the assumption that the above belief is true (insofar as it is meaningful), what difference does granting that assumption make to the critical appraisal of the argument?

2. Are there passages in the *Phaedo* on the basis of which one can clarify the meaning of the claim that the soul bears life? If so, does such clarification lead to a different conclusion concerning the soundness of Plato's argument?

3. Does the critical appraisal of Plato's argument of essential opposites provide a reason for claiming that the term "soul" is useless in philosophy?

4. Are the properties of bodies separable from those bodies? If not separable, in what sense could the properties be said to "inhere in" or "belong to" bodies? If in one's consideration of a thing one abstracted from the thing all its characteristics, what, if anything, would remain to be considered?

XI

ARISTOTLE

THERE IS A PRIME MOVER, ITSELF UNMOVED

ARISTOTLE'S ARGUMENT

Did motion itself ever come into existence, never having been before? And will it in like manner cease to be, so that nothing will move thereafter? Or did it never begin to be and will it never cease to be, so that there always has been and always will be motion, belonging to all things as their deathless and never-failing property and constituting a kind of life for everything that is constituted by nature?

To begin with, all who have discoursed on nature admit that there is such a thing as motion.

*   *   *   *

Let us start from the points established in the earlier part of our Physics. We said that motion is the actualizing of the potentiality of the mobile as such. The necessary presupposition of motion of any kind, then, is that things capable of motion of that kind should already be in existence. And apart from the definition, everyone would admit that what is in motion must be that which is capable of movement in the particular sense of the word in point —if the movement of modification, then the modifiable, if of transference, that which is capable of changing its place—so that there must be something combustible before there can be combustion and something that can burn before there can be burning. And so these things capable of movement either (a) *must have come into existence at a definite moment, not previously having been there, or* (b) *must always be there eternally.*

Now if (a) *every one of these 'movables' came into existence, there must have been some other change or movement, prior to the one under consideration, which prior movement marked the coming into existence of this very object, capable of experiencing or causing movement, which we have seen must itself be prior to movement.*

On the other hand to suppose (b) *that entities capable of being moved and agents capable of moving them had been in existence from everlasting but that no motion had taken place, will at once strike anyone who thinks as unreasonable, and when he goes on to examine it the irrationality will become clearer yet. For if we are to suppose that there was a time when the potentially-moved and potential movers were in existence but all was at rest and no movement took place, and then there came a time when first some potential mover actually moved something movable, there must necessarily have been some antecedent change. For there must have been some cause of that stopping short of actual motion which constitutes being at rest; so before motion could take place, there must have been some change which prevented that cause from any longer hindering motion. Thus before the supposed first change there must have been another change.*

For some moving principles can only cause movement in one direction, while others can reverse the direction of their action: thus fire can heat but cannot chill, whereas it seems that one and the same mental skill may act in opposite directions. There appears, however, to be something analogous to this reverse action even in the former class, since coldness may cause warmth by turning away and departing, just as the expert may do mischief on purpose if he reverse the direction in which to exercise his skill.

At any rate, nothing that 'has the possibility' of producing motion or of being moved or, more generally, of acting or being acted on, can actualize these potentialities under all circumstances but only when they are suitably disposed and approximated to each other. Motion takes place, then, when there exists a mobile and a potential motor and they are so approximated that the one really is able to act and the other to be acted on. So if they had been there eternally but without motion, it must obviously have been because they were not in such relations as to make them actually able to cause motion or to be moved. For motion to supervene, therefore, it must be necessary that one or the other should experience a change, for this must be so where we are dealing with any pair of related factors—for instance if A is now twice B and was not so before, either one or both must have changed. So there would have to be a change anterior to the supposed first change.

And besides this, how could there be any before or after at all if time were not, or time itself be if there were no motion? For surely if time is the numerical aspect of movement or is itself a movement, it follows that, if there has always been time, there must always have been movement. . . . Well then, if it is impossible for time to exist or to be conceived without the 'present now,' and if this 'now' is a kind of midmostness, which combines beginning and end—the beginning, to wit, of future and the end of past time—then there must always have been time; for however far back you go in time past, the extreme limit you take must be a certain 'now' (for in time there is nothing else to take except a 'now'), and since every now is an end as well as a beginning, it follows that time stretches from it in both directions. And if time, then motion, inasmuch as time is but an aspect or affection of motion.

The same line of argument further shows that movement is imperishable. For as we have seen that if we suppose movement to have had an origin we shall have to suppose that there was a change anterior to the first change, so also if we suppose it to cease we shall have to admit a change posterior to the last change. For what is movable does not cease to be movable because it is no longer being moved, nor does that which is capable of causing

motion cease to have that capacity because it is not moving any-
thing; for instance the combustible if it is not being burnt (for it
may still be combustible all the same) or the potential agent of
local shifting when it is shifting nothing. And so, if all the destruc-
tible were destroyed that would not destroy the destroying agent,
which would remain for destruction in its turn, and when it was
destroyed its destroyer would remain; and being destroyed is a
kind of change. And if all this is impossible, it is evident that
movement is eternal, and is not something which now was and
now was not. Indeed to assert the opposite is very like a contra-
diction in terms.

Nor does it help matters to say that that is how thing were
made and that we must take that as a principle, as Empedocles
seems to imply that the alternating power of attraction and repul-
sion effectively to move things was always there of necessity and
the periods of rest between. And one may take it that those who
believe in one active principle only, such as Anaxagoras, would
take the same line. Well, but nothing natural or accordant with
nature is without order; for nature is the universal determinant of
order. And the unlimited bears no proportion to the unlimited,
whereas all orderly succession implies proportion. Thus for there
to be an unlimited period of rest, and then at a certain point for
motion to supervene, there being no principle of distinction to
determine its 'now' from any previous point, so that all orderly
succession is excluded—this, I say, by the mere statement is
excluded from the works of nature. For what is natural is either
absolute, not now thuswise and now otherwise (just as fire always
tends upwards, not sometimes so and sometimes not) or, if not
absolute, is determined by some intelligible principle. Thus Empe-
docles (or others who may adopt his theories) has the advantage
of Anaxagoras, in that he alternates cessation and recurrence of
motion, for this at least gives us an ordered succession. But even
so it is not enough for anyone to assert that this particular succes-
sion actually takes place unless he can point out its determining
principle: he must not lay down or claim as an axiom a ground-
less assumption; on the contrary he must produce some inductive

or deductive proof of his assertion. Now the principles alleged by Empedocles do not in themselves determine an alternation of activities, nor is any such alternation included in the essential notion of either, since the action of one (attraction) is to draw together and of the other (repulsion) to thrust apart. So that if you are to add an explanation of their alternation, you must give instances where such a thing occurs; just as you can show that there is such a thing as 'attraction' because you can see men drawn together by it, and in like manner can see 'repulsion' at work when men mutually avoid each other, and since this obtains in some cases, you propose to apply it to the universe. But even if you had shown that attraction and repulsion alternate, you would have to explain why each acts over an equal length of time. Nor yet (to take a more general ground) is it sound reasoning to conclude that you have reached a fundamental principle when you have shown that this or that always is, or always occurs, thus and no otherwise. Democritus, it is true, held it to be enough for the establishing of determining principles to have shown that this or that has been so in all former times, and did not feel bound to seek any deeper principle behind what has always been. But this took him right in certain cases only, and not in all. For instance the angles of a triangle are always equal to two right angles, but a reason can be assigned for the eternity of this property that lies behind the fact itself. But a first principle can have no such other cause behind it, since principles are eternal on their own merits.

Let this suffice to demonstrate that there never was nor will be a time when movement was not or will not be.

[From *Physics*, Book VIII, Chapter 1, by Aristotle (384–322 B.C.); translated by Philip H. Wicksteed and Francis M. Cornford.*]

Now the thing moved may be moved by the true agent either directly or by some intermediate which itself is moved by the true

*Edition used: Harvard University Press and William Heinemann Ltd., 1952.

agent directly. And the true agent may immediately precede the intermediate agent which acts directly upon the patient, or there may be a chain of several intermediates.

*   *   *   *

If then everything that is in motion must be moved by something, and that something must either be moved in its turn by something else or not, and in the latter case it is the true agent and we need go no further, but in the other case we must run it back until we do reach a primary mover not moved by something else (for it is impossible to run back to infinity through movers that are themselves moved by something else, for there is no beginning at all of such an unlimited series)—why then it follows that if everything that is in motion is moved by some agent, and if the primary agent itself is in motion but is not moved by anything else, *it must be moved by* itself.

Or (reversing the order of the demonstration) we may repeat the argument in this way. Every mover sets something in motion by some instrumentality, either its own or other than its own: the man for instance either by the instrumentality of his own hand or by that of the staff, and the wind either by its own impact or by loosening a stone that moves whatever it may be. And when the primary mover employs an instrument sejunct from itself, that sejunct instrument cannot act without the primary mover that moves by its own instrumentality. But the primary mover can apply its own instrumentality without having to employ any other; whereas an instrument sejunct from a primary must (to be in action) have somewhere behind it some primary agent (or the search for one would run back with no limit). If, then, the agent of motion is in motion itself, we must come to stand somewhere and not go on without limit; for if the staff moves the load because it is itself moved by the hand, the hand indeed moved the staff, but if the hand itself is moved by something else, what moves the hand is in turn a distinct thing. However long the chain, therefore, of things that produce motion by an instrumentality other than their own, there must lie behind it an agent that produces the movement by its own instrumentality. So that if this primary agent is in motion, and there is no agent behind it to set it in motion, it must of necessity be moving itself. So this line of argument again leads to the conclusion that if anything is in motion it must either be set in motion by a self-moving agent immediately, or must send us back through a chain of intermediaries until we come to such an agent.

*   *   *   *

In conclusion, then, it is false to say that everything in motion is moved by something else that is itself moved by something else; and it is true to say that such a series must terminate. Consequently its first member must be moved either by an agent which is not in motion at all, or by itself. Now (reserving the alternative of the first mover being itself not in motion) it is obvious enough in itself (though we have carefully established it if it were not) that if anyone had to determine whether the cause and principle of movement is to be found in that which moves itself or in that which is moved by something else, he would declare for the former, on the general principle that a cause which is causative in itself must be prior to that which derives its causative power from some other cause which is itself also derivatively causative only.

We must, then, start afresh and examine the question: If there is any self-moving agent of motion, how does it move itself and with what kind of motion? Well then, all divisions of a mobile must themselves be divisible without limit; for it has been shown already, in our general treatment of the principles of Physics, that whatever can, primarily and on its own account, be in motion, must be continuous. Hence it follows (1) that if a thing moves itself it cannot do so integrally in both capacities; for that would amount to saying that, being one and indivisible specifically, it was, in its integrity, both agent and patient of the same identical transference, or both the modifier and the modified in respect of the same modification, so that it might be teacher and taught simultaneously, or agent and patient of the same healing. Moreover, it must by definition be some mobile that is set in motion, and the mobile, as such, is potentially, not actually, in motion; and the potential is still only on its way to actuality (movement being an actualizing, though not a complete one), whereas the mover must already be actualized; that which heats, for instance, must already be hot, and, universally, the generator must already be in possession of the characteristics to be conferred upon the generated. Thus the 'self-heating' would have to be both hot and not hot at the same time and in the same respect. And so in all other cases in which producer and produced bear the same denomination. It follows, then, that if anything moves itself, the factor that causes the movement is distinguishable from the factor that is moved.

But (2) that such a case cannot be regarded as one of reciprocal action and passion between the factors concerned may be shown as follows. There would not really be any primary motor at all if each moved the other, for the primacy of causation falls to the agent that is prior to the next most primary and is therefore entitled better than it to be called the source of motion; for we have seen that 'causing motion' may be assigned to an agent in two senses, to wit to the agent that is set in motion by something else or to the one set in motion by itself, and that one further back from the object ultimately moved is nearer to the principle of movement than is an intermediate between it and that object. Moreover, there is no necessity for either moving factor to be put in motion by anything but itself; so it would only be by incidental concomitance that the other moves it in return. I choose then hypothetically to exclude this contingency, and we are left with one element that is set in motion and another that moves it but is not itself in motion at all. Moreover the established fact of the eternity of motion cannot be appealed to as establishing in its turn any such reciprocal action; for all that it establishes is that there must be either some unmoving cause of motion, or some self-moving one. And yet again, if there were such a reciprocal causation of movement it would have to be of the type 'that which is causing heat is, qua cause, receiving heat.'

But in truth there cannot be, in that which primarily moves itself, either a single part that moves itself or a number of parts each of which moves itself. For if, as we are assuming, the whole is self-moved, it must be either (2) moved by some part of itself or *(1)* moved as a whole by itself as a whole. If then *(2)* its motion is due to the self-motion of one of its parts, this part would be the primary *self-mover;* for if isolated from the whole this part would still move itself, while the whole would do so no longer. But if *(1)* the whole is moved by itself as a whole, the self-motion of the parts will be an accidental circumstance; and since it is not necessary, we are at liberty to suppose that they do not move themselves.

All the other alternatives being exhausted, then, we conclude that one factor of whatever is self-moved causes motion without being in motion and the other is moved, for only so is self-movement possible.

*   *   *   *

It is evident, then, from all that we have said that the primary motor is not itself a movable; for the thing in motion under some agent other than itself can always trace back its motion either to a primary unmoved mover or to an agent that is indeed moving but can itself initiate its movement or arrest it, and either way alike the primary motor of anything that is in motion is found to be unmoved.

Now this conclusion is only what we should have expected; for in the three links of mover, instrument of motion, object moved, the last must experience motion but need not cause it; the middle term must be in motion itself as well as causing motion in something else (for it accompanies the changes of the thing it moves and keeps pace with it—patently so in the case of local movement where the instrument and the load must remain in (partial) contact somewhere); and so if the first term (which by hypothesis causes motion) is to be distinguished from an instrument, it cannot also be itself in motion. And since we find as the last term of the series entities (inanimate objects, to wit) capable of being moved but not of initiating motion, and other entities (living organisms, to wit) including in themselves a factor capable of initiating motion and also one capable of being moved, does not analogy suggest—not to say insist—that there is a third order of entities capable of initiating motion but incapable of being moved?

So Anaxagoras did well to say that 'Intelligence' was unaffected (by the material universe) and free from admixture, since he regarded it as the principle of movement, and it could only be so if itself motionless, and could only control it if itself unmingled with it. [From *Physics*, Book VIII, Chapter 5.]

We have shown that motion must be eternal and can never cease; so there must be some prime mover, whether singular or plural, that is eternal and not itself movable. The contention that all *unmoved movers are eternal is not to our present purpose, but the following considerations will show that there must be* something *that is not itself susceptible of any movement in the way of external change, either primarily or incidentally, while it is capable of causing movement in something else.*

Let us grant (if anyone chooses to urge it) that there may conceivably be things which sometimes are and sometimes are not, without any process of becoming or perishing (indeed if anything that has no parts exists at one time and not at another, it may be a necessary conclusion that it does so without undergoing any process of change). Further, let us grant the possibility that some *of the principles that cause motion but are not themselves susceptible of movement belong to this class of things that now are and now are not. But in no case can this be true of* all *such principles; for it is evident that the coming and going of these intermittently present and not present self-movers must have some cause. For anything which moves itself must have magnitude* qua *mobile (for nothing that cannot be divided can be made to move), but nothing that we have said shows that a cause of motion as such must have magnitude. Accordingly the (prime) cause of the continual genesis and dissolution of the things that come into being and pass out of it cannot be found in any of the unmoved movers whose own existence is not eternal, nor in any group of causes some of which produce motion in certain things and others in certain other things. Neither (as is obvious) can any one of such be the cause of the everlasting and uninterrupted process, nor can the whole sum of them; for that the process should be everlasting and uninterrupted is an eternal necessity, whereas the whole sum runs back without limit (so that we never come to a prime cause at all) and is not coexistent but successive. It is clear, then, that though certain unmoved principles of motion may come and go any number of times, and many self-moving things may perish to be succeeded by others, one unmoving principle moving this mobile and another that, nevertheless there must be something which embraces them all and is distinct from any one of them, and is the cause of the others coming and going and of the continual change. This something, then, is what causes the movement of the first set of moving things, and they pass it on to the others.*

So, inasmuch as motion is eternal, it follows that the prime mover, if it be single, or the prime movers, if plural, must likewise be eternal. And by preference we should regard it as one principle rather than many or as a limited rather than an unlimited plurality; for if the consequences are the same it is always better to assume the more limited antecedent, since in the things of nature the limited, as being better, is sure to be found, wherever possible, rather than the unlimited. And a single principle is adequate, which as the first of the unmoved entities and eternal will suffice as the principle of motion for all the rest. Another proof that there must be some single and eternal first mover is the following. We have shown that eternal movement exists of necessity. And for such movement to be eternal it must be continuous, for what constantly exists at all times is as such continuous, whereas the successive is discontinuous (and therefore not eternal). But for movement to be continuous it must be unified; and for it to be unified it must be produced by a single motor in a single mobile, for if the movement were to be produced now by one thing now by another, the whole movement would not be continuous but successional.

So from these considerations one would be led to believe that there is a prime mover, itself unmoved. . . .

[From *Physics,* Book VIII, Chapter 6.]

Now it moves in the following manner. The object of desire and the object of thought move without being moved. The primary objects of desire and thought are the same. For it is the apparent good that is the object of appetite, and the real good that is the object of the rational will. Desire is the result of opinion rather than opinion that of desire; it is the act of thinking that is the starting-point. Now thought is moved by the intelligible, and one of the series of contraries is essentially intelligible. In this series substance stands first, and of substance that which is simple and exists actually. (The one and the simple are not the same; for one signifies a measure, whereas "simple" means that the subject itself is in a certain state.) But the Good, and that which is in itself desirable, are also in the same series; and that which is first in a class is always best or analogous to the best.

That the final cause may apply to immovable things is shown by the distinction of its meanings. For the final cause is not only "the good for something," but also "the good which is the end of some action." In the latter sense it applies to immovable things, although in the former it does not; and it causes motion as being an object of love, whereas all other things cause motion because they are themselves in motion. Now if a thing is moved, it can be otherwise than it is. Therefore if the actuality of "the heaven" is primarily locomotion, then in so far as "the heaven" is moved, in this respect at least it is possible for it to be otherwise; i.e. in respect of place, even if not of substantiality. But since there is something—X—which moves while being itself unmoved, existing actually, X cannot be otherwise in any respect. For the primary kind of change is locomotion, and of locomotion circular locomotion; and this is the motion which X induces. Thus X is necessarily existent; and qua necessary it is good, and is in this sense a first principle. For the necessary has all these meanings: that which is by constraint because it is contrary to impulse; and that without which excellence is impossible; and that which cannot be otherwise, but is absolutely necessary.

Such, then, is the first principle upon which depend the sensible universe and the world of nature. And its life is like the best which we temporarily enjoy. It must be in that state always (which for us is impossible), since its actuality is also pleasure. (And for this reason waking, sensation and thinking are most

*pleasant, and hopes and memories are pleasant because of them.)
Now thinking in itself is concerned with that which is in itself
best, and thinking in the highest sense with that which is in the
highest sense best. And thought thinks itself through participation
in the object of thought; for it becomes an object of thought by the
act of apprehension and thinking, so that thought and the object
of thought are the same, because that which is receptive of the
object of thought, i.e. essence, is thought. And it actually functions
when it possesses this object. Hence it is actuality rather than
potentiality that is held to be the divine possession of rational
thought, and its active contemplation is that which is most pleasant
and best. If, then, the happiness which God always enjoys is as
great as that which we enjoy sometimes, it is marvellous; and if
it is greater, this is still more marvellous. Nevertheless it is so.
Moreover, life belongs to God. For the actuality of thought is life,
and God is that actuality; and the essential actuality of God is life
most good and eternal. We hold, then, that God is a living being,
eternal, most good; and therefore life and a continuous eternal
existence belong to God; for that is what God is.*

[From *Metaphysics*, Book XII, Chapter 7; translated by Hugh
Tredennick.*]

AN ANALYSIS OF ARISTOTLE'S ARGUMENT

1. THE BASIC CLAIM

We are considering the argument which Aristotle designed
to support the claim that "there is a prime mover, itself unmoved
. . . ." The philosopher argues that the prime mover is "eternal,"
that it is "one principle," that it is "not itself movable," and that
it moves by being actual and by being necessarily existent; the
prime mover—as thought which thinks and enjoys itself as the
object of thought—"causes motion as being an object of love,

*Edition used: Harvard University Press and William Heinemann Ltd.,
1947.*

whereas all other things cause motion because they are themselves in motion."

2. THE BASIC ARGUMENT

We have attempted to abstract from Aristotle's *Physics* and *Metaphysics* the argument which the philosopher used to show that there is an unmoved, unmovable, eternal prime mover. In its totality the argument is even longer than is indicated by the selections included here, but we have attempted to include every passage essential to the argument, even though the edited version may lack some of the alternative defenses which contribute to the over-all persuasive power of Aristotle's complete argument.

The basic argument we are considering, then, as presented by the passages quoted, may be regarded as composed of the following fundamental claims and arguments:

1. ". . . all who have discoursed on nature admit that there is such a thing as motion."
2. ". . . motion is the actualizing of the potentiality of the mobile as such."
3. "The necessary presupposition of motion of any kind, then, is that things capable of motion of that kind should already be in existence."
4. ". . . these things capable of movement either must have come into existence at a definite moment, not previously having been there, or must always be there eternally."
5. "Now if every one of these 'movables' came into existence, there must have been some other change or movement, prior to the one under consideration, which prior movement marked the coming into existence of this very object, capable of experiencing or causing movement, which we have seen must itself be prior to movement."
6. ". . . if we are to suppose that there was a time when the potentially-moved and potential movers were in existence but all was at rest and no movement took place, and then there came a time when first some potential mover actually moved something movable, there must

necessarily have been some antecedent change. For there must have been some cause of that stopping short of actual motion which constitutes being at rest; so before motion could take place, there must have been some change which prevented that cause from any longer hindering motion. Thus before the supposed first change there must have been another change."

7. "The same line of argument further shows that movement is imperishable. For as we have seen that if we suppose movement to have had an origin we shall have to suppose that there was a change anterior to the first change, so. also if we suppose it to cease we shall have to admit a change posterior to the last change. For what is movable does not cease to be movable because it is no longer being moved, nor does that which is capable of causing motion cease to have that capacity because it is not moving anything . . . ."

8. "And if all this is impossible, it is evident that movement is eternal, and is not something which now was and now was not. Indeed to assert the opposite is very like a contradiction in terms."

9. ". . . the thing moved may be moved by the true agent either directly or by some intermediate which itself is moved by the true agent directly."

10. "If then everything that is in motion must be moved by something, and that something must either be moved in its turn by something else or not, . . . in the latter case it is the true agent . . . , but in the other case we must run it back until we do reach a primary mover not moved by something else (for it is impossible to run back to infinity through movers that are themselves moved by something else, for there is no beginning at all of such an unlimited series) . . . ."

11. ". . . if the primary agent itself is in motion but is not moved by anything *else,* it must be moved by *itself.*"

12. ". . . the mobile, as such, is potentially, not actually, in motion . . . whereas the mover must already be actualized.

... It follows, then, that if anything moves itself, the factor that causes the movement is distinguishable from the factor that is moved."

13. "But . . . there cannot be, in that which *primarily* moves itself, either a single part that moves itself or a number of parts each of which moves itself. For if . . . the whole is self-moved, it must be either moved by some part of itself or moved as a whole by itself as a whole. If then its motion is due to the self-motion of one of its parts, this part would be the *primary* self-mover . . . . But if the whole is moved by itself as a whole, the self-motion of the parts will be an accidental circumstance; and since it is not necessary, we are at liberty to suppose that they do not move themselves."

14. ". . . we conclude that one factor of whatever is self-moved causes motion without being in motion and the other is moved . . . ."

15. "It is evident . . . that the primary motor is not itself a movable . . . ."

16. "We have shown that motion must be eternal . . . ; so there must be some prime mover, whether singular or plural, that is eternal and not itself movable."

17. ". . . by preference we should regard (the eternal prime mover) as one principle . . . for if the consequences are the same it is always better to assume the more limited antecedent, since in the things of nature the limited, as being better, is sure to be found, wherever possible, rather than the unlimited."

18. "So from these considerations one would be led to believe that there is a prime mover, itself unmoved . . . ."

Let us now simplify the statement of the argument and prepare for the construction of a diagram of the argument's logical form. Because of the complex nature of Aristotle's argument, we shall use *titles* as reminders of the propositions or propositional elements symbolized in the diagram. (Conclusions will not be inserted separately.)

Thus, to symbolize the proposition that there is motion and motion is natural, we use:

(1) √ *Motion* is *natural*

and we then relate the term "motion" to its definition (as given in proposition 2: "the actualizing of the potentiality of the mobile as such"):

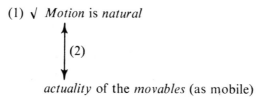

(1) √ *Motion* is *natural*

(2)

actuality of the *movables* (as mobile)

The proposition (4) that *movables either came into existence or are eternal* is diagrammed as an alternative relating to the movables:

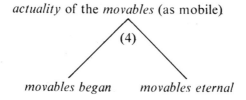

actuality of the *movables* (as mobile)

(4)

movables began   *movables eternal*

(Proposition 3 is an intermediate conclusion, presumed to follow from premises 1 and 2.)

Proposition 5 states, in effect, that *if every movable began to exist, then if there were a first movement (of the movables) it would not be the first movement, for there would be the prior movement of the coming-to-be of the movables.* We label this proposition "5.1" on the diagram. (See diagram facing p. 320.)

Furthermore, there cannot be the first movement of the coming-to-be of the movables, for a movement is a motion, and a motion entails the existence of a movable. To simplify the diagram we simply show (as 5.2) that *if there is the first movement of the coming-to-be of the movables, then there is no such movement.*

Proposition 6 is condensed to read that *if eternal movables at one time first moved, then the first movement (of the movables) was* not the first movement, for there must have been the first movement consisting of the removal of the cause of the immobility of the movables.

Proposition 7 follows the "same line of argument." Here it is maintained that *if there were a last movement of the eternal movables, it would not be the last movement, for there would have to be the subsequent "movement" (or action) consisting of the sustaining of the immobile movables.*

Proposition 8 is the stated intermediate conclusion (not diagrammed independently) that since there can be neither a first nor last movement of the movables that are eternal, *the movement of the eternal movables is eternal.*

Aristotle has argued that motion is to be found in nature, that motion involves movables, and that motion is eternal. We now state proposition 9.1 as follows: *If there is eternal motion (of movables), then there are movers.*

And as 9.2 we have: *Movers are either intermediate (moved by another) or not-intermediate.*

Proposition 10 states, basically, that *since there are intermediate movers* (for example, a staff moved by a man or a stone moved by the wind) *and since all intermediate movers are ultimately moved by some primary mover, there is at least one primary mover.*

Aristotle's remark (central to the argument) that "it is impossible to run back to infinity through movers that are themselves moved by something else, for there is no beginning at all of such an unlimited series" is interpreted as an assertion of the necessity of a "beginning," a first cause or principle by reference to which one accounts for the motion of intermediate movers.

Thus, we understand Aristotle to be claiming that (10.1) *there are intermediate movers;* (10.2) *if there are intermediate movers, then there is a beginning* (a first cause or principle) *of their motion;* (10.3) *if there is a beginning of their motion, it is provided by a primary mover;* hence (not shown independently in the diagram) *there is at least one primary mover.*

Aristotle next argues that self-movers move because of an unmoved factor. He first of all states that it is necessarily the case that (11) *any agent in motion but not moved by anything else is moved by itself.* Aristotle then maintains that (12) *since whatever moves must be actualized—while whatever is moved is only potentially in motion—there must be two factors involved in self-motion: a motion-causing (actualized) factor, and a moved (potentially-moving) factor.* But (13) *no self-mover moves because of the action of a self-moving part, for if there were such a part, it would itself be the primary self-mover (which is impossible).* Hence (14) *the motion-causing factor of a self-mover is an unmoved primary mover.*

Proposition 15 is the conclusion that *the primary mover is not a movable;* that is, if anything is a primary mover, it is unmovable (whether it be the prime mover that directly provides motion for the intermediate movers or a self-mover that has as its motion-causing factor an unmoved primary mover).

Proposition 16 is the argument that *if motion is eternal, then if there is an unmovable prime mover, that mover is eternal.*

Aristotle then offers various reasons for claiming that there is but one unmovable eternal prime mover, but we include only the persuasive comment that "it is always better to assume the more limited antecedent . . . ." We show (as 17.1) that *if there is an eternal prime mover, it is a limited principle; and* (17.2) *if it is limited, it is one.*

Proposition 18 is the conclusion that *there is a single eternal unmoved prime mover.*

It must be understood that the following diagram, despite its complexity, should not be regarded as reflecting *all* the features of Aristotle's argument. After all, the propositions diagrammed are drawn from passages which say more than the diagrams indicate; the excerpted passages are drawn from a rich context; the chapters considered are part of a complex, subtle book; the book is but part of Aristotle's work and is closely related to other books not here examined; and, finally, Aristotle's argument is most meaningful and effective to one who can place it within its own cultural and linguistical context. Nevertheless, an effort has been made to present enough of the argument to give Aristotle's reasoning fair expression, and we have sought to retain whatever is central to the argument. The kind of examination we are undertaking is the sort that a critical reading of the work of any philosopher demands, and it would be no improvement to abandon critical reading because of the difficulty of attending to every possibly relevant feature of what is read.

3. CRITICISM OF THE BASIC ARGUMENT

Let us examine the logical character of the argument as it now stands.

Intermediate conclusion 3 (that there are movables) follows validly from the definition of motion (2) and the claim (1) that there is motion in nature.

Proposition 4 sets forth an alternative: either movables began to be or they are eternal. The first alternative is validly eliminated by argument 5, a *reductio ad absurdum* (later to be appraised materially). It follows that movables are eternal (in the sense that there has never been a time when there were no movables).

Three alternatives are considered: that there was a first movement of the movables, that there shall be a last movement, and that motion is eternal. The first two are eliminated by *reductio ad absurdum* arguments (6 and 7). It follows, then, (8) that motion is eternal.

It is then claimed (9.1) that if there is eternal motion (or any motion), there are movers. Two kinds of movers, the intermediate and the "true agents" or not-intermediate movers, are mentioned (9.2), and it is claimed (by examples) that (10.2) there are intermediate movers (10.1). If there are intermediate movers, then there is a beginning or first cause of their motion; (10.3) if a first cause, then a primary mover. The assertion of a primary mover is validly inferred.

The possibility that primary movers are movable is explored. The denial of this possibility follows from the argument (11) that if the primary mover moves, it is a self-mover; but (12) the self-mover (although moving as a whole) is moved by a motion-causing factor which is fully actualized and, as such, is the primary unmoved (unmovable) mover. In any case, (13) if the motion-causing factor moved, it would itself be the self-mover (and this is incompatible with the original assumption of a *primary* self-mover). Thus, (14) the motion-causing factor is unmoved.

The conclusion (15) that every primary mover is unmoved (unmovable) follows, for if the primary mover were to move, it would have to be a self-mover; but the primary mover would then be not the presumed primary mover but the actualized (and hence unmoving) motion-causing factor of the self-mover. Thus, whether the intermediate mover is moved by a self-mover or (ultimately) by an unmoved prime mover, it is moved by an unmoved primary mover. (Compare to Aristotle's defense of this conclusion: "It is evident, then, from all that we have said that the primary motor is not itself a movable; for the thing in motion under some agent other than itself can always trace back its motion either to a primary unmoved mover or to an agent that is indeed moving but can itself initiate its movement or arrest it, and either way alike the primary motor of anything that is in motion is found to be unmoved.")

It is then claimed (16) that since motion is eternal, an unmovable prime mover is eternal; and it has been concluded that motion is eternal and that there is at least one unmovable primary mover. Hence, the conclusion follows that there is an eternal unmovable prime mover.

Aristotle's first argument (17) in support of the claim (18) that there is but one (a single) eternal unmoved prime mover is valid, for he established at the outset the naturalness of motion; and he now argues that whatever is natural is limited, and that it follows that if there is an eternal prime mover, there is but one such mover.

The second argument for the singleness of the prime mover —an argument not diagrammed—is also valid, for Aristotle concluded in 8 that motion is eternal; and he argues that if motion is eternal, then it is continuous; if continuous, then unified; if unified, then there is but one eternal unmoved prime mover.

Aristotle also argues validly (in an argument not diagrammed) that if there are noneternal unmoved principles of motion, there must be an eternal unmoved prime mover which serves as the prime cause of the genesis and dissolution of such noneternal principles; for everything natural is either absolute or determined by some absolute principle, and the coming into existence or going out of existence of noneternal unmoved principles could not (so he suggests) be absolute.

In our analysis and appraisal of the premises of Aristotle's argument for the necessity of an unmoved prime mover, let us attempt to make explicit the extent to which each philosophical claim involves a claim or stipulation about language. Every philosophical claim in nonlinguistical form is about the world, in that the effort is made to describe the "world" of our experience in some novel and illuminating way, and the "world" of our sense experience is thus broadened by imagination and theory. But although philosophical descriptions are about the world—sometimes the world of sense experience, sometimes the world of numbers, sometimes the world of our ideals—they are also about the language we use to talk about our "world" or "worlds." Thus we have claimed that *philosophical statements, whatever their explicit and grammatical form, have a linguistical function* (at least in part).

We shall attempt to show, although in a somewhat more abbreviated form than exhaustive analysis would yield, how Aristotle's claims involve some linguistical claims; and we shall appraise each of the premises in detail until we are able to make a defensible critical judgment of Aristotle's argument.

A review of some of our terminology will help our appraisal:

Pragmatical statement: A statement which has as its function the expression of a claim or stipulation with regard to the *use* of an expression.

Semantical statement: A statement which has as its function the expression of a claim or stipulation with regard to the *meaning* of an expression.

Logical statement: A statement which has as its function the expression of a claim or stipulation with regard to the *structure* of an expression in some language.

Metaphysical statement: A statement which has as its functions

(1) the expression of the logical claim that a certain linguistical statement is *contingent* (neither tautological nor self-contradictory), (2) the expression of the logical claim that an *empirical investigation* of the factual matter with which the statement is concerned is *not possible,* and (3) the expression of the "metaphysical" faith that the statement in question is a *true* statement.

A philosophical statement is the expression of a linguistical *claim* insofar as the statement functions as a *report* of the *actual* use, meaning, or structure of an expression in use. A philosophical statement is the expression of a linguistical *stipulation* insofar as the statement functions as a *recommendation* of a *possible* use, meaning, or structure for an expression.

We now appraise the premises of Aristotle's argument by considering, in each case, the linguistical function of the statements which compose his argument. (By using the term "proposition" to name a premise or conclusion of an argument we have suggested that a philosophical or linguistical point may be stated in more than one way.)

Let us adopt the following analytical procedure: (1) each premise (and conclusion) considered will be stated in a form approximating its original expression; (2) each premise will then be stated linguistically (as a statement *about* some linguistic expression); (3) each premise will be classified according to its philosophical function; and (4) the acceptability of the premise will be considered.

PREMISE 1

(Original statement): ". . . all who have discoursed on nature admit that there is such a thing as motion."

(Linguistical restatement): The term "motion" has been *used* (by those who discourse on nature) *ostensively* (that is, to call attention to certain cases of what is called "motion").

(Philosophical type): Pragmatical claim.

(Appraisal of proposition): We are not at all inclined to deny that there are instances of what is called "motion." Premise accepted.

(Original): ". . . motion is the actualizing of the potentiality of the mobile as such."

(Linguistical): The term "motion," as it has been used by those who discourse on nature, *means* the actualizing of the potentiality of the mobile as such. Or, a case of what is denoted as "motion" is definitively described as a case of the actualizing of the potentiality of the mobile as such. Or (informally) what we call "motion" is that which constitutes the difference between what is able to move but is not moving and that which is moving.

(Type): Semantical claim.

(Appraisal): If what Aristotle says technically is what we indicate informally—that the word "motion," as we use it in describing moving things, means the *actual moving* of the things—we accept his claim. The point of the definition, it appears, is that a moving thing, as moving (mobile), is always about to come to a place at which it has not yet arrived; a thing has *motion* insofar as it is continually realizing the possibility of coming to and passing through places. What is especially relevant to the argument is the claim that motion is an *actual* process, not a mere possibility or potentiality; or, linguistically, the term "motion," as used in the manner exhibited, means *natural change of some sort.* The semantical claim (so understood) is judged to be reasonable; the account is in accordance with the use of the term and serves the function of semantical claims in that it provides a general description of that to which the term in its ordinary use calls attention. (However, we shall have more to say about motion as the "principle" of "actuality.")

PREMISE 3

(Original): "The necessary presupposition of motion of any kind, then, is that things capable of motion of that kind should already be in existence."

(Linguistical): The statement "Wherever there is motion there are things capable of motion" is a *tautology* (an analytic truth).

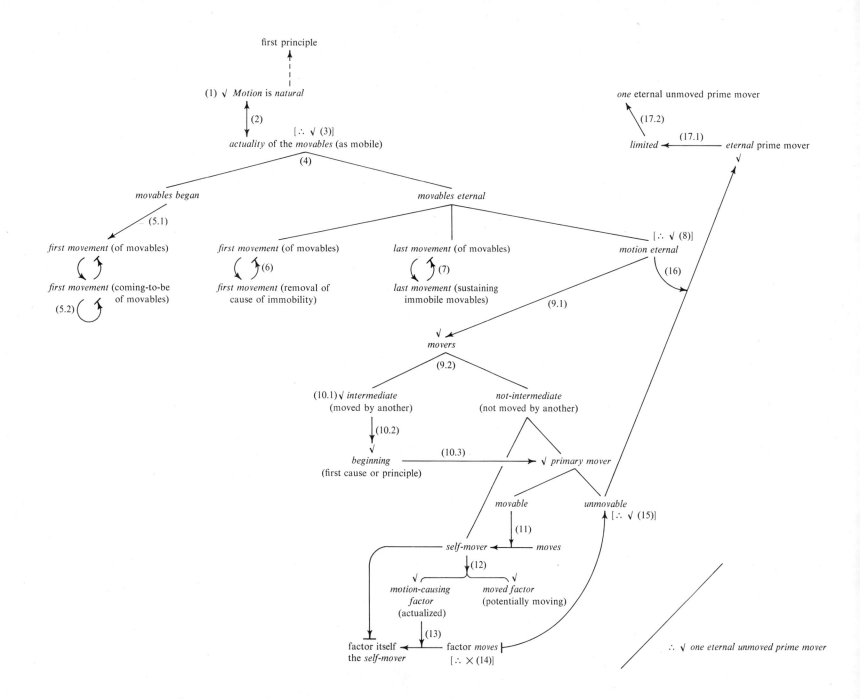

(Type): Logical claim.

(Appraisal): Aristotle has defined "motion" as the actualizing of the potentiality of the mobile as such. The "mobile as such" is that which is moving, and to attribute what is called "potentiality" to the mobile is to describe the mobile as capable of further motion: as *movable*. Thus, the statement "Wherever there is motion there are things capable of motion" may be understood to mean "Wherever there is the actualizing of mobiles capable of motion there are things capable of movement," which involves the proposition that "Wherever there are things capable of movement there are things capable of movement," a proposition which, by its logical form, is true; hence, analytically true; hence, tautological.

Aristotle's logical claim is in accordance with his semantical claim, which is, in turn, in accordance with his pragmatical claim, which fits the use exhibited. Hence, we find the logical claim acceptable.

The only objection that might reasonably be made to the logical claim is that mobiles are not "things." The critic may be thinking that what we call "things" are *nothing but* complex systems of energy; and he might conclude that we cannot, strictly speaking, say that a system of energy, even when moving in relation to some other system, is a moving "thing," propelled, as it were, by a static "substance" of some sort which bears energy.

But in calling something a "moving thing" we need not—and, in fact, we do not—suggest that, behind all appearances, there resides the static bearer of energy. To object to the use of a term on the ground that some metaphysicians have misused the term is not a reasonable procedure.

Precisely because we speak of "moving things," it is proper to claim that where there is motion there are moving things capable of motion.

PREMISE 4

(Original): ". . . these things capable of movement either must have come into existence at a definite moment . . . or must always be there eternally . . . ."

(Linguistical): The statement "Movable things neither came into existence nor are eternal" is a contradiction in terms.

(Type): Logical claim.

(Appraisal): The argument here is taken to mean that either the movables (as a class of potentially mobile things) at one time began to be, or else there never was a time when there were no movables. Stated linguistically, the claim (in condensed form) is that the following statement is tautological: "Movables either began to be or did not begin to be." Premise granted.

PREMISE 5

(Original): ". . . if every one of these 'movables' came into existence, there must have been some other change or movement, prior to the one under consideration, which prior movement marked the coming into existence of this very object, capable of experiencing or causing movement, which we have seen must itself be prior to movement."

(Linguistical): The statement "Every movable came into existence and there was a first movement which was the first movement of the movables" is self-contradictory, for (1) the coming into existence of the movables would itself be movement prior to any movement of the movables, and (2) the movement of the coming into existence of movables would require, as does any movement, the existence of movables. Or (to present the entire argument in linguistical form): The statement "Every movable came into existence, and there was a first movement which was the first movement of the movables" is self-contradictory, for the compound statement "There was the first movement, which was the movement of a movable; and there was the first movement, which was the coming into existence of the first movable" is a contradiction; and it is also self-contradictory to state, "There was the movement of the coming into existence of the first movable," for from "There was . . . movement" it follows that "There was a movable," and hence from the statement "There was the movement of the coming into existence of the first movable" it would follow that "There was a movable prior to the first movable," a statement which is obviously self-contradictory.

(Type): Logical claim.

(Appraisal): Aristotle's argument is not a denial of the proposition that *individual things* all have a beginning and end *as such;* the argument is directed against the claim that at one time there was nothing and then movables began to be. Thus, the argument amounts to a denial of the claim that creation *ex nihilo* is possible. If motion is always the motion of something (a movable), and creation involves motion, then creation requires a movable; but if the creation being considered is the creation of *first* movables, then the creation of a first movable, at a time when there were no movables, would have involved the existence of a movable. It might be argued in further support of this claim (5) that a so-called "no movable," the motion of which would be what might correctly be described as "the creation of the first movable," would not be what we would persist in calling "no movable"; for that the movement of which would yield what we would call a "movable" is itself something capable of creative use, or movement, and thus is what we would call a "movable."

We accept the argument that if there were a first movement, it could not be the first movement of a movable that came into existence; and we also agree that the first movement could not be the coming into existence of a movable. The conclusion—that movables are eternal in that there has never been a time when there were no movables—is granted.

PREMISE 6

(Original): "[If movables are eternal] and then there came a time when first some potential mover actually moved something movable . . . there must have been some change which prevented [the cause of immobility] . . . from any longer hindering motion. Thus before the supposed first change there must have been another change."

(Linguistical): The statement "Movables are eternal, and there was a first movement which was the first movement of a movable" is self-contradictory; for if it is true that "There was a first movement of movables," it is true that "There was a prior movement consisting in the removal of the cause of immobility";

hence, from the first statement mentioned it follows that "There was a first movement which was not the first movement."

(Type): Logical claim.

(Appraisal): It may be argued that a change which consists in a removal of the cause of immobility may alternatively be described as a change which consists in initiating mobility. Suppose I keep a pencil from falling by resting it on the palm of my hand: there is a cause of the immobility, the maintenance of the state of rest, of the pencil. Suppose, then, that I quickly drop my hand: the pencil falls; the removal of the cause of immobility is a change which initiates mobility.

But suppose we consider a different kind of situation. A bicycle is chained to a rack which is immovable. We remove the chain, which has kept the bicycle from being moved. (The rack keeps the bicycle from falling.) Now we move the bicycle. There is a difference between removing the cause of the immobility of the bicycle and providing a cause of the mobility of the bicycle.

But, it may be argued, the chain cannot be described as *the* cause of the bicycle's immobility, for even when the chain is removed there remains a cause of the bicycle's immobility; namely, the state of affairs consisting in the absence of any cause of mobility. Thus, to remove *the* cause of immobility and to provide mobility is one and the same.

These reflections suggest that if there is a philosophical reason for objecting to the argument Aristotle provides in Premise 6, it is a *pragmatical* reason. The problem becomes that of deciding *whether we ought to call* the absence of a motion-inducing cause a "cause of . . . being at rest."

Suppose, first, that we *agree to describe the absence of a cause of motion* as the "presence of a cause of immobility." So interpreted, is Aristotle right in claiming that prior to a first movement of any movable there would have to be *another change,* consisting in the removal of the cause of immobility?

If what is called the "presence of a cause of immobility" is nothing more than what may alternatively be called the "absence of a cause of mobility," then, if there is a change in the one, there is a change in the other, for the two descriptions cover the same circumstance. Thus, if there is the removal of the cause of immobility in any given case, there is no longer what has been called "the presence of a cause of immobility" and, hence, no longer what has been called "the absence of a cause of mobility." But if there is no longer the absence of a cause of mobility, there is the presence of a cause of mobility; and wherever a cause is present, the effect follows. Thus, there is mobility once there is the removal of the cause of immobility.

Aristotle is wrong, then, *as so interpreted:* it *could not be* [logical claim] that *prior* to the first movement of a previously immobile movable there would have to be *another* change, consisting in the removal of the cause of immobility; for the expression "removal of the cause of immobility" is *pragmatically* equivalent to the expression "provision of the cause of mobility," and, hence, to do the one is to do the other, and neither can be prior.

If, then, in the effort to explore modes of interpretation favorable to Aristotle, we *decide not to call* [pragmatical decision] the absence of a cause of motion the "presence of a cause of immobility," then again Aristotle is mistaken, for there would be no logical necessity of a change *prior* to a presumed first movement.

The word that causes the trouble is the word "prior." We are asked to consider the possibility that, from all eternity, the movables were immobile. Then there was a first movement of the movables. The first movement would be what we *agree to call* [pragmatical decision] a "change" in the state of affairs previously obtaining. But Aristotle claims that prior to *that* change there would have to have been *another* change—some other event we would call a "change"—consisting in the removal of the cause of immobility. But we have argued that if it makes sense to describe the *absence of a cause* of mobility as the "presence of a cause of immobility," then the removal of such a cause and the operation of a cause of mobility is one and the same "change," although differently described; and we have also argued that if we do not describe the absence of a cause of mobility as the "presence of a cause of immobility," then the change consisting in the first movement of the movables and the change consisting in the termination of the immobility of the movables is one and the same change, although differently described. In either case, it makes no sense to say that the one change is "prior" to another.

Nevertheless, we contend that Aristotle was right in claiming that if the movables were originally immobile, there could not have been a first movement. But the reason for contending this logical point is not the reason that Aristotle gives. The reason why there could not have been a first movement is *not* that prior to the first movement there would have to have been another change consisting in the removal of the cause of immobility, but that prior to the first movement there would have to have been an event consisting in the imparting of motion to the movables; and the necessity of such an event is expressed by the logical claim that movement could not have come from nothing, for what we call "nothing" is precisely the absence of any "actuality": what we call "nothing" is (in the respect in which it is nothing) whatever could not give rise to anything. Thus, to say that movement came from nothing, or "ex nihilo," would be to contend that movement came from what could not give rise to anything. (To say that the subject of discourse "could not" give rise to anything is to mean that the subject of discourse *would not, under any circumstances,* give rise to anything.)

If, then, a first movement would have to have been initiated by a change consisting of the imparting of motion, and if we decide to call [pragmatical decision] a change imparting motion a "movement," then prior to a so-called "first" movement there would have to have been a movement—but that is impossible (that is, the proposition stated is self-contradictory).

Let us, then, without further consideration of premise 6, grant that there could not have been a first movement of eternal movables.

PREMISE 7

(Original): ". . . if we suppose [movement] to cease we shall have to admit a change posterior to the last change. For what is movable does not cease to be movable because it is no longer being moved, nor does that which is capable of causing motion cease to have that capacity because it is not moving anything . . . ."

(Linguistical): The statement "Movables are eternal, and there is a last movement which was the last movement of a movable" is self-contradictory, for if it is true that "There is a last movement of the movables," it is true that "There is a movement posterior to the last movement, the posterior movement consisting in the persistence of a cause of immobility"; hence, from the first statement mentioned it follows that "There is (will be) a last movement, which is not (will not be) the last movement."

(Type): Logical claim.

(Appraisal): If we make the pragmatical concession that the cause of the maintenance of a state of affairs may be described as a "change" or "movement"—and there is some justification for doing so, since an enduring rest is certainly a change from a state of restlessness, and the effort to maintain rest may, relative to that which opposes it, be said to be a "movement"—Aristotle's logical claim is acceptable.

In fact, the same kind of logical point made in support of proposition 6 may be constructed to serve in support of proposition 7. If *something* (the moving movable) can come to *nothing,* if that which is justifiably called "something" (and, hence, is that which has an effective presence in the world) can come to what we would call "nothing" (or the absence of effective presence), then that which has an effective presence (something) is that which does not have an effective presence—a contradiction. Hence, there cannot be a complete elimination of the moving movables; but if we presume an elimination of the motion of the movables, we find that not all motion has been eliminated, for there must continue to be that "motion" by which the aforementioned motion is opposed and by which the movables are sustained as movables.

PREMISE 8

(Original): ". . . movement is eternal, and is not something which now was and now was not. Indeed to assert the opposite is very like a contradiction in terms."

(Linguistical): The statement "There is movement but movement is not eternal" is a contradiction in terms.

(Type): Logical claim.

(Appraisal): What we here call premise 8 is, as previously noted, an intermediate conclusion. It follows from the previous premises, to which, given certain qualifications, we have assented.

PREMISE 9

(Original): ". . . the thing moved may be moved by the true agent either directly or by some intermediate which itself is moved by the true agent directly."

(Linguistical): The statement "If a thing is moved, it is moved by a true agent; and if it is moved by a true agent, it is moved either directly or indirectly (and, if the latter, by some intermediate)" is a tautology.

(Type): Logical claim.

(Appraisal): We agree with Aristotle's pragmatical decision to use the term "agent" to designate any mover. By a "true agent" is meant a mover not itself moved by another agent. But although it makes sense to speak of a man as initiating an action "on his own" and, in that respect, as not influenced by any other "agent," in Aristotle's account the term "agent" is used in a much broader sense, such that any mover whatsoever—say, a moving branch of a tree—may be said to be an "agent." Hence, there is some question as to whether any mover, other than the totality of movers prior to a given time, could be said to be a "true" mover or agent; for everything that moves (unless it has been moving eternally, and we need not suppose there is any such mover) is moved by something.

Thus, we deny that it is tautological to state, "If a thing is moved, it is moved by a *true* agent," although we agree—because of the use of "indirect" as the logical complement of "direct"—that *if* something is moved by a true agent, it is moved by that agent either directly or indirectly.

But if we deny that there must be true agents or at least one true agent, we break the logical chain by which Aristotle seeks to move to the conclusion that there is a prime mover, itself unmoved.

We shall conclude our analysis of the premises with the analysis of premise 10, although we could terminate our criticism of the argument as unsatisfactory after rejecting premise 9. Premise 10 is interesting because it appears to be an argument that does not depend on the premise that there is at least one true agent.

(Original): ". . . we must . . . reach a primary mover not moved by something else (for it is impossible to run back to infinity through movers that are themselves moved by something else, for there is no beginning at all of such an unlimited series). . . ."

(Linguistical): The statement "There is a primary mover not moved by something else" is logically true, for the statement "There is a primary mover in the series of movers moved by something else" is contradictory.

(Type): Logical claim.

(Appraisal): We grant that it is not possible to find a primary mover in a series of intermediate movers, for the use of the term "primary" to mean a first mover that, as first, could not be intermediate guarantees the logical conclusion. But we deny that from the logical truth that there is no primary mover in a series of intermediate movers it follows that there is a primary mover outside that series. The claim that *if* there is a primary mover, it is not in the series of intermediate movers is true. But although we agree that it would not be possible to have a prime (first) mover in a series of intermediate movers, we do not agree that a first mover is necessary. Linguistically, there is no contradiction involved in the claim "The series of intermediate movers is infinite and there is no first mover."

Aristotle anticipates the kind of criticism here made when he writes, "Nor does it help matters to say that that is how things were made and that we must take that as a principle, as Empedocles seems to imply . . . ." Aristotle argues that "what is natural is either absolute, not now thuswise and now otherwise . . . or, if not absolute, is determined by some intelligible principle"; and the suggestion is that the "absolute" is itself an intelligible principle and a first cause.

But we deny that everything in nature has to be accounted for by reference to some "intelligible principle." If some feature of the universe has always been the case, there is no need to explain that feature unless it *happens* to admit of an explanation. Thus, if energy is without beginning, there is no need (or possibility) of accounting for its origin. If motion is eternal, it is "absolute" only in the sense that it is not the product of determination; no "first principle" is needed to account for the origin of the unoriginated.

Again, Aristotle remarks, "Democritus, it is true, held it to be enough for the establishing of determining principles to have shown that this or that has been so in all former times, and did not feel bound to seek any deeper principle behind what has always been. But this took him right in certain cases only, and not in all. For instance the angles of a triangle are always equal to two right angles, but a reason can be assigned for the eternity of this property that lies behind the fact itself. But a first principle can have no such other cause behind it, since principles are eternal on their own merits."

What we deny is that a "reason" must be found to account for whatever is eternally the case. A reason can be found for whatever *must* eternally be the case, for the term "must" is used legitimately (in ordinary discourse) only with reference to some determining factor (perhaps linguistical, perhaps not) which could be described as a "reason" or "cause"; but we need not assume that whatever *is* eternally the case *must* be eternally the case. It is not self-contradictory, although contingently false, to state, "There is no energy" or "There is no movement"; and it is not tautological, although (as we have claimed) contingently true, to state, "There has always been energy" or "There has always been movement."

Our summary conclusion, then, is that even if motion is eternal, it does not follow that there is a primary mover, itself unmoved.

COMMENTS ON THE ANALYSIS OF ARISTOTLE'S ARGUMENT

Aristotle's argument in support of the claim that there is a prime mover, itself unmoved, is a logical argument based on the fact of motion and involving the underlying assumption that whatever is natural is either an absolute principle or determined by an absolute principle. The contention that everything that is moved is moved by a prime mover, either directly or indirectly, reflects Aristotle's basic presupposition that there is a beginning—a principle or cause—of every series. But in referring to true agents Aristotle concerns himself with *movers,* and there is nothing surprising in the claim that some agents—for example, men—may be said to be "true" in that they are not (or are not obviously) moved by something else. What is central to the argument is the claim, explored as premise 10, that "we must . . . reach a primary mover" because there must be a beginning to the series of intermediate movers—and *the beginning could not be within the series,* for no primary mover could be intermediate.

We have conceded (on logical grounds) that a primary (hence, *not*-intermediate) mover could not be part of a series of intermediate movers; but we have denied that eternal motion must have a cause—a beginning, a first principle. With Democritus, we have claimed that at least some eternal features of the universe—and motion is one of them—need no "ultimate" explanation, for they admit of no explanation. Only if we accepted Aristotle's version of the claim which, in the time of Leibniz, came to be called "the principle of sufficient reason," would we be inclined to insist that an infinite, eternal series of intermediate movers—although infinite and eternal—must have a "beginning" in the sense that it must be capable of being related to a "first cause" or "first principle," itself absolute (not determined by an intelligible principle).

The assumption that every contingent feature of the universe (that is, every feature that is not necessary) can be accounted for by reference to a cause, principle, or "reason" sufficient to have endowed the possible with actuality is an assumption that derives whatever plausibility it has from a limited use or definition of the term "contingent," such that if a feature of the universe is "contingent," it is determined by some intelligible principle. But "contingent" need not mean, and usually does not mean, "dependent upon a cause or principle"; it simply means "not necessary."

We agree with Aristotle in contending that motion is not itself absolute or necessary, for semantical analysis of the meaning of the term "motion" does not provide any ground for claiming that the statement "There is no motion" is contradictory. Thus, in at least one sense of the term "contingent," motion, even though eternal, is contingent, in that no logical inconsistency is involved in the proposition that the universe is motionless. But if, in this sense of the term "contingent," motion is contingent, it does not follow that motion has a cause. In fact, if motion is eternal, it could not have had an efficient cause; that is, no event—itself a movement—could have initiated eternal movement. It is not possible, finally, to appreciate intellectually or enjoy in faith the belief that eternal motion is to be accounted for by interpreting all motion as an irresistible convergence upon an eternally attractive God (pure intellect and actuality). The argument is not persuasive because it involves an unacceptable assumption; and when the assumption is extended metaphysically, the argument becomes not only unintelligible but also bizarre.

Aristotle's argument is significant in that it illustrates the seductive power of a logical argument developed to a great degree of complexity. Once drawn into the vortex of the argument, the critic, concerned as he is with the uses of terms and with consequent meanings and logical implications, may fail to find the origin of the argument's power—the assumption that everything, even the eternal and the given, must be accounted for by reference to an "absolute," a "first principle." But once the assumption has been isolated, the critic is able to come quickly to the conclusion that the assumption is not defensible—either empirically, logically, or metaphysically—and with the rejection of the assumption comes the justifiable rejection of the argument.

QUESTIONS FOR DISCUSSION

1. Aristotle's argument begins with the claim that there is motion. The critic contends that the claim is pragmatical. Is it possible that the claim is empirical? Could it be metaphysical?

2. The critic suggests that motion is "contingent" in the sense that it is not logically necessary—that is, the term "motion" does not designate a feature of the universe the denial of which would be self-contradictory. But surely, it might be claimed, "contingent" *means* "dependent upon something"; hence, how could motion not be dependent upon something for its existence if motion is contingent?

3. If the arguments against the claims that there was a first movement of movables and that there will be a last movement of the movables depend upon peculiar or, at least, unusual uses of the term "movement," are the arguments to that extent defective? Is it possible that the argument can be made more persuasive (in English) by using some word other than "movement"?

4. The critic suggests that physical things can be described as "complex systems of energy." Would the claim that physical things are nothing but complex systems of energy be a metaphysical claim?

5. Is the claim that there is substance always a metaphysical claim? Is it ever a metaphysical claim?

6. Criticize the following argument: Creation *ex nihilo* is impossible because if nothing could yield something, the so-called "nothing" would really be something and hence, not be nothing.

7. Is the claim that, under certain conditions, we "would" or "would not" use a certain term in a certain way pragmatically equivalent to the claim that we "ought" or "ought not" to use the term in that way? If so, what are the conditions?

8. Criticize Aristotle's argument that if there is a prime mover and if motion is eternal, then the prime mover is eternal.

9. Criticize Aristotle's argument that if there is an eternal mover and if that which is limited in nature is better, then the prime mover is single.

10. Criticize Aristotle's argument that an eternal prime mover is needed to account for noneternal unmoved movers.

INDEX